Calvin
and the
Duchess

Calvin and the Duchess

F. Whitfield Barton

WJKP

Library of Congress Cataloging-in-Publication Data

Barton, Florence Whitfield.
    Calvin and the duchess / F. Whitfield Barton.
        p.   cm.
    Bibliography: p.
    ISBN 0-8042-0874-3
    1. Calvin, Jean, 1509-1564—Correspondence. 2. Renée de France,
Duchess, consort of Ercole II d'Este, Duke of Ferrara, Modena, and
Reggio, 1510-1575—Correspondence. 3. Reformation—Italy.
4. Reformation—France. 5. Italy—Church history—16th century.
6. France—Church history—16th century.   I. Title.
BX9418.B16   1989
284'.2'0924—dc19
[B]   88-38612
                                                                  CIP

Westminster/John Knox Press
Louisville, KY 40202-1396

Acknowledgments

A number of years ago while working on a semibiography of Robert Estienne (1503–59), French printer who fled the wrath of the Sorbonne to become printer to John Calvin in Geneva, I came across a reference to Renée of France, who welcomed Estienne's son Henri (1528–98) to her court in Ferrara. Intrigued by the idea of a daughter of Louis XII, exiled to a small Italian duchy, sponsoring a foyer of Protestantism in the bosom of Catholicism, I tried to find out more about the lady.

In a scholarly encyclopedia I read that her father incarcerated her in a convent because of her heresy. Not so! Her father died when she was four years old. In a noted biographical dictionary, I read that she was brought before the Inquisition and imprisoned. Well . . . not quite. And in a biography of Margaret of Angoulême, I read that *she* and Renée were brought up together. But Margaret married and left the court for Alençon the year before Renée was born. There was nothing to do but find out for myself. Eventually I discovered a great deal about this woman with whom I came to identify, but I was not sure how I should treat her.

Meanwhile, as daughter and granddaughter of Presbyterian ministers and—more significantly—daughter of an ultra-

Calvinist mother, I began studying the life of John Calvin, whom my mother ranked only slightly lower than St. Paul. When I happened upon Jules Bonnet's letters of Calvin and found those addressed to Renée, everything fell into place. This book is the result.

It would be impossible for me to list the many persons to whom I am indebted for help in research and for encouragement. Such a list would have to include two eminent scholars no longer living: Dr. Winfred E. Garrison, longtime literary editor of *The Christian Century*, and Dr. Samuel Ives, for many years Curator of Rare Books at the University of Wisconsin. How could I name the reference librarians at the Library of Congress, the Iowa Historical Society, Zion Research Library, Princeton University, McCormick Theological Seminary, Louisville Presbyterian Theological Seminary?

I do not know the names of the courteous attendant in the Ariosto Library in Ferrara and the very knowledgeable lawyer who made the way easy for me in Modena; but I am well acquainted with Betty Lawhon of the Doniphan, Missouri, Public Library, who never seemed to weary of ordering books for me through Interlibrary Loan.

I cannot begin to express my appreciation to Dr. Nancy Hardesty, my editor at John Knox Press, for the time and effort she expended in readying my manuscript for publication and for her belief in its possibilities.

On a more personal level, I must express my gratitude to my son, Dr. Thomas Barton, who insisted that I take off from Toulouse on my own to go to Paris, Blois, and Montargis, Modena and Ferrara, in search of Renée; to my daughter Ann Sciba, who listened to my interminable stories about Renée and worked up the genealogical charts; and to my *belle fille* Betty Burton Barton, who gently prodded me on.

F. Whitfield Barton
Doniphan, Missouri

Preface

This account of the almost lifelong friendship of John Calvin and the duchess of Ferrara has been reconstructed in large part from Calvin's letters, synchronizing his life as revealed therein with that of Renée of France. Émile Doumergue surmised that only about half of Calvin's correspondence survived.[1] We have eleven of his letters to the duchess although references in these and in letters to his fellow theologians indicate that he wrote her more often.

Unfortunately, we have only one long letter from Renée to Calvin, written in March 1564. It has previously been assigned to 1563, but internal evidence proves conclusively the correctness of the later date. Evidently Calvin acceded to her request that he burn her letters. We know, too, that much of her correspondence was intercepted by her husband.

There is some disagreement as to dates assigned to two other letters. Williston Walker dated Calvin's first letter to Renée as having been written in 1537, since Calvin refers to a letter he had written Louis Duchemin in that year, and since Calvin sent the duchess a tract "recently published."[2] This was the *Traite de la Cine*, which he indeed wrote in 1537 but which he revised and issued again in 1540. François Richardot, the object of Calvin's warning, was employed by Renée as almoner late that year at a salary of 720 livres. He remained with her for several years in that capacity. Herminjard placed the letter in 1540.[3] Jules Bonnet dated it 1541.[4]

Since in 1540 Calvin was engrossed in affairs of the Strasbourg church, giving lectures, attending meetings, and torn with the necessity of deciding whether or not to return to Geneva, I have felt it quite reasonable that immediately after making that move and before becoming too involved in his multitudinous new duties, he would write this woman he had visited five years before and had found so receptive to his ideas. He was already a correspondent of one of the duchess's ladies of honor and had been kept informed of conditions at her court.

The undated letter which Bonnet assigned to February 1562, in which Calvin warned the duchess about her daughter Anne's acts destructive to the Reformed, could not have been written at that time since Anne was in Joinville then with her husband the duke of Guise and her sons, awaiting the birth of her third child, *before* the Vassy massacre, for she had done nothing to call forth such a letter. I have placed this letter after Guise's murder when Anne was doing everything possible to have Coligny sentenced for her husband's assassination.

I have presupposed that readers will have some acquaintance with events and personalities of sixteenth-century France; therefore I have confined myself as far as possible to events narrated in Calvin's letters to his friends. I have also kept at a minimum the tangled threads of political alliances made by the dukes of Ferrara with or against the Emperor Charles V (1500–58), to whom they owed fealty for Modena and Reggio; their papal suzerains, ever eager to seize Ferrara; and the kings of France, who owed the dukes more money than they would ever be able to repay and needed Ferrara as a buffer between Germany and Spain and a staging area for their invasions of Italy.

Renée's husband Ercole II d'Este was the son of Alfonso I and Lucrezia Borgia, a marriage forced upon the Este prince by Lucrezia's father, Pope Alexander VI (1431–1503). Renée was the younger of the two viable children born to Louis XII (who had secured the annulment of his marriage to the daughter of

Louis XI—a union of twenty-two years' duration—through the good offices of the Borgia pope) and Anne of Brittany, widow of Charles VIII, whose previous marriage, like that of her husband, had been forced.

Renée and her sister Claude were crippled like their mother, and her husband was agreeably surprised that none of their five children was similarly deformed. Emanuel Stickelberger wrote that the duchess always wore a high collar and a ruff to hide her misshapen shoulder,[5] but the portraits by Corneille de Lyon and Clouet show her in low-necked gowns.

Sixteenth-century Ferrara was a glittering Renaissance city, famous for its industry, wealth, and university. The dukes were patrons of artists, poets, musicians, and scholars. Ercole's grandfather had torn down a broad swath for his Addizione Ercole, with the Corso Ercole I running from the north wall to the north entrance of his terracotta castle, which still dominates the Old Town. Though much damage was wrought to the city during World War II bombardments, today it looks singularly undamaged, the Renaissance palaces still lining the Corso Ercole I.

After four hundred years there are still reminders of Renée. Much of the castle is open to visitors: the ballroom where in 1543 Pope Paul III received her, her bedroom, her terrace garden with potted orange trees surrounded by a marble railing, her chapel. Around the corner, past the statues of Borso and Niccolo, is the entrance to the palace courtyard, where a flight of marble steps leads up to what are now municipal offices. On these steps Isabella, duchess of Mantua and Ercole's aunt, stood to welcome her nephew's unwilling French bride.

The cathedral across from the palace, has been "improved" since Renée's time, yet one can still see Jeanetto striding out of the great central door uttering blasphemies on Good Friday while John Calvin was there. Inside one can imagine Renée and her ladies listening raptly to the sermons of Bernardino Ochino, whom the duchess would rescue from the fires of the Inquisition. It was from the cathedral steps that the duke announced to his subjects the happy news that his consort had agreed to give up her heretical beliefs.

The Palazzo San Francesco, to which Renée retired after her

trial, was not the convent of that same name, nor was she ever incarcerated in a convent. It is now the administration center of the university. Where the Corso Biagno Rossetti crosses Corso Ercole I stands the Palazzo Diamente, completed by her son Luigi, the pleasure-loving prelate who constructed the Tivoli Gardens. The Piazza Ariosto commemorates the court poet who included stanzas in praise of the duchess in his *Orlando Furioso*. The Palazzo Schifanoia, now a museum, was a favorite of Renée and her ladies during her early years in Ferrara.

At Modena, where the bridal party stopped for two weeks of celebration on the way from Paris, the site of the ducal palace is now occupied by the military academy. But the cathedral, where Ercole's father insisted a second wedding mass be performed, is much the same as it was then except for empty spaces where images of saints were removed and carried off to France by Napoleon. There are a number of books once belonging to Renée, a few musical instruments, a few letters in the Estense Museum, all brought to Modena in 1598 when the papacy finally absorbed Ferrara, the legitimate Este line having expired. Though Alfonso II married three times, he produced no legitimate sons.

Goethe said, "The traveler must know what he has to see." At Blois guides were interested only in showing the apartment where Renée's grandson was murdered and pointing out the cupboards where, they said, Catherine de' Medici kept her poisons. They knew nothing of Louise of Savoy or Claude of France or Margaret of Angoulême; or if they knew, they did not tell. Nevertheless, Renée was there in the Francis I wing where her sister died in her arms and in the Louis XII wing, hanging on the words of old Jacques Lefèvre.

At Paris, many of her letters are preserved in the Bibliothèque Nationale, letters to courtiers of Francis I and to the king, almost undecipherable. At Montargis the castle has been destroyed. Her portraits are at Versailles, at Chantilly, at the Hermitage, but court painters were notorious flatterers. I have tried to show her as she was.

Dedication

To my dear children Ann, Tom, and Betty

—in gratitude for their patience and forbearance,
without whose loving encouragement this book
would never have been written

Abbreviated House of

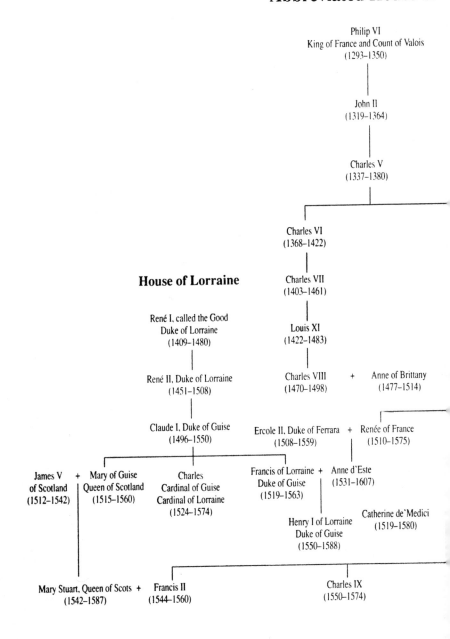

Philip VI
King of France and Count of Valois
(1293–1350)

John II
(1319–1364)

Charles V
(1337–1380)

Charles VI
(1368–1422)

House of Lorraine

Charles VII
(1403–1461)

René I, called the Good
Duke of Lorraine
(1409–1480)

Louis XI
(1422–1483)

René II, Duke of Lorraine
(1451–1508)

Charles VIII   +   Anne of Brittany
(1470–1498)   (1477–1514)

Claude I, Duke of Guise
(1496–1550)

Ercole II, Duke of Ferrara   +   Renée of France
(1508–1559)   (1510–1575)

James V   +   Mary of Guise   Charles   Francis of Lorraine + Anne d'Este
of Scotland   Queen of Scotland   Cardinal of Guise Duke of Guise   (1531–1607)
(1512–1542)   (1515–1560)   Cardinal of Lorraine   (1519–1563)
                                         (1524–1574)
                                                             Henry I of Lorraine   Catherine de'Medici
                                                             Duke of Guise   (1519–1580)
                                                             (1550–1588)

Mary Stuart, Queen of Scots + Francis II   Charles IX
(1542–1587)   (1544–1560)   (1550–1574)

Valois and Satellites

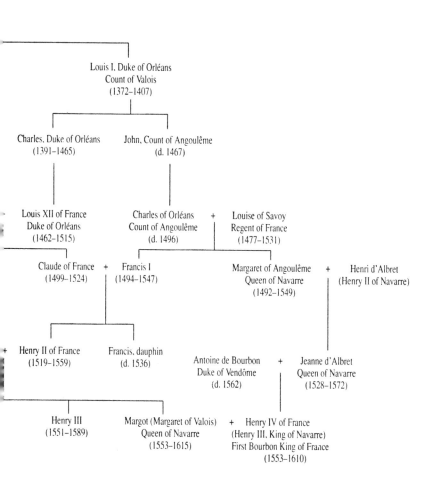

Louis I, Duke of Orléans
Count of Valois
(1372–1407)

Charles, Duke of Orléans
(1391–1465)

John, Count of Angoulême
(d. 1467)

Louis XII of France
Duke of Orléans
(1462–1515)

Charles of Orléans + Louise of Savoy
Count of Angoulême   Regent of France
(d. 1496)   (1477–1531)

Claude of France + Francis I
(1499–1524)   (1494–1547)

Margaret of Angoulême + Henri d'Albret
Queen of Navarre   (Henry II of Navarre)
(1492–1549)

Henry II of France
(1519–1559)

Francis, dauphin
(d. 1536)

Antoine de Bourbon + Jeanne d'Albret
Duke of Vendôme   Queen of Navarre
(d. 1562)   (1528–1572)

Henry III
(1551–1589)

Margot (Margaret of Valois) + Henry IV of France
Queen of Navarre   (Henry III, King of Navarre)
(1553–1615)   First Bourbon King of France
                                (1553–1610)

Contents

PART ONE

The Spark Is Struck

I

Alias Charles d'Espeville

All of John Calvin's (1509–64) biographers mention his visit to Ferrara in the spring of 1536, but even Theodore Beza (1519–1605) called that period a "blank page in the Reformer's life." Calvin himself said of Italy only that he came and went. We do not know what impelled his journey to the court of Francis I's sister-in-law. Beza wrote, "He felt an inclination to visit Renée, duchess of Ferrara, a daughter of Louis XII, whose piety was greatly spoken of."[1]

Stickelberger said that the duchess of Ferrara (1510–75) invited Calvin to visit her at the instigation of Clément Marot (c.1497–1544).[2] Other writers have surmised that Margaret of Navarre (1492–1549) sent him to Renée. Fontana's allegation that he came to Italy to set up a foyer for Protestantism at Ferrara is absurd since the young scholar had at that time not the faintest intention of dedicating his life to spreading the gospel according to John Calvin.[3]

We do know that following the tumult over Nicholas Cop's inaugural address in November 1533, Cop fled to Basel and his friends were sought for arrest. Calvin hurriedly left the city before his rooms were ransacked for incriminating evidence. Margaret, queen of Navarre, the king's sister, invited Calvin to visit her, interceding with her brother on Calvin's behalf. Her court at Nérac had become a sanctuary for those attacked by the Sorbonne and she herself had been accused of heresy.

He stopped for a while with his friend Louis Du Tillet, also a suspect, in Angoulême, where he began work on the treatise which would become his *Institutes of the Christian Religion.* The following April he went with Du Tillet to Nérac, Margaret's court, where he found Jacques Lefèvre d'Étaples (c.1455– 1536), most notorious of all the early French reformers, whose "heretical" writings antedated those of Luther.

Deeply religious, Lefèvre had never entertained a thought of leaving Holy Mother Church. All he had worked for and hoped for was purification of the institution, eradication of superstitions, and reformation of the clergy. He saw in young Calvin an instrument of God's work, though there was little in Calvin's background pointing to his future leadership of French Protestantism. His early translation of Seneca's *Of Mercy* was simply a literary composition, not a plea for toleration of the Evangelicals whom, in fact, he rather looked down upon. But his theological and legal education had fitted him preeminently for authorship of the work which would become the basis for French Protestantism.

The date of his conversion to Protestantism has been pushed back by recent biographers to some time between 1526 and 1531, and the legend that he was author of Cop's sermon has been discounted. Certainly the influence of his closest friends— François Daniels of Orléans, Nicholas Cop in Paris, and his cousin Pierre Robert ("Olivétan")—had a part in shaping his thoughts. He was profoundly influenced by his study of Augustine. Mathurin Cordier taught him more than Latin; Melchior Wolmar more than Greek. "Through you," Lefèvre told his visitor at Nérac, "God will erect his kingdom in our land."[4]

Back in France, Calvin resigned his benefice in Noyon and in Paris became spokesman for the new doctrines. Years later he wrote that all interested in the new ideas came to him. One Michael Servetus (1511–53), a Spanish doctor/theologian, made an appointment to argue with him the doctrine of the Trinity but failed to keep the engagement until twenty years later.

In October 1534 the "Placard Affair" erupted, with crude and obscene posters reviling the papacy pasted up in Paris and even on the door of the king's bedchamber at Amboise. A net for all suspected heretics was flung far and wide, with twenty captured and executed in short order and hundreds arrested. Calvin and Du Tillet escaped, first to Strasbourg, then on to Basel.

There for more than a year he was associated with other reformers, spent his time in writing French and Latin prefaces for Olivétan's translation of the Bible, and correcting the New Testament section. Meanwhile he continued working on the *Institutes*, his personal confession of faith, writing a long introductory letter to Francis I (1494–1547), defending the Reformed from their slanderers. He completed the work in August 1535. Immediately after its publication the following March, he set out with Du Tillet for Ferrara.

Either Margaret of Navarre or Clément Marot might logically have suggested that Calvin visit Ferrara. Renée's welcome to French refugees for any and every reason was widely known and had continued even after Pope Paul III had written the duke that he would no longer tolerate the duchess's sheltering of those suspected of harboring Lutheran opinions (the term was used of all who opposed Catholicism).

It is not possible to say whether or not Renée had any direct contact with Marot either at the French court or at Nérac before her marriage, though it is possible. His father had been brought to Queen Anne's court by Michelle de Saubonne, baroness of Soubise, four years before Renée's birth, bringing with him his little son. The boy became a valet de chambre to Francis I, was later at Margaret of Navarre's court, and in 1527 succeeded to his father's post as court poet. In that capacity he wrote the epithalamium, or wedding hymn, at the time of Renée's marriage to Ercole d'Este.

Considering the long relationship he had enjoyed with the French royal family and the friendship between his father and Madame de Soubise, he might well have expected to find a sanctuary in Ferrara. Imprisoned twice in Paris, the first time for eating bacon during Lent (an offense for which C. A. Mayer, in his study on Marot, says the poet risked being put to death[5]), he is thought to have played a role in the "Placard Affair." At any rate, he fled to Nérac for safety until January 1535, when his name appeared on the list of those in France condemned to death for contumacy. Even the king's beloved sister was unable to protect him longer. Margaret sent him on to Ferrara, where he was welcomed and enrolled on the list of the duchess's servitors as a secretary.

When Calvin reached Ferrara in March 1536, he was accepted as another French scholar come to pay his respects to Italian learning. He was introduced to Ercole II, duke since the death of his father two years before, as Charles d'Espeville, a cognomen he would use in all his correspondence with the duchess as well as with other chosen ones. And he brought Renée the first copy of his *Institutes of the Christian Religion.*

"When the Lady Duchesse of Ferrara saw and heard Calvin," wrote Beza, "she knew of whose spirit he was; and as long as he lived, she remained for him a special instrument of God, faithful in love and devotion."[6] She was all the more ready to receive him, to hold long, private conversations with him, because of the widening rift between her and her husband caused by his recent banishment of her beloved companion, Madame de Soubise.

Calvin felt himself at home among the erudite professors of the University of Ferrara, the liberal churchmen, the wandering scholars frequenting the duchess's court. Yet he was cautious in his remarks when others expressed themselves freely about the church and its need for reform, questioning, criticizing, even ridiculing the system they yet felt obliged to go along with.

During the weeks he spent in Ferrara he made friends: Jean de Parthenay, the son of Madame de Soubise, who would later be a leader in the Protestant army during the Wars of Religion; Anne de Soubise, now Madame de Pons; Françoise Boussiron and the young German professor Johann Synapius, whom Erasmus had persuaded to go to Ferrara from Heidelberg with his brother Chilian, both of whom held Reformed beliefs.

Calvin was still in Ferrara on 14 April when the first open breach between the duke and duchess over the matter of religion came to a head. On Holy Friday Jeanetto, one of the duchess's singers, walked out of the cathedral at the time of the adoration of the cross, uttering blasphemies. If his act was intended to cause a riot, it was a failure. The service continued, and it was only that night that the boy was arrested.

While Jeanetto's protest was seemingly a childish and insignificant act, both duke and duchess immediately dispatched letters—Renée to the French court, Ercole to the pope— defending themselves. Renée also sent an urgent message to the bishop of Lavaur, French ambassador in Venice, begging him to claim jurisdiction of Jeanetto as a subject of the king.

Six days previously Ercole had been warned that the pope was taking a very jaundiced view of the duchess's activities, having heard of her asylum for Lutherans. Perhaps that warning made him react too quickly, but his wife's independence in matters religious and political kept him walking a tightrope, afraid of the French king, Renée's brother-in-law; afraid that the pope, avid for his duchy, would excommunicate him and bring an army against Ferrara as popes had done in his father's day.

This matter of Jeanetto was the duchess's fault. The boy had been condemned in France for his part in the placard business, but Ercole had listened to his wife's pleas and agreed that Jeanetto might remain in Ferrara so long as he lived as a good Catholic. This flagrant insult to Holy Mother Church could not be glossed over.

When, at the third drop of the estrapade (a form of torture in which a person is hoisted to top of gallows by the wrists, which are tied behind the back, and then dropped just short of the ground), Jeannetto confessed that his act was a failed attempt to lead a protest against the church, naming most of the duchess's servitors as his cowardly accomplices, the duke found himself in a dilemma. To arrest so many so long associated with Renée, implying that the duchess had knowingly harbored heretics, would undoubtedly bring down upon him the wrath of the French king; not to act quickly and firmly would arouse the wrath of the Holy Father. He made a token arrest—Jean de Bouchefort, for years one of Renée's most devoted retainers. The other suspects, after loudly declaring their innocence before the inquisitor, fled. In July Marot, who had brought the young singer with him to Ferrara, wrote the duchess from Venice, but it is not known when he arrived there.

During the examination of witnesses, a Franciscan monk testified that one night during Lent he had heard a Frenchman in the duchess's palace speaking against the Holy Faith, especially against the authority of the church and against the pope, and declaring that humanity had no free will but to do evil. The witness went on to say that, when reproved, the speaker defended himself by saying the duchess's almoner preached those things publicly, with her approval. It is impossible to *see* Calvin in this injudicious Frenchman, however much we may *hear* him.

The imbroglio continued, Renée's attempts to free her servitors only making matters worse. Ercole's ambassador to the French court found nothing against Bouchefort and reported that Jeanetto had been pardoned by the king. The bishop of Lavaur intensified his efforts to have the prisoners released to him. The duchess, unable to browbeat the inquisitor of Ferrara into releasing them, implored the pope to help her. Paul III, only too willing to interfere, ordered the inquisitor to deliver Jean de Bouchefort *and those arrested on the same charge* to the bishop of Bologna for greater security.

The duchess congratulated herself that the prisoners would soon be out of her husband's hands, but Ercole refused to admit defeat. Since the French ambassador, in the name of Francis I, and the bishop of Bologna, in the name of the pope, each claimed the miscreants, it was impossible to obey one without disobeying the other. Therefore he would keep all prisoners under guard. To discipline his wife for interfering, he arrested her treasurer and longtime confidant, Cornillau.

Renée wrote to the bishop of Tournon insinuating that her husband intended to take her life since he had deprived her of her servants and all authority.[7] (Ercole had refused to allow the bishop of Lavaur to speak to her.)

To Margaret, queen of Navarre, she wrote, "I am sure that Madame de Soubise has told you of the terrors and even assaults made against me since she left. I cannot bear any more. Without the help of the Lord I could not have. Daily my vexations increase. . . ."[8]

When the duchess's frantic calls for help to cardinals, the queen of Navarre, and the king himself did indeed bring His Majesty into the affair (though the French court considered the matter blown out of all proportion, simply a ploy by the duke to deprive his wife of all her French servitors), Ercole appealed to Paul III for guidance. His Holiness suggested three options: free the prisoners, banish them, or turn all of them over to the French ambassador.

Choosing the third course, the duke was horrified to find only Jeanetto and Cornillau in confinement. What had become of Bouchefort, the only one mentioned by name in the first papal brief? How and when had he escaped? Was the Bouchefort named in the brief indeed the duchess's servitor of that name? The Ferrarese ambassador in Rome reported that the missing prisoner was a well-known heretic, arrested previously in Paris, who had been counted upon to reveal all the details of the plot before he escaped there.

The mystery of the missing prisoner has never been solved. The escape was discovered on 14 July. Marot wrote the duchess on 15 July from Venice, where he had been for two weeks. Calvin was back in Paris in May, preparing to go to Strasbourg. It has been suggested that the fugitive was a fourth person, so important that his name in all documents relating to the trial was erased and many papers destroyed.

Fontana wrote that it was impossible to conclude definitely that the escapee was *not* John Calvin, hypothesizing that Calvin could have taken the name of Bouchefort when he was arrested. Fontana maintained that if the prisoner had really been Bouchefort, he would not have been permitted to return to Ferrara, when, as a matter of fact, Bouchefort served the duchess for years to come.[9]

Lodovico Muratori (1672–1750) stated unequivocally that the man was Calvin, that only his incarceration would have been grave enough to explain the agitation of the duchess. He was convinced that a party of horsemen, sent by Renée and the

French ambassador, had rescued Calvin as he was being transferred from one prison to another, and then spirited him out of Italy.[10] Is this simply a scenario of the antiquarian-archivist of Modena, the "Father of Italian History," or is it based on documents since lost, especially those collections taken to France by Napoleon, to which Muratori had access?

The legend persists, and in Tirraboschi's *Storia della Literatura Italiana*, we read: "Calvin's stay at the court of Ferrara brought more damage to Italy than all the emissaries of Luther."[11]

II

Renée of France

She was born at Blois on 10 October 1510, the second of two surviving children of Anne of Brittany (1477–1514) and Louis XII (1462–1515), both daughters and both misshapen like their mother. Renée was only a little past three years old when her mother died, to be followed in less than a year by the king. The queen's closest friend, Michelle de Saubonne, baroness of Soubise, Renée's governess and guardian, took the place of her mother.

She retained vivid memories of the year following her mother's death: the long journey to Paris and on to Saint-Denis in the litter, with the coldly forbidding Louise of Savoy, her mother's enemy, part of the endless funeral cortege; the wedding ceremony of her sister Claude (1499–1524) and Francis of Angoulême (1494–1547), Louise of Savoy's son, with Renée and all of the court still dressed in black, and Claude weeping for their mother.

On New Year's Day she was told that the king, her father, was dead, and his young English wife was sent back to Henry VIII. Then Francis of Angoulême became king, and Claude, still crying, became queen. Madame Louise, wanting to rid everyone of all reminders of Anne of Brittany, banished Madame de Soubise

from court. Even Brantôme, so flattering to royalty, spoke of the
harsh treatment accorded Queen Anne's daughters by the king's
mother,[1] an accusation Louise of Savoy in her diary protested
much too much.

Not that the sisters were completely ignored. In between his
amours, his tournaments, his hunts, and his wars, Francis spared
time to father seven children in the ten years before pious, dull
little Queen Claude died in her sister's arms; and he made good
use of Renée to further his political alliances. As an infant, she
had been betrothed to Gaston de Foix, her cousin, and after his
heroic death in battle, to Charles of Austria; then, when Francis's
newborn daughter took her place, to Charles's brother Ferdinand. That treaty abrogated while Francis was vying with
Charles and Henry of England for the empire, he promised her to
the son of the elector of Brandenburg in exchange for the elector's
vote. Double-crossed there, other offers were considered. The
duke of Bourbon's suit was rejected; the king of Portugal's seriously entertained. Cardinal Wolsey was putting forth feelers on
his master's behalf, Henry casting covetous eyes on Brittany,
when Anne Boleyn appeared on the scene and Renée was, happily, forgotten.

Until she was almost fourteen, Renée lived close to her sister,
both taking only nominal part in court activities, and that only
on official occasions. The king's mother Louise set the model of
immorality and extravagance while his sister Margaret played
the role of queen on all but state occasions.

We have glimpses of Claude and Renée: watching tournaments at the Field of Cloth of Gold; with Louise and Margaret in
Meaux to observe the reforms Cardinal Briçonnet was introducing in his diocese with the help of Jacques Lefèvre and his
ardent young disciples; going with the king and his sister to visit
the imprimerie of Robert Estienne and waiting until the royal
printer finished correcting proof.

After Claude's death, Renée attached herself emotionally to
Margaret, the only person to show her any affection. This
remarkable woman certainly had a share in the girl's spiritual
development. Devoted to her brother, she could make no public

avowal of her Protestant leanings (though the Sorbonne wished to condemn her writings), leaving the final break with Rome to her daughter, Jeanne d'Albret (1528–72), mother of Henry IV (1553–1610).

Renée fades from view in the cataclysmic events after Francis's defeat at Pavia: his imprisonment in Spain, Margaret's mission to Madrid, Louise of Savoy's regency and the fires lighted at her direction to rid the kingdom of heresy and so avert the further wrath of God. Renée went to Bayonne with the court to welcome the king home and to see her two small nephews, Francis and Henry, hurried off to Spain as hostages in their father's stead. She rode with the king and Margaret when he made his entry into Paris after weeks of riotous celebration.

To please Margaret, the king granted amnesty to a number of heretics, among them the reformers who had fled from Meaux during the heretic hunting, particularly hotheaded Guillaume Farel (1489–1565), who refused to return from Switzerland, and Jacques Lefèvre, archheretic in the eyes of the Sorbonne, whom the king made librarian at Blois and tutor to his children and Renée.

Renée became a voracious reader and devoured Lefèvre's theological writings. She imbibed the new doctrines. The relationship of teacher and pupil continued until her marriage. In 1527 the widowed Margaret of Angoulême married Jean d'Albret, king of Navarre, and took Lefèvre and Renée with her to Nérac. They were still with her that winter at Blois, and at Saint-Germain-en-Laye with the court in the spring, when Ercole d'Este, son of Alfonso, duke of Ferrara, arrived to marry the French king's sister-in-law.

Ercole was not a willing party to the union. Though there was no question of love in any royal marriage, and though he had been prepared, he was still shocked at the appearance of the bride-to-be. Her carefully designed shoe could not disguise the fact that one leg was appreciably shorter than the other, causing one shoulder to protrude as though humped. Nevertheless, he obeyed his father's instructions. The interest of the duchy must come first. (His father had been forced by political necessity to marry Lucrezia Borgia, daughter of Pope Alexander VI.) Later, flattered by Louise of Savoy and Margaret of Navarre, Ercole became reconciled, captivated by Renée's apparent intelligence, the pure oval of her face, her long blond hair, and seduced by the perquisites promised him by the king.

By this alliance, the Estes would secure a powerful protector in their constant struggle with the Holy See. Since the emperor's sack of Rome, public opinion had turned against him, and the prestige of Francis I was once more in the ascendant throughout Italy. With his help, the Estense princes might aspire to greater glory.

On his part, Francis recognized Alfonso's military acumen, his skill in manufacturing cannon, and his willingness to lend money to a spendthrift prince. The geographical position of Ferrara made the duchy a perfect staging area for future French attempts on Milan and Naples, that obsession so disastrous to Charles VIII, Louis XII, and more recently Francis himself. Most of all, Francis's choice of son-in-law was dictated by the fact that married to a second-rate duke and far from the scene, Renée would not be likely to assert her claim to the duchy of Brittany, a claim she had a right to by terms of the marriage contract between Anne of Brittany and Louis XII. To make assurance doubly sure, Francis had her sign a document giving up her rights.

The wedding ceremony was performed with great pomp at the Sainte Chapelle on 28 May 1528, with balls, tournaments, and feasting continuing for several weeks, in spite of the bride's migraines and the groom's empty purse. On 28 June Renée and her new husband accompanied court and king to Paris, where Francis led an expiatory procession and replaced an image of the Blessed Virgin in a shrine vandalized by "Lutherans," where he dedicated himself anew to ridding his kingdom of heresy.

Because of plague in Ferrara, the newlyweds delayed their departure until September, allowing time for Renée's beloved childhood governess Madame de Soubise to come from Brittany and become one of the ladies of her retinue.

Besides her innumerable chests, her costumes and jewels, her ladies of honor and servitors, and her promise of pension and dowry, the young bride, stubborn as her Breton mother, carried with her the conviction that she was going into exile, an exile bearable only by the knowledge of her royalty—she made her formal entry into plague-devastated Ferrara in a crimson velvet robe lined with ermine and wearing a crown on her flowing tresses, when her rank dictated only a coronet—and by the belief that by this marriage, this exile, she was serving the king.

All her life she had lived in the shadow of his splendid presence. How could she have failed to worship him as her sister had done, as his mother and sister did? To her he was indeed the Lord's anointed. He had arranged this union for his own purposes. In Ferrara she would serve him as he had told her to do.

From the beginning Ercole d'Este (1508–59) considered the French marriage a mistake. His wife set up a queen-size court, lavished gifts on her attendants, multiplied alms—especially to the hordes of French soldiers stumbling home after the Neapolitan debacle. Criticized, she retorted that except for the hated Salic law of France, they would be her own subjects. Her extravagance was even harder to accept since the pensions promised by her brother-in-law failed to materialize.

The Estes, father and son, could not fault her for not producing an heir in the spring of 1529—her pregnancy resulted in a miscarriage. But in November 1531 the child she bore was well-formed, much to their relief, and christened Anne (1531– 1607) in a magnificent ceremony at which Pope Clement VII acted as godfather, by proxy. In November 1533 the whole duchy joyously celebrated the birth of Alfonso (1533–97), Ercole's first legitimate son, at which Francis, by proxy, served as godfather.

On the surface the marriage seemed to be successful. In public Ercole and his wife displayed conjugal affection and respect. They often dined together, witnessed theatrical performances, listened to concerts. Yet in each there was a rising tide of discontent. From her first days in Ferrara, Renée wrote to the king, to Margaret, to the grand master, Montmorency, complaining of her loneliness, her husband's "mistreatment." Even during the celebration over the birth of her son, her letters show that she felt herself in need of help from the French court. To all appearances she was not mistreated. Ariosto, the court poet, idealized her in his poems praising the Estensi; ambassadors expressed their admiration of her; she administered her court as she chose. Yet the domestic quarrels went on.

In January 1534 Francis I sent a gentleman of his bedchamber, Antoine de Pons, count of Marennes, to Ferrara, with orders that he be married to Anne de Soubise. Ercole, having no desire to take part in the magnificent nuptial celebrations, went to spend the carnival season in Venice, to escape having anything to do with the Soubise family, especially the mother.

Already Duke Alfonso and his son had identified Madame de Soubise as the source of their dissatisfaction with the French bride. She supported Renée in her refusal to learn Italian, her insistence on wearing Spanish fashions (*de rigueur* at the French court), in her making of her court a French enclave.

Alfonso credited Madame de Soubise with more serious offenses: of leaning toward the new religious opinions too openly herself and encouraging Renée in making her court a foyer for the discussion of every kind of opinion. He had been forced to make lame excuses to Pope Clement VII about those meetings in his daughter-in-law's court.

He was inclined to gloss over the pope's hints, since nowadays there was open criticism of the church everywhere. Mazolli, his own physician, had dedicated to him a book deriding monks and depicting Luther as a hero. The duke was more concerned with Madame de Soubise's injury to his purse. Taking advantage of her position, she was importing goods from France for resale without paying custom dues. Worst of all, he was convinced that she was acting as secret agent for the king, supporting Renée's interference in Valois/Este politics.

He began a correspondence with Francis urging His Majesty to recall the lady, a correspondence which was still underway when the duke died in October 1534. Ercole was more impatient than his father. He saw in his wife's favorite the source of the rumors about his mistreatment of Renée. He intercepted her letters accusing him and believed they were written at his wife's dictation.

After months of correspondence with Francis over the situation, during which time Ercole's hatred of the woman intensified, he directed the Ferrarese ambassador to "demand" Madame de Soubise's recall. At the same time that lady, tired of the duke's animosity, petitioned the king to the same effect, and on 8 September His Majesty agreed that she should return to France immediately after the birth of the duchess's child, due in December.

Renée, in the sixth month of her pregnancy, seethed with indignation but to no avail. (It was during this time that Clément Marot wrote his poem to the queen of Navarre, lamenting the duchess's sorrows.) To escape her tears and rage, her husband set out for Rome to pay homage to his suzerain, the newly elected pope, Paul III, and to go on to Naples, where he would try to ingratiate himself with the emperor, Charles V.

His meeting with the emperor was highly successful. On his way home, again in Rome, he wrote the duchess in late November and again in December, exulting about the reception accorded him by the emperor. French influence in Italy was definitely declining, and the Estensi changed political partners whenever expediency dictated.

Letters from his secretary in Ferrara told the duke of the birth of his second daughter, Lucrezia (1535–98), in mid- December, and he expressed his pleasure that this one also was well-formed. He did *not* express pleasure at hearing of the surprise his wife and Madame de Soubise were preparing for him: the French court was to be in Lyon in March; Renée had been invited by the king himself to meet him there. She would accompany Madame de Soubise as far as Lyon. Ercole returned to Ferrara determined to assert himself.

The projected journey was not simply a whim, and Renée would not lightly relinquish it, having set foot beyond the bounds of the duchy but once since her marriage. She was convinced that her journey would serve her king and the duke: it would show the emperor that Ferrara was still in the French orbit. The duke knew only too well how the emperor would take the visit to France. Coldly furious, he forbade her to go.

In January the king wrote him from Lyon, insisting that the duchess be permitted to come and see her kin. Angry letters proliferated. Francis twice sent a gentleman to view the situation and tell him what was going on. Margaret of Navarre sent the bishop of Rodez from Venice to report the facts. The quarrel was the topic of conversation in all the courts of Europe. In Rome Rabelais warned that the duchess was in grave danger.

Certainly the reputation of the Estense dukes made such an expectation believable. Everyone knew of Ercole's ancient uncles, still imprisoned after years in a castle tower. Everyone recalled the tragic story of Parisina and her stepson/lover, beheaded in the castle dungeon. An Este was capable of any horror.

The duke tried to keep from arousing the king's ire, making excuses at first: his wife was too frail; the weather was too inclement; an Italian mother would never dream of leaving her newborn child. Finally he simply put his foot down and Madame de Soubise departed without the duchess in a carriage given her by Renée.

John Calvin arrived in Ferrara a few days after Madame de Soubise's departure. On 13 April, the bishop of Carpi wrote Cardinal Gonzaga: "Madame the duchess has not appeared in public since the departure of her companion, nor put foot outside her apartment where she is served by her maids of honor and where no one is permitted to see her."[2]

The gossip-loving bishop was wrong. Before that time John Calvin had been welcomed into the duchess's inner circle and had been accorded a number of private interviews with her. No one can say when he left Ferrara. He was still there on 14 April when Jeanetto walked out of the cathedral blaspheming. When and how did he leave?

III

Trial and Error

The dozen years before Calvin's arrival had witnessed a violent upheaval in Geneva, a thriving trade center since the fourteenth century. Victim of a three-cornered struggle for control by bishops, counts, and the dukes of Savoy, by the sixteenth century the canton was an island surrounded by Bern, Savoy, and France.

In 1523 the canton of Zurich adopted Zwingli's doctrine. The year following, Bern was host to a convocation of theologians to dispute Zwingli's twenty-one theses. Three years later, Bern's inclination toward Protestantism was strengthened by Guillaume Farel's arrival, and in 1528 that canton severed connections with the Roman church.

Reformed opinions could not be confined within Bern's walls. Farel, filled with missionary zeal, carried the message to Geneva, barely escaping with his life from an enraged crowd in September 1532 and again the following May. Taking advantage of the unrest in Geneva, Savoy besieged the city. Bernese troops forced Savoy's withdrawal. Geneva refused to accept Bern's sovereignty but did accept Protestantism, which Bern insisted upon as part of a treaty of alliance.

Farel and Pierre Viret (1511–71) came to Geneva to preach

the Reformed doctrines, contested by Dominicans who warned the populace against Bern and Lutherans, the two factions keeping the city in an uproar which continued for some time. In November 1533, of the four syndics elected for the coming year, three were Reformed. Since the syndics appointed the members of the Petit Council, it was evident that Geneva would eventually be Protestant.

Farel was unceasing in his denunciations of the papacy. When Ami Perrin, scion of an influential family, fired by Farel's preaching led a crowd of young men to take over the pulpit of a convent, the council condoned the act. Then when a Perrin-led mob vandalized St. Peter's (after another of Farel's sermons), the magistracy abolished the mass. Canons and nuns left the city. Franciscans and Dominicans were ordered to conform or leave.

Geneva's revolt against Savoy was more political than religious, but Bern's assistance brought in the religious element. On 26 February 1536, the magistracy (of which all four syndics and solid majorities of both the Petit Council and the Council of 200 were now Reformed) voted to "live in this holy evangel, law, and word of God, desiring to abandon all masses and images and all that may pertain thereto."

Farel was deputized to set up the social/religious organization necessary to transform a fiercely independent, pleasure-loving populace into one whose chief end was "to glorify God and enjoy Him forever." His sole assistant for this herculean task was old, half-blind Eli Courault, a former chaplain of the queen of Navarre and like Farel a refugee from French persecution.

Such was the situation when John Calvin and his party arrived in Geneva on the way to Basel on an August evening. The difficulties Farel had encountered in the five months since he had accepted his assignment had convinced him that he must have help. He was a preacher, not an administrator. He saw in Calvin—lawyer, theologian, author of *The Institutes of the Christian Religion*—God's answer to his prayer.

The threadbare story must be repeated. The shy, intense young man refused Farel's plea; he was going on to Basel to live quietly in the company of scholars, where he would study, read, and write in peace. Farel, bitter and disappointed, rose to leave. At the door he turned, "I tell you," he cried, "in answer to this excuse of your studies, in the name of Almighty God, if you will not devote yourself to the Lord's work, he will curse you as one seeking not Christ but himself!"

Years later Calvin wrote, "It was as if God had stretched forth his hand from on high to stop me."[1]

After a severe bout of sinusitis, for which he was bled four times in the ensuing month, Calvin began his work on 5 September, lecturing daily on the Pauline epistles, meanwhile beginning work on a French translation of *The Institutes* and, with Farel, drawing up a Confession of Faith. This document was submitted to the council in November. Those citizens refusing to subscribe to it were to be excommunicated. That demand was too great and made too soon. Although those who opposed swearing to the Confession were subject to banishment, the requirement could not be enforced.

Opposition to the ministers intensified in January 1537 when Calvin and Farel brought to the council their recommendations for the organization of the church of Geneva. The magistracy was not at all willing to carry out their regulations. The Lord's Supper was to be celebrated every Sabbath and not to be partaken of by those who "do not belong to Jesus." Dancing, card-playing, and gambling were forbidden. Sumptuary laws were to be enforced. Attendance at Sabbath worship was compulsory. Punishment for fornication and adultery was most severe. Education was to be compulsory for all children. Students were to memorize the catechism that Calvin was writing.

There were other suggested regulations, most of which the magistracy finally approved. The one they jibbed at was the demand that the ministerial council or consistory should have the power of excommunication. Overseers throughout the city were to report the serious faults of their neighbors to the ministers, who would then broach the sinners, urging them to repent. If that measure failed, the matter would be brought before the congregation. If the sinner remained impenitent, he or she would be expelled from the society of Christians and refused the Eucharist, though she or he might still attend sermons.

The magistracy admitted that the process was based squarely on Scripture. But the final step, they insisted, should be in the hands of the magistracy, not the church. This was the practice in Bern.

Though he had been defeated on the matter of excommunication, a battle which he would eventually win after many years, Calvin felt that progress was being made. The formal break with Rome had encouraged the Anabaptists of Geneva to come out of hiding and attempt to spread their beliefs. In March the magistracy permitted a public disputation between the Anabaptist leaders and the Reformed ministers, but so great was the agitation among the populace produced by these verbal jousts that to prevent anarchy the council declared the Anabaptists defeated and banished them.

Other opponents of the new regime were not so easily dismissed. Resistance came from three overlapping groups: the libertines (not to be confused with those persons castigated by St. Paul) who refused to accept the authority of the consistory; many devout Catholics who had no intention of relinquishing their faith; and nationalists, dismayed at seeing the church take over powers which should belong to the magistracy and seeing in the ministers an opening wedge for French conquest of the little republic.

With one accord the members of these groups blamed Farel and Calvin for all the strictures imposed on their personal freedom, although there were already sumptuary laws on the books and although in 1490 Genevans had been prohibited from gambling in taverns or on the streets during the hours of mass. Two years before Calvin's arrival the magistracy prohibited indecent dancing on the street and in February 1536 the playing at cards or dice during hours of sermons and after 9 P.M.

Each group of dissidents made use of men who attacked the reformers on doctrinal grounds. The first of these was Pierre Caroli, whose enmity disturbed Calvin soon after his arrival in Geneva. Farel had censured the man because of his loose morals, yet the Bernese magistracy had supported him and appointed him chief pastor at Lausanne. There Caroli sought to undermine the work of Pierre Viret. At a meeting of the synod of Lucerne, Calvin and Farel supported their friend, accusing Caroli of advocating prayers for the dead.

Counterattacking, Caroli accused Calvin of Arianism because Calvin had not used the Athanasian Creed nor the words "Trinity" or "Person" in the Genevan Confession of Faith. Calvin refuted that charge and others so ably that Caroli was deposed and banished.

From this first altercation to the final one with Joachim Westphal years later, Calvin refused to ignore attacks on his doctrine. Having drawn it inexorably from Scripture, he regarded an attacked on *The Institutes* as an attack on God. His readiness, his passion, in defending the "Honor of God" led to bitter and endless battles.

In spite of his defeat of Caroli, rumors spread that the reformers could not agree on doctrine and that Calvin was antitrinitarian—an epithet that could send a sixteenth century person-in-the street into apoplectic arguments as to whether Christ was of the *same* substance or of *like* substance as God.

But in Geneva in the fall of 1537, what the average citizen resented most was this hauling of folks before the consistory for dancing and playing cards in their own homes or for a little gambling. They did not want marriage feasts forbidden or neighbors snooping and informing against each other.

When in December the ministers again petitioned for the right to administer excommunication, the reply was a thundering "No!", for the newly elected syndics and their appointees to the Petit Council were overwhelmingly libertine/nationalist.[2] In January 1538 when Calvin and Farel appeared before the Council of 200 to defend six men unjustly accused of plotting with France, they were advised to content themselves with preaching the gospel and to leave politics to the magistracy.

Now many of the General Council were advocating the expulsion of *all* French refugees, including the ministers, and they announced that the Genevan ministers were to follow the order of worship devised by the church of Bern, as the magistracy of Bern had requested. At a meeting of the synod of Lucerne immediately after, Calvin declared his willingness to use unleavened bread in the Lord's Supper and to follow all other Bernese practices, even to the observance of the four ancient festivals of the Roman church, including the Feast of Circumcision, since those were what St. Paul called adiaphora, "matters of indifference." What he resented profoundly was the highhanded act of the Genevan magistracy in accepting Bern's directive without so much as consulting the Geneva ministers.

Back in Geneva, Calvin and Farel went to the hôtel de ville to voice their complaints before the council. They were refused admittance. Matters between church and state worsened.

On the Monday before Easter, the ministers were served with orders forbidding them to continue preaching until further notice. When Eli Courault ignored the order, he was imprisoned. Calvin and Farel were followed in the streets and mocked. In their public lectures they were jeered at and heckled. Nightly, shots from harquebuses were fired outside their dwellings.

On Easter St. Peter's was packed with people come to see if the ministers would defy the magistracy. Calvin preached as usual and at the close of his sermon announced that he would not profane the Lord's Supper by celebrating it in a city in a state of anarchy. A riot erupted in the cathedral, spilling out into the street. The militia was called out to restore order. On Monday Farel and Calvin were banished from Geneva.

IV

To Strasbourg and Back

Though Bern interceded for the exiles and the Synod of Zurich supported them stoutly, the Geneva magistracy was adamant: neither Calvin nor Farel might set foot again in the city. The summer passed in indecision, Farel being called to Neuchâtel in July, Calvin without plans. On 10 July 1539 he wrote Louis Du Tillet, "the Lord himself will direct us. . . . there is nothing I dread more than returning to that charge from which I have been set free."[1] Two years afterward, looking back on his Geneva experience with anger, frustration, and humiliation, he would write another friend, "After that calamity, . . . I had determined in my own mind never again to enter upon any ecclesiastical charge whatever, unless the Lord himself, by a clear and manifest call, should summon me to it."[2]

That call came through the lips of Martin Bucer (1491–1551) who, with Wolfgang Capito (1478–1541), persuaded Calvin to come to Strasbourg, securing him a post in the university early in September and soon urging him to organize a church for the growing number of French refugees. As he had with Farel, Calvin at first demurred, until Bucher accused him of trying, like Jonah, to escape the hand of God by flying from God. Again Calvin felt that hand of God directing his life.

For almost three years to the day he remained in Strasbourg, a city already called "The New Jerusalem," lecturing, writing, preaching four times weekly, corresponding with other theologians, attempting with Bucer to work out a compromise on the Lord's Supper satisfactory to all Protestantism, doing all in his power to aid those Protestants in France persecuted for the faith. Yet all the time he was passionately concerned for the well-being of the church in Geneva. Little more than a month after he was settled in Strasbourg, he wrote a long letter to his former congregation, assuring them of his remembrance and affection.[3] Banishment of Calvin and Farel had not restored peace to the city, and already Genevans were beginning to talk of his recall.

His personal life was dismal. He was racked by dysentery and constant migraines. His stipend from the university was infinitesimal, and he could ask nothing from the refugees in his church, most of whom were as poor as he. He sent his brother back to Geneva to sell his books and meager household furnishings. Antoine and his half-sister Antoinette then opened a boarding house in Calvin's lodgings.

His friends, particularly Bucer and Capito, concerned over his ill health, urged him to marry so that someone would look after him. Farel and Viret agreed with them on the necessity of finding him a wife. Several candidates were rejected on various grounds: this one could speak no French; that one was too frivolous; another had no money at all. In May 1539 Calvin wrote Farel what he was looking for: "Always keep in mind what I seek to find in her; for I am none of those insane lovers who embrace also the vices of those they are in love with, where they are smitten at first sight with a fine figure. This only is the beauty which allures me: if she is chaste; if not too nice or fastidious, if economical, if patient, if there is any hope that she will be interested about my health."[4]

He was not utterly selfish nor a chauvinist. He knew his condition and that life with him would not be easy. In June, again to Farel, he wrote that he had not yet found a wife and "frequently hesitate as to whether I ought any more to seek one."[5]

He set aside the halfhearted search in September 1539 when

he responded to the request of the Geneva magistracy to reply to a letter from Cardinal Sadoleto trying to woo Geneva back to the Catholic fold. Calvin welcomed the opportunity again to attack the Roman church in doctrine and dogma. His *Letter to Cardinal Sadoleto* was published and spread far and wide, giving his supporters further hopes for his return. It became part of the Protestant arsenal. The Catholic church had no hope of reclaiming Geneva after Calvin's letter.

By this time there was a ground swell of pleas that Calvin consider returning. Viret, and even Farel, joined the chorus. When, in January 1540, violent dissension broke out in the church at Geneva, with disorder spreading through the city, the magistracy tendered him a formal invitation to return. It was too soon; his wounds were still bleeding. But his letters at that time show his inner turmoil.

". . . rather would I submit to death a hundred times than to that cross, on which one had to perish daily a thousand times over," he wrote 29 March 1540 to Farel. "Set yourself to oppose the measures of those who shall endeavor to draw me back thither."[6] In May to Viret: "I read that passage of your letter, certainly, not without a smile where you shew so much concern about my health, and recommend Geneva on that ground. Why could you not have said at the cross? for it would have been far preferable to perish once and for all than to be tormented again in that place of torture."[7]

Farel could not desist. The work at Geneva could not go for nothing. In spite of what he and Calvin had suffered at the hands of their enemies, Calvin must return and carry on the work to which God had called him. In June Farel went to Strasbourg to argue the case, bringing Calvin a letter from his old teacher, Mathurin Cordier, begging him to reconsider.

Meanwhile Bucer had at last found a wife for his friend, and Farel came to Strasbourg in August 1540 to perform the wedding ceremony, uniting Calvin and Idelette de Bure, frail and pious widow of one Jean Stordeur, an Anabaptist from Liège, whom Calvin had converted, with Idelette, to the Reformed faith.

Within a month, the bride had the opportunity of showing

care for his health when her husband was overwhelmed by a combination of those illnesses that plagued him all his life: bronchitis, sinusitis, indigestion, drenching sweats, with frequent lapses into unconsciousness. After ten days in bed and barely on the road to recovery, he was appalled to see Idelette collapse under the strain of nursing him night and day. It was an unhappy beginning for what would be a happy, though brief, marriage. Idelette had two small daughters by her previous husband, and Antoine and his wife, as well as his half-sister Antoinette, were living with Calvin now.

In Geneva, on 15 September, the Petit Council deputized Ami Perrin to use every effort possible to persuade John Calvin to return to Geneva and impose order on the church. In October the General Council voted his recall. It was late that month when Calvin, still feverish and coughing, set out with Bucer as delegates to the Diet of Worms, missing by a few days the embassy from Geneva led by Ami Perrin. The delegation followed him to Worms to present the document, "praying earnestly that Monsieur Calvin would return to his old place and former ministry."

The four syndics chiefly instrumental in banishing the ministers were gone: two banished for corruption and immorality, two dead. In a long letter to Farel, written at Worms, Calvin described his mental and emotional state during and after his interview with Perrin, torn between repugnance and what he feared was his duty. Twice, he wrote, he had been compelled to leave the room to regain control of himself—this Calvin who has been painted as austere and unfeeling.

"While I call to mind," he continued to Farel, "by what torture my conscience was racked at that time, and with how much anxiety it was continually boiling over, . . . I dread that place as having about it somewhat of a fatality in my case." He called upon Farel to witness that no tie could have held him there other than his recognition that he could not cast off the yoke of God's calling. "Now that by the favor of God I am delivered, should I be unwilling to plunge myself once more into the gulf and whirlpool which I have already found to be so dangerous and destructive, who would not excuse me? . . . how can I have any reasonable expectation that my ministry can be of any use to them? ... And yet ... the more that I feel disposed to turn away with abhorrence ..., I am the more inclined to suspect myself."[8]

To the magistracy he could not return a definite answer. Instead he put them off, saying that he was committed to serving the church at Strasbourg, but he would consider their proposal. When he had time, he would come to Geneva and explore the situation.

Letters to his friends show his indecision, a state of mind that accentuated his migraines. "Since I waver somewhat myself ... I am utterly unable to arrive at any settled determination, except that I am prepared to follow fully the calling of the Lord, as soon as he shall have opened it up before me."[9]

Before going to Worms he had secured Nicholas Parent to fill his pulpit during his absence. If he accepted the call to Geneva, it would be necessary that Bern approve Parent as a permanent replacement. In December he wrote Parent: "I am so perplexed, or rather confused in my mind as to this call from Geneva, that I can scarce venture to think what I ought to do,—that whenever I enter upon the consideration of this subject, I can perceive no outlet by which to escape. Wherefore, so long as I am constrained by this anxiety, I am suspicious of myself, and put myself into the hands of others, to be directed by them. In the meantime, let us beseech the Lord that he point out the way to us."[10]

In February 1541 he wrote the Geneva magistracy that while the church at Strasbourg was willing to consider the dismissal, he was still not able to give a definite answer since now he must attend the diet at Ratisbon, thus serving both churches. "Seeing that I am at the disposal of God," he ended, "I am always ready to employ myself thereto in whatsoever it shall seem good to him to call me."[11]

Convinced of the futility of the coming meeting, he gave it little thought. Instead, his mind continued to circle constantly about his deferred decision, quartering like a hound on the trail, its nose to the ground. He reread Viret's letter begging him not to desert the Geneva church since only Calvin's return could end the crisis caused by his banishment.

He knew what he had to do but continued to kick against the

pricks. "Whenever I remember those days," he replied to Viret, "I can only shudder, alarmed at the idea of exposing myself again knowingly to that kind of conflict." He reminded Viret of the personal hatred he had experienced from powerful men in Geneva, of the insurmountable difficulty of hauling unruly men and women into the fold by their heels. Yet, he defended himself, he had not refused irrevocably to return. "Somehow," he seems to have been musing as he wrote, "I cannot tell how it has happened, but I am beginning to feel more inclined to take the helm again if circumstances require."[12]

On the same day he wrote to Farel: "If I had a free choice I would prefer to do anything else in the world, but I am not my own master. I offer myself to the Lord. When I have overcome my spirit and am in control of it, I shall be subject to Him alone."[13] He would drink the cup, he said, and with God's help would do what God required of him.

These letters were written in February. Still in Ratisbon in April, he received a letter from the pastors of Zurich pleading that he not refuse the call of the Lord. His long reply, written in May, gave a detailed account of the events leading up to the banishment of Farel, Courault, and himself and the refusal of the magistracy to hear their defense. Again he protested the alarm he felt at the thought of taking up this burden again.[14]

Plague was rife in Strasbourg that spring, and his family fled the city. He did not return until July. By August he had made up his mind. To Farel he wrote: ". . . as to my intended course of action, this is my feeling at present: had I the choice, nothing would be less agreeable to me than to follow your advice; but when I remember that I am not my own man, I offer up my heart as a sacrifice to the Lord. . . . It is God with whom I have to do . . . therefore I submit my will and affection, subdued and held fast, to His obedience."[15] He would go back, but with tears of foreboding and anxiety of heart.

On 16 September he wrote Farel from Geneva: "I am settled here. May God overrule it for good."[16]

The magistracy paid to bring his family and a few bits of furniture from Strasbourg; gave him a dwelling, a bolt of black velvet for clothing, a tun of wine, a promise of twelve measures of grain, a salary of 500 florins, and—most important— assurance of complete support in enforcing ecclesiastical ordinances "as prescribed to us in the Word of God and as was in use in the ancient church."[17]

His work was cut out for him. There were church ordinances to revise and work up, conferences to be held with the magistracy, ministers to be secured and some to be dismissed, defense of Farel to be undertaken in Neuchâtel. His household had to be set up. He wrote to Bucer in mid-October, "You cannot imagine in what state of frenzied confusion I am living, with constant interruptions. . . . I am entangled in so many affairs that I am almost beside myself!"[18]

In the midst of all the chaos, he sat down to write a letter to the duchess of Ferrara. He was not interested in her as a woman: he was concerned with her immortal soul.

PART TWO

The Tow Is Ignited

V

Ferrara
1536–41

After such long-sustained conjugal conflict within the space of a single year, one reads with amazement a note from the Ferrarese envoy dated 10 August, soon after the remaining prisoners had been handed over to the French ambassador, saying that the pregnancy of the duchess could not have come at a better time. The duke's announcement seems to have been a bit premature since Leonora (1537–81) was born in June 1537. Whatever the date of reconciliation, if such it was, Ercole seems to have been following the advice of Cardinal Trivulce, who saw in the long-continued strife only a domestic quarrel which the duke could solve by "spending a night with his wife."

Nevertheless, Ercole continued to mistrust Renée, refusing again in the fall to permit her to go to France, this time for the wedding of her niece Madeleine and James V of Scotland. Although he had rid her court of some dangerous persons, there were others he could not touch without just cause, particularly Anne de Parthenay, Madame de Soubise's daughter, and her husband, Antoine de Pons, whom the duchess had made her confidants and constant companions.

To counteract the poison she seemed to have imbibed, the duke invited Vittoria Colonna (1490–1547), marchesa di Pes-

cara, to Ferrara to be company for his wife during her confinement. The marchesa was the epitome of learning and piety. He
could not have chosen a better—or worse—companion.

Vittoria Colonna, twenty years older than Renée, had at 17
married Ferdinando Davalos, Marquis of Pescara, to whom she
had been betrothed since infancy. Though she rarely saw him
after their first two years of marriage (since he was one of the
emperor's generals), after he died of wounds received at Pavia,
she devoted herself to writing sonnets in his praise, performing
works of piety, going on pilgrimages, becoming intimate with
cardinals, writers, and artists. By now she had become a legend, a
model of piety and conjugal constancy. What better person could
be found to lead the duchess back into the right path?

Ercole was not aware that the marchesa had been for more
than a year part of the company clustered about Juan de Valdés
in Naples. Writers, churchmen, nobility—they were a select
group, profoundly influenced by this man, wholly Lutheran in his
beliefs but still hoping for reformation of the church from within.
Cardinals Gasparo Contarini and Pietro Carnesecchi (both of
whom would be victims of the Inquisition); Peter Martyr (Ver-
migli), Bernardino Ochino, Galeazzo Caracciolo (all of whom
would flee to Geneva); Marcantonio Flaminio, deeply religious
poet who would refuse to act as secretary at the Council of Trent
and who, like Vittoria Colonna herself, would later be claimed by
Protestants and Catholics alike—these were only a few of the
disciples of Juan de Valdés.

Pietro Giannone, who spent twenty years writing his *Istoria
civile del regno di Napoli*, said:

> In Naples not only had the poison penetrated the breasts of some of
> the nobility, it had reached the ladies, and it was believed that the
> highly celebrated Vittoria Colonna and Giulia Gonzaga (judging
> from the intimate terms on which they lived with Valdéz), had
> become contaminated with these errors.[1]

Private meetings, Giannone went on to say, took place in the
Colonna and Gonzaga palaces.

The emperor, in Naples at that time, disturbed by the spread
of ultramontane beliefs, issued an edict threatening loss of life

and property to anyone consorting with persons infected with the German heresy. Yet he understood so little of what the "German heresy" was that Peter Martyr, long-time student of Bucer's commentaries on the Scriptures, lectured openly to bishops and nobility on Paul's epistles, and John Mollio preached the Reformed beliefs in the church of San Lorenzo.

Most remarkable was the acclaim, one might say veneration, accorded the Franciscan-turned-Capuchin monk Bernardino Ochino (1487–1564), who preached—again we have Giannone's report—in an entirely new way, referring to the authority of the Scriptures, leading his hearers to consult the Bible for themselves on such disputed points as justification by faith, monks, images, even the papacy itself, and all so eloquently that churches could not contain the crowds that pressed to hear him. The emperor himself heard Ochino's Lenten sermons in San Giovanni and said, "This man preaches with a spirit and devotion to make the very stones weep."

In Ferrara the next year, the marchesa was given her own palazzo, where the litterati and members of the hierarchy from northern Italy came to converse and admire, and where she continued writing her *Rime Spirituale*, for now she had turned from the theme of earthly to heavenly love.

What would one expect these two women to talk about during the countless hours they spent together? Vittoria arrived in May 1537. She served as godmother for Leonora, born in June. She left Ferrara in February 1538. The two took their meals together, listened to music, applauded the dancing of little Anne, heard sermons—and talked. Alike in their deep desire to see the church reformed, they differed in that the poet's religion was mystic and otherworldly, while that of Renée was theological and practical.

So flattered was the duke that the marchesa was honoring his wife with her friendship that in July he was easily persuaded to become, like her, a patron of the noted preacher all Italy was flocking to hear. He invited Ochino to come and preach in the cathedral, gave him a house in the suburbs as a convent for his disciples, invited him to come later to preach the Advent sermons, and was overjoyed that his wife spent hours in conversation with the holy man.

Immediately after the marchesa's departure, Ercole's aunt, Isabella, the dowager duchess of Mantua, came for a visit. She had welcomed Renée as a bride to Ferrara ten years before, and a warm friendship had developed between the two through correspondence. Balls, theatrical performances, banquets and horseback riding followed in quick succession. The duke was so pleased with Renée that he broke off his affair with the Countess Calcagnini (temporarily) and made his wife pregnant again. The couple seemed completely reconciled. Yet when his aunt asked that Renée be permitted to visit Mantua, he refused to let her go. Renée swallowed her disappointment. She was not entirely alone: always she had her beloved Anne de Parthenay and Antoine de Pons, especially the latter—handsome, charming, deferential, considered by her court and by herself as her "servant-knight."

On Christmas day she gave birth to her last child, Luigi (1538–86). Paul III agreed to be godfather and sent Cardinal del Monte in his place to hold Luigi at the baptismal font the following April. Although Renée wrote a note thanking the pope for so honoring her and her husband, signing herself his very devoted daughter (since she was courteous and a politician), she took little interest in the christening, for the duke, hoping to repair his fences, had decided to send Pons to Paris.

Francis I had shown his displeasure at the duke's tying himself more closely to emperor and pope, both enemies of France. When the king ordered Pons home for a new honor, Ercole seized the opportunity to have the young French lord try to convince His Majesty of the duke's continued devotion. The duchess made no attempt to conceal her dissatisfaction at her servant-knight's departure.

Was the "mission" a ploy of Ercole's to separate Pons and Renée? The duke wrote his ambassador in Paris to keep Pons there as long as possible. One of Montmorency's secretaries met Pons in Lyon, sent Renée's letters (in which she begged His

Majesty to treat her "cousin" as he would treat her) on to Paris by special courier, since, he wrote, they concerned the good of the kingdom. He added that the Italian relatives of the duchess wanted nothing in the world so much than to separate her from Monsieur de Pons, "from whom she receives an infinite number of services."[2]

The duke must have been aware of the intimacy of Renée and her servitor before he intercepted their letters. Was their relationship more than platonic? Probably not. Even though the king's mother had promoted the "gallantry" of her daughter's would-be lovers, Margaret had refused to tarnish her reputation, and early on, Margaret had been Renée's role-model. For one as conscious of her rank as Renée, to have stooped so would have been unthinkable, but she certainly enjoyed and encouraged his open attachment.

It would not have taken an overt act to arouse the half-Este/half-Borgia duke to the enormity of the insult to him and to his house. He could not afford the scandal of sending his wife back to France. Instead, he sent Pons until he could make plans. So, for eighteen months, Renée wrote to her friends begging them to do whatever was necessary to expedite her "cousin's" mission, ending her letters (as that to Monsieur de Roches): "You know how this touches me and that his return is necessary to the king's service and to my own."[3]

The duke intercepted most of her letters, filed copies of the ones he sent on. Twice papers in the ducal archives were destroyed, but one long letter and fragments of others remain. The twelve-page one is not what one would expect from a duchess writing to her servitor and must have shocked her husband. It gives a graphic picture of Renée at this time. Because of its prolixity and almost complete absence of punctuation, it is summarized and excerpted here:[4]

The day after the accouchement of my cousin [Madame de Pons], the Basque arrived, who I promise will bring you a great joy, seeing that our Lord has arranged things so happily for you and will do so still more in the future. It is all the more necessary for us to humble ourselves and pray for pardon and grace that the loving face of the gracious Father, which he has ever shown you may never turn toward you in wrath, which I pray may never be and that you may continue in his grace. . . .

I am sure that he is with you and will guard you, for which care I cannot sufficiently praise him. We have pitied you, my child, your "sister" and I, considering the troubles you have had to undergo. Before we received your letters, we often said that you pass over your troubles lightly. [She then warns him about talking too much to the Constable, Montmorency, and advises him to ask advice of Ippolito, the duke's brother.]

If this letter is badly written, it is because I am writing it in bed, and it is early morning. I began it before I could hardly see and will continue it a little at a time until the Basque leaves. I began it yesterday morning before his arrival. Your little dog came to give me a thousand caresses between the covers and took the pen from my hand with his little mouth and came to lie down on my arm with the pen under his head, and he slept, and I also to keep him company. I don't know which of us had more need of it. He raised his head to look at me and then went back to sleep—it was too early for him.

[She goes on to tell of a practical joke played on a "monsieur of Montpellier" who had come to see the duke; of sickness in the city; his wife had been sick but was now recovered and his baby was well. She describes the little boy, his mouth and chin like his father's, a sweet face, everyone enjoyed looking at him, precious as a little puppy, one had to kiss him. The cardinal of Ferrara and the constable would be his godfathers. The bishop of Avranches would serve as the constable's proxy.] He is a good person. I believe that what he says comes from his heart. [She had gone with the bishop to the mountain, where] Monsieur the duke was supping with La Noyant [the Countess Calcagnini].

[The day after the Pons's baby was born, she had had supper with the cardinal of Ravenna and her husband, and the next day a picnic in the woods with Ercole and the bishop. Another time she had dined with Ercole and the cardinal of Ravenna in the city, and had gone to visit her father-in-law's old mistress, Laura Dianti.] That is all the air I have had since you left, but I attend your "sister" when she gets up, and we go on to take the air together and wish that you were with us. I have received no letter from you other than through the muleteer and the Basque.

[The child was baptized in the chapel before dinner and then brought to her chamber, where his mother, the bishop, Renée, and her children dined. The bishop had inquired about her "ally" in

France, and she had replied very discreetly. He said it felt like her court was empty now that Pons was no longer there.] He is not the only one who says so. [Again she begs him to return as soon as possible.] The Basque will tell you all about our little company, of the health of your "sister" and of the little dogs that always sleep with me and don't want to leave me. I have them brushed and defleaed every morning and night. . . .

I assure you we need you to come home to give joy to our little company. Your wife is accustomed to having you with her always, and since your leaving she has a stomachache. She has no fever and always gets up in the morning, but Brasavola [a physician] says it is caused by a melancholic humor. So far, thank God, it seems to be nothing serious, but if you should remain very long in France, it would be very bad for her, the doctors think. [Again she begs him to return soon], as much for your wife's sake as for my own. [But he must not consider her ennui if his affairs are going well, for which she prays daily to God and also for his health. All the children have had fever except his little boy who is never sick and so heavy he tires his nurse's arms; already he raises his little head from his pillow, and he nurses well.

Her little girl, Leonora, is the prettiest of all her children, and always so happy. Anne, now eight, takes care of the younger ones always. She sleeps in Madame de Pons's chamber. Renée had put her other children in the chamber of the duke's secretary, because the ceiling in the large room was about to fall.

She and Madame de Pons may go to Saboncello, a village on the Po, a few miles from the city,] but Monsieur does not want me to go yet; I know he does not intend for me to go at all. He does not care that the doctors say I need a change of air. I have an opilation [?] and often a migraine prostrates me.

[There is a paragraph in code here, followed by the cryptic admonition] I pray you, my child, to come back as soon as possible and do not forget to bring with you the little god of love. I read what you say about the death of poor Cornillau, for which I am very sorry. I am giving his office to Lyon Jamet for love of you. . . .

Your good and faithful cousin, Renée of France.

On her arrival in Ferrara, Renée had set up a private courier service, securing the help of officials in Bologna and other towns on the route to France and employing faithful servitors to carry her letters. Now the duke, grown suspicious, watched her more closely. In one of her letters she warned Pons that the duke had asked her if she had any letters to send to France and she had assured him she had none. She added that there was no one she could trust. Certainly not her husband, for he intercepted this letter and many of Pons's replies until she finally realized why she received so few letters from her servant-knight.

But Pons could not be kept in Paris indefinitely. As he was the king's not-so-secret agent, the duke could not banish him without sufficient reason. Wounded pride, though painful, was not reason enough. It was necessary to put into operation his plan of action. On 8 July he signed an "Act of Donation made by Don Ercole d'Este, Duke of Ferrara, to Madame Renée his wife, of the house and palazzo of Consandolo, in the duchy of Ferrara, as much because of the sacred tie which unites them as testimony of their mutual love and of the perfect harmony which reigns between them."[5]

When Antoine de Pons reached Ferrara in September, Renée's court celebrated joyously for ten days; after which, without warning, the duchess was ordered to retire to Consandolo, fifteen miles from the city, gift of her husband to demonstrate their perfect harmony.

VI

The First Letter

The duke had removed his wife from her cavalier and from some of those critics of the church who had infested her court, but he had not erased their influence and seemed unaware that some committed Lutherans remained with her: her physician, Johann Sinapius, whose marriage had been arranged with Françoise Boussiron, one of Renée's ladies of honor, through correspondence by Calvin, whom the young couple had taken as spiritual adviser; Chilian Sinapius, teacher of Greek to the Princess Anne; Perigrino Morato, in whose house in Ferrara Lutherans gathered for theological conversation, and whose daughter, the erudite Olympia, had just been brought to court as tutor-companion for Anne; Anne de Parthenay, Madame de Pons, true daughter of Madame de Soubise, who followed her mother's Protestant predilections. And there was the new almoner brought to his wife by the duke, a devoutly religious man with whom Renée held long conversations after learning he had been in Paris an intimate friend of Calvin. This François Richardot had already convinced the duke that he was profoundly attached to Holy Mother Church.

Renée found at Consandolo opportunity for study and meditation, ordering books from the Aldine press in Venice and buying religious tracts from itinerant peddlers. She lamented that she had no opportunity to serve her king, but her isolation made easier her sending and receiving letters.

She had been at Consandolo only a few weeks when a letter was brought her by a stranger, the first letter she received from John Calvin:[1]

Madame,

I humbly beg you to take in good part my boldness in writing you. If you consider me too outspoken, I assure you that I am not actuated by presumption or conceit but only by concern for your service in our Lord.

Although I acknowledge myself an unprofitable servant of the church, nevertheless I am employed in that capacity according to the grace the Lord has bestowed upon me. Therefore I have felt it incumbent upon me to write to you, if I would do my duty, not merely because I feel myself obliged to seek your welfare as far as I am able (though that alone would be enough to motivate me) in consideration of the eminent position you occupy. It seems to us whom the Lord has called to be ministers that we should keep you in special remembrance and do all in our power to help you, because you, more than most princely persons, are in a position to advance the kingdom of Christ.

Besides this, I observed in you such fear of God and disposition to faithful obedience, that regardless of your high rank I would think myself accursed if I left undone any profitable service presented me. I say this without intending any flattery but with a sincere heart, speaking as in the presence of the One who knows our secret thoughts.

Madame, in conversation with certain persons who have passed through this city, I have been given to understand that one Master François [Richardot] whom you have appointed preacher to your household, after having acquitted himself well in preaching--at least as well as could be expected of him—has persuaded you that it would not be a bad thing if you, after having heard mass, would partake of some sort of communion or Lord's Supper.

I was told that one of your ladies, because of the knowledge she has received of God, did not wish against her conscience to engage in a practice she considers wrong in itself; and for her stand Master François has turned you against her who was formerly one of your favorites; that the disagreement has reached such a point that you have intimated that those who support her are creating a scandalous dissension among the faithful. Considering this of such importance that it should not be glossed over and seeing that you have been told [by Richardot] that things are quite different from what the Lord has revealed to me through the Scripture, I think it my duty to set you straight.

While I was deliberating about what I should do, I was told by Madame de Pons that you very much wish to be more fully instructed, seeing the many quandaries in which you find yourself. Her message confirmed my belief that I should try to give you a faithful exposition so that you may judge of these matters for yourself, and when you have fully understood God's truth, to follow it in all obedience, since your zeal is not such that rebels against it but receives the truth in love.

Nevertheless, Madame, before I begin my exposition, I beseech you not to be suspicious of me as though I were put up to this by anyone in your household or to favor some particular person. As God is my witness, I do this of my own accord, not having been requested by anyone to write to you. I am writing only because the facts of your ambiguous situation were reported by certain persons who had no idea that I might be able to communicate with you. . . .

To be perfectly frank, concerning Master François, I must warn you not to give yourself too unreservedly to his teachings. If I do so, I do not need to be afraid that you will entertain a bad opinion of me, as though I were speaking from envy or hatred of this person. I have no reason or occasion to envy him; and the hatred I have felt for him up to the present is such that I have, to the best of my ability, tried to guide him into well-doing.

But when I see someone with an ill-formed conscience setting himself to subvert the word of God and extinguish the light of truth, I cannot pardon him, not even if he were my very own father. As for this individual, I have been aware, from long acquaintance with him, that whatever small understanding of Scripture God has given him, he has always made use of it to his own profit and ambition, preaching whatever he saw would be helpful to his avarice, and forbearing to preach if it began to be troublesome to him. Not only so, but wherever he could procure worthy persons to sponsor him and the wealthy to fill his purse who required him to glorify God, he has worked to satisfy them by selling them his words.

But whenever he has met with trouble or persecution, he has ready a denial to escape from it, to such a degree that one cannot know whether or not he is making the sacred word of God a sport and a mockery. He has turned his ministry into a farce, playing one role at one time, its opposite at another, according as the occasion demands.

I say nothing about his personal life except that I could wish it better in a minister of God's word. I know, Madame, that a Christian should not defame his neighbor. I do not wish to do so, because if I wanted to speak ill of him, I could say much. But our Lord does not mean that when we see a wolf in a shepherd's disguise scattering the flock, we should remain silent for fear of speaking ill of him. Instead, God commands us to reveal the perversity of those who, like the pox, corrupt by their infection and mar the face of the church.

I would not have used that method here [Geneva] if I had had any better remedy, considering the mortal fury of that kind of people which I provoke against myself. I have today no warfare so fierce as with those who, under pretense of preaching the gospel, wear a rough garment outwardly toward princes, amazing and entertaining them by fine subtlety, enshrouded as it were in some cloud, without ever leading them to the right end.

But how could I have acted otherwise? If I do not confront them, it is because I see their hearts so divested of all fear of God, that when I warn them of divine judgment, that is no more than a fable or an amusing tale to them. But when I tell them plainly what they are, to convince them that they can carry their abuse no further, I find them more restrained.

This person [Richardot] I have often attempted to bring back into the right path, even to make him confess his iniquity. However, he excused himself impudently before people, though convicted in his own conscience before God. Nevertheless, with a terrible obstinacy and hardness of heart, he persisted in declaring that he could not desist from doing what he knew to be wrong. Though one time, after having read a treatise of mine, with grievous imprecations on himself, he protested that he would never again attend mass because it was such a gross abomination. But I know my man so well that I pay no more attention to his oath than to the chattering of a magpie. . . .

Now, Madame, having done with this person, I come to the crux of the matter. He has given you to understand that the mass is neither so wicked nor abominable, but that it is permissible for him to perform it and for the faithful to hear it, so that those who make this a matter of conscience are the disturbers of the church, stirring up scandals among the weak, whom we are commanded to strengthen.

As regards the first part, I doubt that I should belabor it. I suppose you are already convinced that the mass is the most execrable sacrilege imaginable. I am afraid I would appear ridiculous in taking the time and trouble to prove what you can have no doubt about. Although a letter cannot include matter sufficient for a large book, nevertheless I shall touch briefly on it to make sure that you have no uncertainty. Insofar as the mass is a sacrifice instituted by men for the redemption and salvation of the living and the dead, as the Roman canon states, it is an unbearable blasphemy by which the passion of Jesus Christ is completely obliterated, as if it were of no effect whatever.

In reply to that, we say that the faithful have been purchased by the blood of Jesus, have obtained thereby the remission of their sins, been accounted righteous, and have the hope of eternal life. This belief, therefore, implies that the blessed Savior has offered himself to the Father as an eternal sacrifice by which our iniquities have been purged and cleansed, and we have been received into the grace of the Father and made partakers of the heavenly inheritance, as the Apostle shows fully in the Epistle to the Hebrews.

If, then, the death of Jesus be not acknowledged as the *only* sacrifice, made once for all in order to have an eternal efficacy, what remains but to efface it completely as being altogether ineffectual?

I am well aware that these liars, to cover their abomination, say that they are making the same sacrifice Jesus made, but from that statement arise several blasphemies. That sacrifice could be made by none but Jesus Christ himself. The Apostle says that if he is now sacrificed, it follows that he must suffer still. Therefore, one of two things must take place here: either to acknowledge that the mass is a horrible blasphemy and detest it as such; or by approving it, to trample underfoot the cross of Jesus. How much it is contrary to the Supper of Christ, I leave you to decide for yourself after you have read in the Scripture the words of institution. But their crowning desecration is their idolatry of adoring a creature instead of God. . . .

We can neither perform nor witness such rites without grievously offending God by communicating in such abominations. How can we pretend we are not justly reproved for having countenanced such iniquities when we receive them with greater honor and reverence than we do the word of God? If you want to know how that pleases the Lord God, read what God says by the prophet Ezekiel in the twentieth chapter, where God tells the people of Israel that they love to practice open idolatry like the Gentiles, including God's name with the names of their idols, as wishing to compass their own ends contrary to God's statutes by which God was to be worshipped, and by setting up their own foolish inventions by which they were made to fall away from God's word.

On the other hand, the prophet tells them that the Lord will scatter all those who swear by God's name, avowing him their God while at the same time they witness against themselves by adoring other gods.

Should someone object that externals in religion are matters of indifference, that the only requisite is that the heart be upright, our Lord replies that he will be glorified in our bodies, bought by his blood; that he requires us to confess with our lips; that all our prayers should be consecrated to his name, uncontaminated and undefiled by anything displeasing to him.

Because this subject cannot be adequately treated in a letter, for your fuller understanding I am sending you a treatise in which you will find reasons enough to satisfy your thirst for knowledge.

The scandal still remains, which your almoner says troubles the consciences of the weak, when someone considered a believer holds the mass in such horror that he would not come in contact with it in any way. [Richardot] does not consider that in reference to those things which are either commanded by God or forbidden, although we might offend the whole world, we must not go beyond God's ordinances.

That which is commanded us—to support and strengthen our weak brethren by doing nothing which may wound or offend them— refers to lesser things of no great importance which are of themselves indifferent and permitted in Christian liberty. . . . All those commands about not scandalizing our neighbor tend to his edification in well-doing, as St. Paul points out in Romans 15. It follows that we must not seek to please our neighbor in those things which do not tend to edification but to his destruction.

Thence we have St. Paul's doctrine in First Corinthians 8 and 10, where he says that if by any action of ours our neighbor is encouraged in his wrongdoing, though there were no violations of conscience on our part, we destroy our brother and sin against God. As is here the case: we know the mass to be accursed and execrable; we attend it to content the ignorant; those who see us participating conclude that we approve of doing so, and they follow our example. St. Paul counts that a great crime. . . .

Wherefore, Madame, I do beseech you not to permit that under the fear of "scandal" anyone should beguile you. There is no more pernicious scandal in this world than when a Christian brother or sister by our example is driven forward into error and entrapped in ruin. If we would avoid all scandal, then we must cast behind us Jesus Christ, the stone of offense over which most of the world stumbles. Even so, he was a scandal to the Jews to whom he was sent, as in the past a great part of that nation was offended and stumbled in the worship of their God.

We must hold fast by this rule: that in reference to things either commanded or forbidden by God, it is chiefly required that, in the doing or forbearing, he may not be defrauded of the obedience due him though we should offend the whole world. Since Christ and his gospel are a scandal to the evil-disposed and malignant, we must expect that if we follow him, *they* will always be a scandal to us.

As for things which are free and indifferent, . . . that we can either do or omit, we should suit ourselves to the convenience of our Christian brothers and sisters so that our liberty may be subject to choice. Even in doing so, we must support their weakness so that they may be built up in God, for if we lead them on by our example, drawing them into what they consider wrong, we are the means of their destruction.

Few of those who have experienced the truth of God do not know the iniquity of the mass. Convinced of the kind of thing it is, it is impossible for them not to want to flee from it. While some have scruples and doubts about it, when they see that we communicate, they follow our example without caring to have their doubts resolved. This is the worst scandal that can happen to them: their consciences are killed.

If what I hear is true, [Richardot] would have you believe that the mass is of such small importance that German churches make no question about it; that is, that those of one persuasion let the others alone and permit them to celebrate the mass. By saying this he inflicts grievous injury to the churches of God by charging them with a practice which you will acknowledge to be false when you inquire for yourself.

Not only among all the churches which have received the gospel, but among private individuals as well, it is agreed that the abomination of the mass must not continue. To that effect Capito, one of those who attempt to moderate the zeal of others in this matter, has recently written a book dedicated to the king of England, in which he affirms that it is the duty of Christian princes to abolish such execrable idolatry in their countries. In short, there is no person of any renown who does not agree on this point.

Well then, Madame, since God has been pleased by his goodness and infinite compassion to visit you with the knowledge of his name and to enlighten you to the truth of the holy gospel, acknowledge the calling to which God has called you. For God has drawn us out of the abyss of darkness where we were captives in order that we might follow the light of God's word without swerving from one side to the other, seeking evermore to be instructed by him so that we may profit more abundantly in that holy wisdom wherein God has made a beginning in us. Above all, we must take care not to hinder the Spirit as do those who shut their ears and eyes to the simple truth, content to remain ignorant of what the Lord would have them comprehend.

Nor would the Lord have us do so out of dread that God would punish our contemptuous ingratitude, but that we should study to profit continually in the school of this Good Master until we shall have gained perfection in doctrine, free from the weight of this earthly coil of flesh, praying with David that God would instruct us in the doing of his will.

Surely if we go forward therein with zealous affection, God will guide us so that we will not stray from the narrow way. And although we are still ignorant in many respects, God will vouchsafe complete revelation as there is need for it, knowing the appropriate season better than we.

The main point is to understand how holy doctrine should bring forth fruit in us; that is, when it so transforms us by the renewal of our minds and hearts that God's radiant glory of innocence, integrity, and holiness illumines our souls. If it be not thus with us, we take the name of God in vain by glorifying ourselves, boasting that we know the gospel. I do not intend to admonish you to do what you do not do now, but so that the work of God, already begun in you, may be confirmed from day to day.

. . . I beg you to pardon my simplicity. Should it be your pleasure to have fuller instructions on this subject, and especially on how a person should govern himself in regard to scandals, I shall attempt with the Lord's help to satisfy you. Meanwhile I am sending you a letter which you may desire to spend some time on, and also a small tract which I put together recently. I hope it may serve as a help. . . .

May the Lord care for you in this your infirmity; may God manifest in you the efficacy of the Spirit in such a way that you may be as much honored in his household as God has elevated you in station and dignity among people.

Charles d'Espeville

VII

Geneva
1541–54

Calvin, like the prophets before him, had returned unwill-
ingly to shoulder the load which he was persuaded the Lord
had laid upon him. Determined to force stiff-necked people into
living out the kingdom of God, he set about recodifying Geneva's
constitution and laws dealing with every facet of life, which the
populace must take oath to uphold.

His duties as chief minister were onerous: daily preaching on
alternate weeks, lectures three times a week, reading the Scriptures weekly at public meeting, presiding at weekly meetings of
the consistory, advising the magistrates on legal matters. Late at
night he worked on his commentaries, tracts, and numerous letters, often while he was suffering from indigestion, sinusitis, and
migraines. He had little time for personal affairs. The year after
his return to Geneva, his only child was born prematurely, a little
boy who lived less than four months.

The years from 1541 to 1555 have been called Calvin's "years
of struggle." He fought with the magistracies of Geneva and Bern
and with the libertines of Geneva—those citizens who had engineered his banishment and who welded the discontented into a
political party. His bitterest fights were with violent men who
refused to accept the doctrines which Calvin, with remorseless
logic, had drawn from his understanding of Holy Scripture.

His first theological bout was with Albert Pighius (c.1490–1542) on free will, which ended with Pighius's embracing Calvin's views—his only doctrinal dispute with a happy ending.

His next opponent was Sebastian Castellio (1515–63), a distinguished scholar whom Calvin had appointed rector of the academy. Their antagonism began when Castellio publicly and caustically criticized the ministers of the church. It worsened when Calvin refused to approve for publication Castellio's French translation of the Bible because of its poor grammar and because Olivétan's translation was superior. When the seigneury (magistrates) suggested that Calvin correct the manuscript, he refused to waste his time.

Later he refused to appoint the man to the ministry because Castellio doubted the doctrine of election, doubted that Christ had actually descended into hell, and doubted that the Holy Spirit had anything to do with the "obscene and lascivious" Oriental love song called the Song of Solomon. The hostility between the two men continued throughout Calvin's life.

Did the duchess of Ferrara answer that first letter of Calvin's? In one of his letters to Viret there is a reference to a lost letter from her. Her letters to Pons were not the only ones intercepted by her husband. At any rate, Calvin was kept informed of events in Italy.

When Paul III set up the Roman Inquisition in 1542, Ochino was cited to appear at Rome for preaching justification by faith at Naples and Venice. Renée enabled him to escape from Italy, and Calvin welcomed him to Geneva, appointing him minister of the Italian church and supporting him warmly against doctrinal adversaries—until much later.

Ochino was soon followed by another of the duchess's protégés—Celio Curione, noted theologian who had preached in Ferrara and many other Italian cities. He too was indebted to Renée for his escape from the Inquisition. He too was welcomed but ten years later aroused Calvin's undying enmity.

When the plague came to Geneva in 1542, 1543, and 1544, Calvin was instrumental in setting up a plague hospital in which two ministers who had volunteered for service died. The seigneury refused Calvin permission to work in the pesthouse, saying his life was too important to the republic to be risked. Others thought differently: a Dominican from Savoy came preaching that the plague was the result of the devil's reign in Geneva, and the devil was Calvin.

With each outbreak, the plague was more virulent, until in 1545 the seigneury announced that it was spread by evil persons who had smeared doorknobs with poisonous ointment. The guilty ones were discovered. Fifteen women were burned and "some men [implicated in the plot] were punished still more severely; . . . and twenty-five others imprisoned."[1] After that the plague subsided.

Calvin found great difficulty in procuring ministers of probity for the church. There was much wrangling among the incumbents, and the reputation of the church suffered by the misdoings of two in particular, both of whom were habitués of taverns. In May 1544 Calvin deposed one for flagrant homosexual activity and the other for "irregularities." Sebastian Castellio served as a constant gadfly.

Throughout his life as a minister, Calvin was deeply involved in two concerns: to bring all the Protestant churches together on the subject of the Lord's Supper and to bring an end to the persecutions of Protestants in every land. He was not successful in either, but his multitudinous letters on these two subjects attest to the passion he felt for them.

Clément Marot arrived in the city in the spring of 1543, again a fugitive, and set to work translating the Psalms. Calvin encouraged him, writing an introduction to Marot's book, which was published in the fall. Two of his own tracts were completed and published that year—"On Superstitions" and "On Nicodemites"—while he was busy examining men to be dispatched to churches in France begging for ministers. By now Geneva had become a seminary, drawing theological students from Italy and France.

On 13 February 1546 Calvin wrote a curious letter to "Monsieur Jean Frellon, Merchant Bookseller living at Lyon on the Rue Mercière" in regard to an unnamed Spanish physician living in the nearby town of Vienne—Michael Servetus (1511–53).[2]

That same day he wrote to Farel: ". . . Servetus has lately written to me and has added a long volume of his delirious fancies. . . . If it be agreeable to me, he will undertake to come here. But I will not give him my assurance of his safety, for if he comes, provided that my authority is of any avail, I shall not suffer him to depart alive."[3] Toledo had already condemned Servetus for several of his earlier books, and the Sorbonne for another. Antitrinitarians were heretics everywhere and merited a heretic's end. Calvin added, to Farel, that he would try once more to bring Servetus back to the truth but would do nothing about the man's book. Instead, he filed all the correspondence away and ignored the Spaniard's repeated requests for the return of his manuscript.

That spring Calvin had more pressing matters to attend to than the return of a blasphemous book by a crackpot author. Idelette was now a semi-invalid, and his own health so poor that the seigneury supplied him with a full-time attendant, an ill-favored humpback with a mind for figures, who gradually relieved him of the financial burdens of running a household.

He was still barely convalescent in July when he rushed to the public square in order to quell a riot caused when his friend Michel Cop attempted to put a stop to a morality play being performed by strolling players before an entertainment-starved audience. Calvin himself saw no reason to prohibit the play—it had been approved by the seigneury—but to calm the tumult he supported Cop, with the result that the populace saw him as the disciplinarian denying them a show.[4]

By now the three groups opposed to Calvin were coalescing into one, women as well as men becoming more violent in their rejection of church discipline. They accepted, though grudgingly, laws against drunkenness, profanity, and debauchery, but playing at cards or dancing in one's own home? No holidays except Sundays? Requiring names of infants to be only those found in the Bible? Children imprisoned—and worse—for lying? And as for beheading that little girl who struck her mother—such dreadful things were not to be borne.[5]

At a private dinner party given by a Monsieur Cortelier, the host cursed Calvin roundly. An informer notified Calvin, and the seigneury sentenced Cortelier to six months in prison. Opposition now centered in Ami Perrin, his in-laws the Favre family, and their relations, the Bertheliers and the Vandels. François Favre was a 60-year-old roué, equalled only by his son Gaspard.

In December 1545 Gaspard had been called before the consistory for adultery; the seigneury sentenced him to prison. He was released six months later, in time to play skittles on Easter Sunday. Again haled before Calvin, he refused to answer any questions, finally snarling, "Yes, I know you are above everyone!" A little later he was reported as inciting a group of young men-about-town to play raucous games outside the church where Calvin was lecturing.

Calvin had two names for Gaspard Favre's sister Françoise, Ami Perrin's wife: "Queen of the Amazons" and "The She-Devil." In March 1546 at a wedding celebration in the Perrin home, some of the guests danced. The matter reported, Perrin, now captain of the militia, refused to appear before the consistory, though a guest, Abélard Corne, minister as well as a syndic, admitted his guilt. Both were imprisoned. Madame Perrin, brought almost forcibly before the consistory, called minister Abel Pouppin a "Great Pot-Belly," threatened Calvin, and screamed that the consistory had no jurisdiction over the private lives of the citizenry. Cited to appear before the council, she was imprisoned but bribed the jailer and escaped to her father's estate outside the city walls. At about the same time, her father, summoned for having immoral relations with several women, fled and joined his daughter.

When, the following spring, Ami Perrin, who had served his prison sentence and was now captain of the archers, asked permission from the seigneury for his archers to wear slashed breeches at an approaching festival, permission was granted though Geneva had banned this worldly fashion some years before (as had Zurich, Augsburg, and Bern) and Calvin had incorporated the prohibition into the new laws. Now Calvin protested the council's decision, asking why a one-time exception should be made if slashed breeches were a work of the devil? The council revoked its decision, and Calvin was, of course, blamed.

Shortly after this, Perrin was delegated to head an embassy sent to pay respects from the seigneury to the new French king, Henry II. On his return, Perrin brought his wife and father-in-law back to Geneva, where they were immediately called before the consistory. Asked, for the record, if he had not been imprisoned before for lewd conduct, Favre replied that he had nothing to do with ministers since they were all Frenchmen and he was opposed to France. He was also, he said, opposed to any and all restrictions on his private life.

Excommunicated and deprived of his citizenship, he took his punishment as a great joke, going about the city and convulsing his cronies by grinding his teeth and crying, "Watch out! I am a dog!" (not a sheep of Calvin's flock).

At the treatment meted Favre, Perrin made a scene and was again imprisoned. At the same time he was accused, with one Maigret, of having made a secret pact with Henry II to set up a French garrison in Geneva since on his return from France, Francis, duke of Aumale (later duke of Guise) and Jacques de Nemours, both military leaders in Henry's army, had been seen in Geneva. Perrin was tried and acquitted, his former honors restored. Riding the crest of his popularity, he persuaded the council to take his father-in-law's case out of the hands of the consistory. Calvin himself was forced to appear before the Council of 200 on the charge of being a part of the supposed French plot.

It was no coincidence that the Gruet affair exploded at this time, for the libertines were seizing every opportunity to embarrass Calvin, and Jacques Gruet was an intimate friend of the elder Favre. In June, during the uproar at Madame Perrin's second appearance before the consistory, papers were discovered lying on the pulpit, threatening the ministers with death and declaring that private behavior was no concern of the state, that it was dangerous for a city to be ruled by a foreigner, a man of melancholy temperament, and concluding with a number of scurrilous and sacrilegious diatribes.

The perpetrators were soon discovered: Jacques Gruet, a former canon, and Pierre Vandel, one of Perrin's friends. Vandel was imprisoned for debauchery and for having placed the papers, of which Gruet was author, on the pulpit. Under torture, Gruet confessed. The seigneury condemned him for sedition, blasphemy, and atheism. It was for sedition that he was executed on 27 July 1547.

The libertines were frightened into momentary inactivity, but their underground machinations continued. Rumors of Calvin's death were spread throughout the cantons and France. From Lyon and Burgundy came letters warning him that *Les Enfants de Genève* were offering five hundred crowns for his murder. These harassments he could ignore. What he could not and would not ignore was the malicious gossip spread by Françoise Perrin that his poor Idelette, before their marriage, had been a whore.

From the pulpit he reminded his hearers that at his son's baptism five years before he "had admitted the truth about the fault of his wife and her former husband." In Liège they had been Anabaptists, a sect which denied the authority of the civil powers, and had been joined as husband and wife, handfast by mutual consent, in the presence of their congregation. In spite of his explanations, the slander was gladly received and spread by his enemies.[6]

When Perrin was released from prison in December, a hero to the populace, a riot erupted in the streets and Calvin, who chanced to be passing, was attacked. Beaten, kicked, and buffeted, he was rescued by friends. A few days later he made an impassioned speech before the council, detailing the offenses of the libertines against him and the consistory. His speech was interrupted by a commotion in the council chamber. When order was restored, he finished his roster of complaints and went home.

"I am just now returning from the Senate," he wrote Viret. "I said a great deal, but I might just as well have been talking to the deaf . . . I have not made up my mind what to do, but I can no longer tolerate the manners of this people. . . ."[7]

At month's end, recognizing the state of unrest in the city, the Council of 200 ordered Calvin, with ten other peacemakers, to "quell all dissension in the city" without suggesting how the order might be accomplished. However, the presence of the peace-making committee brought a temporary calm. Calvin took the opportunity of going to Basel to visit Madame and Monsieur de La Falaise, friends from his childhood, to whom he was deeply attached. On his return he went to Bern to defend Viret and three other ministers deposed from churches in Lausanne.

The peacemaker was not left long in peace. Pierre Ameaux, a member of the Petit Council and formerly a manufacturer of dice and playing cards, petitioned the consistory to grant him a divorce from his wife, who had been imprisoned for flagrant adultery. For months the consistory delayed granting the decree, and the matter was still unresolved when Ameaux, half drunk at a dinner party, expressed himself too freely about the consistory and especially Calvin, who, he said, was no better than the former bishop of Geneva.

Informed upon and imprisoned, Ameaux was ordered to apologize to Calvin, but that punishment was unsatisfactory to Calvin. The culprit must show true contrition by apologizing to God. Farel and Viret, upon consultation, supported Calvin, and Ameaux, clad only in his shirt, made a tour of the city, lighted candle in hand, kneeling at the door of every church to ask God's pardon for his sin.

That fall, after a lengthy visit by Monsieur and Madame de La Falaise, Idelette took to her bed, suffering from a recurrence of the illness that had incapacitated her in Lausanne during the summer, where she had gone to attend Madame Viret at her lying-in. At the same time Calvin was prostrated by stomach cramps, fever, and violent convulsions.

He was still shaky when he heard that a letter of his, written to Viret three years before and stolen, had been published and the original brought to the seigneury. Written during one of his disagreements with the council and to an intimate friend, he had poured out his feelings, criticizing council members bitterly, individually and as a group, for their supineness before the libertines. "They judge under cover of Christ," he had written, "but hope to rule without Christ."[8]

He did not wait to be called before the council but strode

unannounced into the hôtel de ville demanding an audience. Taking the offensive, he again poured out a recital of the affronts and injustices he had received, reminding them that he had been promised full support when he returned from Strasbourg. He was ready, he said, to apologize for the contents of the letter if an apology was demanded. Then he left the council chamber.

Expecting to be recalled, he wrote to Farel and Viret, both of whom hurried to Geneva to defend him. But the council was more concerned with the danger posed by the nearby imperial forces and contented itself with administering a mild rebuke to Calvin and returning the stolen letter to Viret.

What he had written Viret was even more true in 1549. The strength of the opposition was formidable. Openly the libertines boasted of "the revolution to come" when Ami Perrin was elected first syndic in February 1549 and Pierre Vandel procurator-general. Throughout the city acts of vandalism and violence took place without provocation or punishment. The council announced that there was no need of so many ministers and sermons, yet they ordered sermons to be given daily and laid down new regulations for the celebration of the Lord's Supper. The Ten Commandments were to be recited "as in the past," and other changes in the order of service as performed by the Reformed were to be made. When Calvin, as spokesman for the consistory, refused to follow the new regulations, Perrin, not yet ready for a confrontation, revoked the orders.

The temporary retreat of his enemies encouraged Calvin. He could laugh at accusations that he was getting rich, but in the spring of 1549 he was not even aware of the accusations, for after a month-long illness Idelette died. Long letters to Farel and Viret show his grief, his recognition of what her devotion and support had meant to him.[9] "The best companion of my life," he called her, telling how her courage and constancy had sustained him in all his trials. He never married again and tried to be a good father to his two stepdaughters, one of whom would disappoint him sorely.

Now he persuaded the seigneury to pass a law that "an annual visitation be maintained from house to house for the examination of men and women as to their faith, in order to discern between the ignorant and hardened sinners and the Christians."[10] So successful was this program that in December the edict was reaffirmed, the council declaring that it had brought great benefit to the city since its promulgation in April.

When Perrin volubly protested this tightening of the screws, Calvin wrote him that the reform of manners and morals was God's will, that the consistory could be no respecter of persons. No matter how worthy or important a person might be, he must obey the laws of God. Even François de Bonivard, who had been for four years a political prisoner of the duke of Savoy in the dungeon of Chillon, was now in the Geneva prison for debauchery.

Calvin was greatly heartened now by new arrivals in the city, men who fled France when Henry II's Edict of Châteaubriand was issued: Theodore Beza (1519–1605) and seven French gentlemen with him; followed later by Charles de Jonvillers, who later became Calvin's secretary, and Robert Estienne,[11] of late royal printer to the king of France, who would print many of Calvin's works. "Robert Stephens [Estienne] is now entirely ours," he wrote Farel, "and we shall soon hear what storms his departure has raised in Paris. The retiring philosophers [the Sorbonne] will doubtless be quite insane."[12] Other refugees joined the fast-growing French colony: Laurent de Normandie, the Colladons, the Budé brothers, William Rabat. Galeazzo Caracciolo, son of the marquis de Vico, arrived from Naples. A former disciple of Juan de Valdés, despite the pleas of his father, his wife, and his children, he fled to Geneva and became an ardent supporter of Calvin.

In September 1551 another person, late of Italy, arrived: Hieronymus Bolsec (d. 1584), former almoner and preacher at the court of the duchess of Ferrara. Like Richardot, he had been chosen for his position by the duke and enjoyed the patronage of both Renée and Ercole before his double dealing was discovered. By malicious lies he had secured the dismissal of the Sinapius brothers, Françoise Boussiron, and Olympia Morata.[13] Banished from Ferrara a few years later, Bolsec had for several months been practicing medicine in a village near Geneva, where he had become personal physician to Calvin's friend de La Falaise.

Bolsec had already caused a tumult in the church at Jussy. Now at a public meeting of the consistory, he protested loudly the doctrine of predestination, declaring that by it Calvin made God out to be tryant, author of all sin. Livid with rage, for it was not his doctrine the man was attacking, said Calvin, but God's own word, he refuted Bolsec, then ordered him seized as a reprobate and blasphemer. Before the council Bolsec refused to recant, arguing that people are not saved because they are elected but are elected because they are saved, that nobody is doomed at the mere pleasure of God, that all Calvin's teachings were lies.

The seigneury agreed unanimously as to the man's heresy but could not agree on his punishment. Heresy in Geneva was not a capital crime but was punishable by banishment. The libertines on the council were quick to defend Bolsec and persuaded the seigneury to seek advice of Basel, Bern, Zurich, and Neuchâtel.

The last two (or rather Bullinger and Farel, to whom Calvin sent urgent letters) declared for severity of punishment; Basel and Bern (the latter ever inimical to Calvin), for gentle measures. "While wishing to preserve the purity of dogma," concluded the magistrates of Bern, "we should not swerve from Christ's love of charity. . . . Jesus Christ loved truth, but he loved souls also, . . . even those who went astray." They added in passing, "The problem of predestination is vexing to all men."[14]

Calvin, again confined to his bed, wrote Farel and Bullinger complaining of his lack of support.[15] He felt that the case was more serious than Basel and Bern realized. It was not, he said, that he wanted the miscreant put to death; but the sentence given him, that of perpetual banishment, was not severe enough.

Bullinger's letter upbraiding him for lack of moderation and humanity wounded him deeply. Sure that he was the instrument of the Lord, he could not brook criticism whatever its source, but worse than Bullinger's criticism was the rupture of his lifelong friendship with de La Falaise, who loyally supported his physician. The relationship ended with a last bitter letter from Calvin defending himself.[16]

The year 1552 was marked by increasing persecution of the Protestants of France. In March Calvin set out, in spite of a bout of painful hemorrhoids, to ride to Basel and plead for the Swiss churches to make a concerted appeal to Henry II on behalf of the Reformed. It was a sleeveless errand, for no appeal could have saved the five young students from Lausanne imprisoned in Lyon or extinguished the fires lighted to the glory of God in Angers, Languedoc and Provence, Brittany and Bordeaux.

The number of Calvin's correspondents had grown so enormously that he suffered greatly with bursitis in his right shoulder, necessitating the employment of a secretary, without whose services few of his letters would have been preserved. In July he wrote the young king of England, Edward VI (1537–53), sending him also a tract of four sermons and his exegesis of Psalm 87.[17] He wrote Archbishop Thomas Cranmer (1489–1556), urging him to purge the English church of "relics of popery,"[18] and replied to the French church in London in answer to their question as to whether they should continue to pray for the pope and call Mary "Mother of God."[19]

For a season the libertines were quiet, although Perrin was now captain-general of the militia as well as first syndic, his friend Philibert Berthelier, auditor, and his brother-in-law lieutenant-judge of the civil court. Increasingly the libertines were gaining control of the Petit Council.

A former monk from Burgundy, one Trolliet, appeared in Geneva calling himself a Protestant and demanding permission to preach. He was turned over to Calvin for examination and was rejected brusquely and finally. The libertines on the council sprang to his defense when Trolliet complained, attacking *The Institutes*, maintaining—like Bolsec—that Calvin's book presented God as the author of all sin.

The council waffled as to what course to pursue; supporting Calvin, yet calling Trolliet a "man of God," they seemed on the verge of naming him a minister in spite of Calvin. Calvin had no intention of submitting to such indignity. Writing Farel and Viret to come to his support, he demanded a public debate. After two months of interminable hearings, in November the weary council issued their decree:

> Having heard in Council the learned and worshipful ministers of the word of God, Master William Farel and Master Peter Viret, and worshipful Monsieur John Calvin, minister of the Church of Geneva, and noble John Trolliet, also of Geneva, in the depositions and replies *now often repeated* touching *The Christian Institutes* of the said Monsieur Calvin; and having well considered the whole, all things well heard and understood, the Council has pronounced the said *Christian Institutes* well and holily written and its holy doctrine to be God's doctrine, and that henceforth no person shall dare to speak against said book nor the said doctrine. We command both parties and all concerned to observe this.[20]

Once again the libertines had been defeated. Now they took a different tack, stepping up their propaganda, uniting with the nationalists against all foreigners, especially the French. Insults and outrages proliferated, with refugees robbed in the streets, pushed into the gutter, hooted at, all their appeals for justice ignored. More rumors spread that the ministers were in league with the French king. Unbridled immorality became rampant, with summons to appear before the consistory ignored.

The council, unable to curb the near anarchy, issued edict after edict which could not be enforced. Amid the turmoil Calvin continued his preaching and teaching, dictating far into the night books, tracts, letters—letters urging certain ones to come to Geneva, letters of encouragement to the weak and the imprisoned, letters to English and Polish royalty, many letters to his friends. He certainly wrote others to Renée than those we have, for in July of 1553 Paolo Gaddi at her court wrote him urging him to write the duchess "for she finds them [the letters] very agreeable and helpful." She begs him to send her a guide, "a counselor, of which she has great need, being surrounded by wicked men whom she cannot send away and having for almoner only a monk who is much more concerned with advancing himself than with serving God."[21]

That same month Calvin inquired of Bullinger about a letter

from Renée which had gone astray. An Italian writing to Curione said he had left a letter from the duchess with Bullinger to be sent on to Geneva. What had become of it? If it were lost, he was anxious that the duchess be informed, for the nobleman whom she had employed for many years as messenger to the French king was about to make a journey thither. "I have requested him to ask you whether anything was done with the packet Paulus left with you, in order that he may inform his mistress of it."[22]

Later in the year Calvin received a courier from Ferrara. These are the instructions Renée had given the man:[23]

Memoir to Louis de Mauray, master of our guard and valet de chambre, to communicate and show to Monsieur d'Espeville:

It is necessary for him to send me two women, if possible, or one at least, for the governance of the girls in our service. We wish them to be widows, as approved by St. Paul; but because in these days such women are hard to find, any past sixty years of age, healthy and strong enough to fill this charge, will do. We will even lower the age to fifty. We desire women who have always been honest and chaste, otherwise we do not want them; although we know that one should receive and esteem those to whom God has given the grace of knowledge of him, and can accomplish through them all the grace which can be found in others, for he gives them as much and to whom it pleases him. But in order that their lives have been and may be exemplary and that one might not find in them customs or gestures which are not holy example, it seems to me that those whose lives have been otherwise ought not to want such a position nor would one wish to employ them.

I have been of this opinion all my life, and I am sure that the said d'Espeville would not wish to do me wrong. Besides their being fearful and loving of God, they must be sober of speech, behavior, conversation, exhortation, and example, as the holy Apostle said, peaceful and not gossiping, nor lovers of men. But if they have daughters of marriageable age, they may bring them. We will make adequate provision for the said girls, who will share rooms with my ladies and eat at the table of my women. . . .

And we do not wish any commerce carried on in the chambers of the said ladies. It is not necessary that the said women be too delicate, for we go outdoors in the country often in comfortable coaches and boats. They will not have a great deal of labor to do.

As for their wages, we will pay them from 40 to 80 francs each. They will not be at great expense as to clothing—decent serge robes with high collars, black caps with tabs over the ears. It is not necessary that they be noble, but above all, they must be *good*, they must love peace and be not desirous of entertaining men, unless the occasion offers and that in my presence, which is not often. They must flee gossip and slander, pushing it away as best they can.

Therefore, we pray the said d'Espeville that he reply if he can find women with such qualifications. And if he can do so, that he let you interview them. I think he will find a safe way to send me his letters, by which way I shall reply. As to the sermons, they are not at all painful. You, Louis, will tell him what you know about it.

From Fonsenere, this 17th day of October, 1553

Renée de France

Before Calvin received de Maury, a letter to Louis de Trie, French refugee and close friend to Calvin, arrived and was about to set in train an event that would put all thoughts of the duchess of Ferrara out of Calvin's mind. In Vienne, near Lyon, Antoine Arneys, de Trie's cousin, wrote begging him to return to his home town and to Holy Mother Church. In his reply, de Trie mentioned a heretic now living in Vienne, one Michael Servetus calling himself Villeneuve, physician to the archbishop there. Arneys reported this information to the authorities, but Villeneuve denied that he was Servetus or author of the heretical *Restitution of Christianity*, recently published anonymously. Because he was vouched for by the archbishop, Matthew Ory, inquisitor for the kingdom, gave him a special hearing and released him.

Now Arneys wrote de Trie demanding proof of his allegations in order to avoid a libel suit, and de Trie sent him seventeen letters in Villeneuve's handwriting, saying,

It took a lot of trouble to get these from Calvin. He wishes blasphemies by this Servetus to be punished but says it is not his place to wield the sword of judgment. He would prefer to check erroneous ideas by teaching rather than by persecution. He finally gave me these letters when I told him that without the proof I would be accused of blackmail.[24]

A month later Villeneuve-Servetus was remanded for trial before Ory. Loudly and vainly he swore that he was not "Servetus," but the letters to Calvin and pages from the manuscript written in the same hand proved his guilt. In April he was incarcerated in the Lyon prison crowded with Reformed prisoners. In June he made his escape and was condemned to death *in absentia*. His effigy was burned, a death he himself would risk wherever he surfaced.

On an August Sunday he arrived in Geneva intending, he said later, to embark for Zurich there, on his way to Naples. Of course there was no boat on Sunday from Geneva, so, paying for a night's lodging at "The Rose," he went forth to attend the mandatory Sunday worship service. He was recognized, arrested, and remanded for trial.

It chanced that Calvin was already involved in another battle with the libertines. Philibert Berthelier had let it be known that he intended to partake of the next celebration of the Lord's Supper. Since he had been refused the sacrament eighteen months before because of flagrant immorality, Calvin announced from the pulpit that the unworthy would be barred from the Lord's table. Berthelier's supporters appealed to the seigneury, and the man's excommunication was annulled. Insult was added to insult when the council appointed Berthelier, auditor of the Petit Council, defense attorney for Servetus.

The situation was critical for Calvin and the church. Would he abandon his apparently unending struggle for the church's right to impose excommunication? "I took an oath," he wrote Viret, "that I had resolved rather to die than profane so shamefully the holy Supper of the Lord."[25]

He demanded to appear before the council. There he pointed out the illegality of lifting Berthelier's ban, but Perrin, again a syndic, had his way. The council refused to countermand its decree. Then, Calvin declared, rather than suffer the authority of the consistory to be trampled upon, he would resign. Bickering, divided, the magistrates finally decided to defer judgment on the Berthelier issue until after disposing of the Servetus matter.

So began the long-drawn-out trial, an oral and written disputation, Calvin and Servetus reviling each other along the way. Calvin called the Spaniard a Simon Magus, a wretch unable to judge what he did not understand. Servetus demanded that Calvin be punished as a false accuser and caused the audience to laugh aloud when he demanded that Calvin's property be awarded him.

The first phase of the trial, debate on the church Fathers, began on 16 August. On 20 August Calvin wrote Farel, "I hope that at least he will be sentenced to death, though it is my wish that he be spared needless cruelty."[26] The second session, to prove Servetus a dissolute and depraved character, was punctuated by the usual exchange of scurrilous invectives, charges and countercharges, and the introduction as evidence of a copy of the Vienne condemnation.

The third and final stage began on Friday, 1 September. On the morning of that day, the council announced that Berthelier had been granted permission to take Communion the forthcoming Sunday. Calvin protested vehemently, and the syndics called an extraordinary secret meeting that night.

On Sunday, when Calvin appeared in his pulpit as usual, he faced a church packed with people, many of whom were there just to see what would happen when Berthelier went forward to communicate. The invitation was given, along with a warning, and Berthelier did not appear. The syndics had warned him not to attend the service, and the feared tumult was averted.

And so the trial proceeded, Calvin writing Farel that he was trying to show the man his errors and lead him to the truth in order to spare him a painful death.[27] Before pronouncing sentence, the judges announced that they would—again—seek the opinion of other Reformed churches. Messengers were dispatched with works of Tertullian and Irenaeus, copies of the questions put to Servetus, with his replies, refutations by the Geneva ministers. Calvin could not let all this testimony speak for itself. He was sure of Farel and Viret, but to Bullinger and

Sulzer he wrote, insisting on Servetus's guilt and necessity of extreme punishment, "which should be a solemn vindication of the truth."[28]

Statements from the churches arrived in mid-October. From Zurich, wholehearted support for Calvin. From Basel, "Try to convince him of his errors. If he persists in his errors, use the power entrusted to you by God to prevent him by force from further injuring the church of Christ." From Bern, "We pray that God may give you wisdom and courage to eradicate this pest from the churches." From Schaffhausen, "Stop the devil; otherwise his blasphemies will eat away the members of Christ." From Lausanne, "No severity is too great to punish such an offense. Our preachers are in total agreement with what Calvin thinks of Servetus' doctrines."[29]

On 26 October the list of Servetus's blasphemies was read before the council, fifteen clauses culled from his various writings, including his early translation of Ptolemy's geography, in which he had pointed out "errors of Moses" and had printed a blasphemous statement by a Dutch scholar to the effect that Palestine, instead of being a land flowing with milk and honey, was a barren, infertile place. There was also an astrological work long condemned by the Sorbonne. His *Concerning the Errors of the Trinity*, published in 1537, and this latest work, *Restitution of Christianity*, not only assailed the doctrine of the Holy Trinity as a devil, a three-headed monstrosity, but called infant baptism the devil's sorcery and denied that Jesus and God were of the same substance!

What sentence other than death could he have received in any country? The council was still divided, some members calling for life imprisonment, others for banishment. Chief syndic Ami Perrin walked out before the judge-advocate read the sentence: "We, the magistrates and judges of this city . . . decree that you, Michael Servetus, be led to the Place Champel to be bound to a stake and with your book be burned to ashes as a warning to all who blaspheme God."[30]

Calvin did not approve the sentence. Death, yes; the man deserved death, but Servetus was a gentleman and gentlemen were executed by the sword. He visited the condemned in his cell, where Servetus begged for forgiveness. To Calvin's pleas that he renounce his errors and ask forgiveness of *God*, which would be followed by the forgiveness of all Christians, Servetus refused. Calvin's God was not his God and the Council of Nicaea did not speak for him.

On the day of the execution, Farel (in Geneva to support Calvin during the trial) walked with Servetus to the stake. Calvin remained in his study, alone and upon his knees, praying for the soul of the criminal. Servetus prayed for himself as the flames reached him, "Jesus, Thou Son of the Eternal God, have mercy upon me!"[31]

Throughout Europe sentence and execution were acclaimed with only an occasional protest surfacing. In Basel a tract by anonymous authors decried death—any death—as punishment for heresy. Calvin attributed the work to his ancient enemy Castellio, aided by the Italian scholar so dear to the duchess of Ferrara, Celio Curione. Indignant, he replied to the pamphlet, then suppressed his reply until later, writing Bullinger, "They [the authors] deserve to be overwhelmed in eternal oblivion."[32]

The affair Berthelier was almost an anticlimax. The council had agreed that the controversy should be resolved by advice of the other churches. Zurich judged Berthelier's excommunication *by the consistory* "necessary to maintain ecclesiastical law and conformable to the Divine Word," though to Calvin himself, Bullinger, ever tender to sinners, urged "moderation, lest we lose those whose salvation is desired by the Lord."[33]

Schaffhausen's reply was pious, judicial, and noncommital. Basel merely sent a copy of their church/state regulations. Bern, whose church was subordinate to the government, replied that excommunication was not practiced in their judiciary. All agreed, however, that since the Geneva church had been expressly charged with regulating morals, no change should be made in its power of excommunication.

But the council was in no hurry to act. Always it had been the place of the civil government to regulate private lives—amusements, dress, morals, whatever. In the other cantons excommunication was a civil punishment. The council felt that the consistory should only recommend to the magistracy the excommunication of a transgressor.

To Calvin, the church's right to excommunicate was vital to church discipline. Excommunication should be the final attempt to correct the sinner, to be used only after private and public admonition had failed, and then to keep the sacrament from being profaned.

The question remained moot until February 1554 when the newly elected syndics, evenly divided between libertine and Reformed, announced that Berthelier's excommunication should stand, ordering his supporters to make their peace with Calvin and "swear not to befriend evil causes."

The decree, however, still did not grant the consistory the right to excommunicate, and the battle over the issue would continue. In the council Calvin announced that he freely pardoned all those who sincerely repented but that he was only one member of the consistory. To Bullinger he wrote that same day, "In Geneva the church is tossed about by as many opposing currents as Noah's ark in the deluge." He was worried greatly, he went on, about what would happen if he were ever compelled to leave again.[34]

Berthelier continued his attempts. He was refused the sacrament that Easter and again in June, his violence the second time resulting in his imprisonment. On 6 September Berthelier and the consistory were summoned before the council for another hearing, and in January the Petit Council voted to uphold the consistory. It seemed that the battle was won.

All during the spring and summer of 1554, while the trouble with Berthelier was still going on, more and more foreigners came to Geneva for refuge. The previous summer, upon the accession of Mary Tudor, English and Scottish Protestants fled to the continent. Calvin heard the details of the plight of John Laski (1499–1560) and his English congregation. They had sailed from London for the Low Countries, but their ship was storm-swept to Denmark, where Christian III's Lutheran councilors prevailed upon him to forbid them sanctuary. Reembarking in the teeth of another storm, they were repulsed at Hamburg and Rotterdam. Welcomed by the Swiss, they joined the scores of Italian and French refugees.

Calvin prevailed upon the seigneury to provide land for four hundred immigrant families, giving the libertine/nationalist coalition yet another reason to hate him. Their suspicions of his participation in a French plot were not allayed by the arrival of John Cheke, former tutor of the late King Edward VI, to visit Calvin, nor of John Knox (c.1513–72), who remained in Geneva for some months observing the organization of the church and working with Christopher Goodman on the Geneva Bible.

In July he had another visitor, one he had known for some time, having met him in Ferrara almost twenty years before and, apparently, receiving him more than once in Geneva. This was Lyon Jamet, ancient friend of Clément Marot, one of the duchess of Ferrara's secretaries often entrusted by her as well as the duke with delicate missions. He was on his way from Paris with urgent messages from Anne, duchess of Guise, to her mother. He remained closeted with Calvin for some time. On his departure, Calvin wrote another letter to the duchess.

VIII

Ferrara
1541–54

Gradually, after the receipt of Calvin's letter, Renée withdrew her favor from Richardot, making excuses for not confessing or hearing mass but continuing to listen to his sermons intently. Though ready to accept Calvin as her spiritual mentor, she saw no ambiguity or hypocrisy in signing herself "Your obedient and affectionate daughter" when thanking the pope for his promise to be Luigi's godfather. Her personal beliefs did not nullify common courtesy. Nor did Calvin's outspokenness in regard to superstition keep her from ordering two shifts made to the pattern of that in the treasury of Our Lady of Chartres, or wearing a cord said to have belonged to St. Francis of Paola, inherited from her mother.

Isolated as she was at Consandolo, she was in a position to assist any who came to her for help, setting up a sort of "underground railway" by which she and her nearest neighbor, Galeatto Pico della Mirandola smuggled heretics to safety, insisting that they were no more heretical than most of the cardinals and bishops she conversed with. The Council of Trent had not yet defined orthodoxy.

She devoted herself to her daughters' educations, employing a singing master, spinet master, dancing master for Anne and Lucrezia, as well as instructors in language and eloquence. With the pope's permission, she secured a nun from a convent in Ferrara to instruct Leonora and Luigi. She continued her correspondence with Swiss reformers, bought theological works from itinerant Swiss and German book peddlers and ordered others from Venice.

It was during the summer of 1542 that she became involved in the scandal of Bernardino Ochino. Paul III had, at the insistence of Cardinal Caraffa, finally set up an inquisition at Rome patterned after that of Toledo. Shortly after, Ochino in Venice preached a sermon in which he expressed his indignation at the imprisonment of one of his disciples, Giulio Terentiano, for preaching justification by faith.

The papal nuncio at Venice suspended Ochino's preaching and reported the Capuchin's insubordination to the pope. In spite of protests from the Venetians, Ochino was cited to Rome and got as far as Florence when friends warned him that death awaited him. Hurrying to Ferrara, he was hidden by the duchess until he could be spirited away and helped to escape to Geneva. Renée's part in the flight could not be hidden for long, and Caraffa's suspicions of her disloyalty to the church hardened into certainty when Celio Curione fled Italy, his escape also facilitated by the duchess of Ferrara.

The duke found himself in a perilous position. He had thought her seclusion at Consandolo would keep his wife out of mischief, if one may apply such a term to her acts. It was essential that he demonstrate Este devotion to Holy Mother Church. Hearing of the coming interview between pope and emperor the next spring in Bologna, he invited His Holiness to stop in Ferrara on his way to the rendezvous. Paul III graciously accepted.

Ercole spent the intervening months preparing for the momentous occasion, following the minute instructions sent him from Rome as to the care and entertainment of the vast retinue that would accompany His Holiness. The city was cleaned, the cathedral completely renovated at great cost, palazzi set in magnificent readiness, streets repaired, food stocked for the feeding of twenty cardinals, forty bishops, foreign ambassadors, and all of their servitors.

After having been welcomed tumultuously by Ercole's subjects in Reggio and Modena, the pope boarded the duke's gilded *Bucentaur* and was transported down the Po to the marble landing stage at the Belvedere palazzo, where he spent the night. On the next morning, 23 April, he made his formal entry into the city *en fête*, borne on a palaquin, cannon stationed along the way (according to the pope's directions) in such a manner that the smoke would not hide His Holiness from the hysterical crowds.

Mass at the cathedral with the duke's choristers excelling themselves, a public banquet, a tour of the duke's hunting lodges and palazzi, vespers—all this culminated in an audience in the great hall of the castle, to which Renée and her ladies were permitted to come and make their obeisances.

The day following was marked by more feasting, races by Jews and naked prostitutes, a tournament which the pope observed from a window with the duchess beside him. By that time the pope was in need of rest. Later, after supper, he witnessed a play performed by the duke's children directed by Olympia Morata, the duchess's protégée.

The duke assured himself that his money had been well spent even though the old pontiff was a little miffed when Ercole refused to advance him 50,000 ecus on his annual tribute and hedged when His Holiness suggested a marriage to unite his "nephew" Horace Farnese with the Estense princess, Anne. Nevertheless, the pope presented the duke with the golden rose and advised him to recall his wife from exile and live with her as a husband should, saying sternly that the scandal of separation must have an end.

In a private audience with the duchess, Paul III assured her that he did not believe the rumors of her disloyalty to Holy Mother Church. As earnest of his sincerity, when she complained of the accusations being circulated against her, he promised to send her a brief that might be of some use to her, and on his departure gave her a diamond ring and his blessing.

He did not forget his promise. The brief, dated 5 July 1543 begins: "The sincerity of your proven faith renders you worthy that we should accord you this, which should assure the peace of harmony of your family and yourself." It goes on to forbid any

jurisdiction of the duchess in matters of the faith to any tribunal
except that of the Inquisition sitting at Rome. No local inquisitors, bishops, papal nuncios, or legates of the Lateran might act
against her. If the privilege given her was not respected, she was
authorized to call upon the secular arm of the law to employ the
gravest chastisements against any infractors.[1]

By now the duke had come to realize that Consandolo was
only a temporary solution. He was faced with the same quandary
as with Madame de Soubise, made worse by the problem of Pons.
He could not rid himself of Pons and his wife without a most
excellent reason. Francis I had made Pons a member of the Order
of St. Michael. He was an idol of the French court, an agent of the
king, and—like his Parthenay wife—tainted with Lutheranism.
Ercole had no intention of accusing the king's sister-in-law of
adultery. He did not suspect her of that, and after all, she was the
mother of his children. He could not afford a scandal. Perhaps he
sighed for the days of the beautiful Parisina, beheaded with her
stepson in the dungeon beneath his feet. He delayed acting.

When French forces were defeated in the north and in Pied-
mont and Milan, he felt the time was ripe for executing a plan he
had finally devised. Pons played into his hands. Always arrogant,
since his return from the French court, the handsome young lord
had become unbearable. His boast that both he and his wife were
of better birth than the duke was reported to Ercole. With all the
gossip about his—Ercole's—mother Lucrezia Borgia's relations
with her brother and her father before she became Duke Alfonso's second wife; and the suppositions, unfounded, of her
relationship with the marquis of Mantua and Bembo during her
life in Ferrara floating in the air, Ercole took that boast as the
veriest vilification of his mother. While he was seething, informers told him that Pons was spreading the rumor that Ercole
was planning to poison the duchess. Who cared if the informer
was lying? Here was the opportunity the duke was waiting for.

The confrontation was oblique, as befitted Este-Borgia genes:
he had François Richardot, the duchess's almoner, thrown into a
dungeon, where he was forced to sign a strangely worded affi-
davit: "Having asked Madame de Pons if it were true that His

Excellency was happier when his wife was sick and sadder when she regained her health, the said lady replied that such was the case."[2]

Only an Este prince could have composed such a thing and drawn from it the conclusion that Anne de Parthenay believed the duke capable of such ill will toward his wife. Moreover, Ercole declared, if Madame de Pons so accused him, it could only be to convince the duchess that the duke was trying to bring about his wife's death by having her physician poison her. If the duchess believed that, the next and logical step would be that she should act first and poison the duke. Tortuous reasoning? Not at all in Ferrara.

At Consandolo the duke confronted his wife, bringing Richardot to make his affirmation. The ensuing scene was frightful, with Madame de Pons sobbing and protesting her innocence, Renée coldly contemptuous and retiring to her bed with a migraine.

Pons, in Ferrara, advised of the charge against Madame de Pons, drove to Consandolo to rescue his wife and child and flee to Venice. The duke made no attempt to stop him, saying that the flight only proved their guilt. He invited Pons to return and defend himself and appropriated Pons' furniture and wardrobe for the man who had informed against him. Then he wrote his version of the affair to the king. When the couple arrived in Paris, they found themselves completely out of favor at court, their disgrace dragging down Madame de Soubise with them.

Still at Consandolo, Renée was profoundly depressed. A note written to Ercole soon after the Pons affair, while he was in Rome, reflects the state of her mind. It is coldly formal, giving him news of the duchess of Camerino, asking him to kiss, in her name, the feet of the Holy Father and ending, "Praying to God, Monsieur, to give you a very good and long life, Your very obedient wife, Yours very humbly, Renée of France."[3]

She wrote the queen of Navarre to send her another companion. Margaret chose for her a young woman of Renée's age who had been at her court for some years. The Ferrarese ambassador examined her credentials and approved of her, and Madame de La Roche, warned to keep her ears open and her mouth shut, came to Ferrara in fear and trembling, having been told of the sword that had fallen on the heads of her predecessors. Her employment lasted just six months before the duke, recognizing her as a Lutheran, sent her packing. There would be no more French companions for the duchess.

During Richardot's tenure as almoner, the Swiss theologians were much concerned with his influence. Viret wrote Calvin, "May God direct our pious duchess by his Spirit, that she may not do as so many others who, after having professed the Gospel, turn aside."[4] He had far more cause for concern when Ercole brought his wife the man who replaced Richardot: Hieronymus Bolsec, whom we have already met in Geneva. Bolsec was a consummate actor. To Renée he presented himself as an ardent secret Protestant and gradually took over her letter-writing as well as her alms-giving. One letter from Consandolo, written to Calvin, recommends in her name an Italian refugee going to Geneva. Bolsec saw to the distribution of her alms in Geneva as well as in Ferrara. To the duke he was a devout Catholic and a faithful informer concerning the duchess's activities.

More and more Rome was concerned with the "Lutheranism" spreading like a blight over Modena and Ferrara. Yet the jurist Alciati (once Calvin's professor of law at Orléans) wrote Amerbach that Ferrara was a paradise after the treatment he had received in Germany, and Baldassar Altieri found sanctuary with the duchess for a time. When Cardinal Morone attempted to stamp out heresy in Modena, Renée invited Francesco Porto, noted Greek scholar, to come and teach her daughters. The duke delayed ridding Ferrara of heresy because of more important personal affairs.

When Francis I died in March 1547, to be followed shortly by his beloved sister Margaret, Renée felt herself more than ever bereft of all those she had known and loved. She remembered the new king, Henry II (1519–59), as she had last seen him, a frightened seven-year-old child on his way to a Spanish prison. She had no idea how his experience had shaped him, how his father's indifference to him, including the marriage the boy had been forced into with Catherine de' Medici (1519–80), a woman beneath his rank, had embittered him. What help could she expect of the stranger, should she need it?

Ercole, too, was worried about what he could expect of this new king. He had known where he stood with Francis I, but Henry was an unknown quantity. Politician that he must be, Ercole went to Turin to meet the new ruler and congratulate him. There was no thought of his wife's accompanying him. He was going to engage in delicate negotiations, and she had just been indiscreet enough to involve herself in a failed attempt to overthrow Andrea Doria in Genoa, thinking she would thus be helping France.

Of the two rulers, Ercole was the more adroit. Each sought a favor. Henry was dreaming of another invasion of Italy, that *fata morgana* that had led the last three French kings to disaster. He wanted to use Ferrara as a staging area, the Ferrarese cannon, and the duchy as a commissary. Ercole wanted to show his good intentions without committing himself. Despite the king's glittering promises, Ercole refused to become a tail to his kite.

Henry then offered another lure: marriage for one of the duke's daughters to a French lord, Ercole's choice of four. This offer was more to the duke's liking. Anne was sixteen, past marriageable age. He had already been in contact with Sigismund of Poland on the subject, and the French court had reacted with alarm. Paul III was still pressuring him to give him Anne for his grandson, but for an Este to marry a bastard and son of a bastard was unthinkable. He would choose one of the French lords but not too quickly. Eventually, after consultation with the duchess, the choice was made: Francis of Guise, duke of Aumale, of the royal house of Lorraine, the favorite of Henry II, against whom Henry's father on his deathbed had warned him.

Negotiations were long-drawn-out. Ambassadors from the bridegroom-to-be came to Ferrara, then said their lord preferred the younger sister, Lucrezia. Unconvinced that Lucrezia was not nubile, as her parents insisted, nevertheless they finally agreed on Anne. In late September the ducal family accompanied Anne as far as Mantua, then hurried back to Ferrara to face the storm brewing there.

While the marriage negotiations were yet in progress, Bonifacio Ruggieri, Ercole's ambassador at the papal court, sent his master a long letter warning him of what was being said about His Excellency and Madame his consort. Cardinal Santa Croce, chief inquisitor for the Holy See, was much concerned about the heretics infesting the duchess's court and the fact that the duke permitted their presence around his wife, "giving," he said, "full details as to what had been reported about Madame your consort and God knows with what foundation." The inquisitor had declared that not a heretic was brought before the Holy Office but had been welcomed and aided by the duchess.

He had defended the duchess, Ruggieri said, arguing that to prefer one political party to another was no heresy; that since the Lutherans preached faith without works and the duchess was noted for her works of charity, giving away more than she had, it was impossible for her to be a Lutheran!

Ercole, advised by his newly appointed inquisitor-general for Ferrara, Girolamo Papino, was more astute. Letters sped back and forth between Ferrara and Rome. Paul III himself wrote the duchess, affectionately chiding her for surrounding herself with courtiers and scholars who took advantage of her credulity. He remained convinced of her innocence until his death the following year.

The cardinals of the Holy Office were less credulous. Jesuits in Ferrara kept the pot boiling. They reported that the university was infected with Lutheranism in every branch. Many of the faculty were openly disciples of Bucer and Melanchthon. The gentlemen of Madame's household ate meat during Lent. Madame no longer frequented the churches. Madame had a private chapel in the castle, where there was neither holy image nor crucifix. Madame had connived with Galeatto Pico della Mirandola to rescue a doctor condemned to the galleys.

At first the duke denied everything: his wife had always been and still was a devoted daughter of the church, as her ancestors before her had been. The Holy Father should know that an Este would never countenance anything not approved by the Holy See. But Santa Croce, inquisitor for the Holy See, with the pope's blessing, became increasingly insistent: the duke must confront his wife, must compel her to dismiss the heretics in her household. The number of known unbelievers was finally reduced to two: Antonio Bruccioli, translator of an Italian Bible dedicated to Renée, and a Greek monk, ostensibly Francesco Porto.

In November after his return from Mantua, Ercole promised to confront his wife and inform her of the pope's demands "in order not to publish that our wife is accused of such things, out of respect for her and our sons." He would see that the two heretics named by Santa Croce were dismissed, proof that he was "not lacking in anything necessary to preserve the divine cult and the dignity of the Holy See."[5]

Yet he delayed. He had gotten rid of Madame de Soubise, of the Pons pair, of Madame de La Roche, partly at least because they were unorthodox. All of them had been favorites of Francis I and/or his sister the queen of Navarre. Both of *them* dead, he had assiduously cultivated a good relationship with Henry II, which certainly would be vitiated (he thought) if he allowed His Majesty's aunt to be openly accused of heresy. It was like the dilemma of Pope Clement VII when Henry VIII of England wanted a divorce from the emperor's aunt. Yet Santa Croce kept harrying him.

Paul III tried his hand: he ordered de Gye, French ambassador at Rome, to return to Paris through Ferrara and plead with the duchess to mend her ways, thinking that she might listen to her countryman. But in Ferrara Ercole refused to permit de Gye to have an audience with his wife, sending instead his own secretary with the pope's message.

After reading His Holiness' instructions to the ambassador, the duchess announced that the secretary might tell Monsieur de Gye, the duke, the cardinals of the Holy Office, and the pope that she would render an account of her actions to God alone (and much more to the same effect), after which she dictated a note to her husband:

> . . . I thank God that I have done nothing for which I can be blamed by people of good will. My confidence is in God and none other. My life and that of my companions is witness enough to those who wish

to blame me. I know their malevolence is turned toward me as to one they can injure. . . . The little people are regarded by God as the greatest and often the better. Jesus Christ said that the merciful will obtain mercy. He does not want me to ask mercy for any who do not deserve it. . . . It is better to obey God. . . .[6]

The letter is long and almost incoherent.

The next attempt to corral her was made at Santa Croce's instigation. The duke sent Claudio Jaio, director of the newly established Jesuit college and his own confessor, to reason with her. Renée refused to hear the man.

Since the duke himself delayed action, suspicion now began to be directed against him also. To protect himself he must show determination and energy in ridding Ferrara of any taint of Lutheranism. He banished all German professors from the university, including the Sinapius brothers and Françoise Boussiron, Renée's lady of honor, who went with her husband. Peregrino Morato had recently died. His daughter Olympia, who had been the darling of the duchess's court, would have suffered more than exile because of accusations brought against her by Bolsec had she not married a young German student at the university and gone to Germany with him. Bruccioli disappeared from the duchess's court, and it turned out that the "Greek monk" wanted by the Holy Office was not Francesco Porto after all. The city was turned upside down in the duke's search for heretics.

Twenty years later when the duchess was beyond reach of the Inquisition, Thomas Palino, testifying in another case, said that he had preached that year, 1548, before the duchess; that though she did not go to mass or take absolution, neither did many other persons; that she had missed one of his sermons during Lent and had come to his convent to have him repeat it and had called him back to Ferrara later to hear him again. He had read *Galatians* before her but had never talked about papal authority, purgatory, indulgences, or the mass; that she had never spoken against the faith, *and when she did he had refuted her!*

So, with his wife's household cleaned and many of his subjects imprisoned, the duke could congratulate himself that attacks against the duchess—and him—would die away. One would have expected the duchess to act henceforth with discretion if not dissimulation, but she could not stand by, assenting to persecution. In June 1549, still at Consandolo, she wrote to Ercole: "I beg you very humbly to free the prisoners you have remitted to the inquisitors of St. Dominic [naming them] for, Monsieur, they are not so guilty, as Monsieur the cardinal your brother tells me. The inquisitors tell me they do not find anything of importance against them, which makes me beg you to grant this request. . . ."[7] If she had contented herself with writing notes to the duke, suspicion of her might have died away. Instead, she acted openly to show her sympathy with the persecuted, especially with Camillo Fanino of Faenza.

This Fanino, a young man of the Romagna, had a few years earlier become infected with Reformed opinions. Armed with a copy of Antonio Bruccioli's Bible, he set out to preach the gospel as he understood it, achieving a great following among the unlettered. He was arrested and imprisoned, and after some time, moved by the tears and reproaches of his mother and wife, recanted, made his penance, and was released. Later, obsessed with guilt, he left home to evangelize the Romagna, was seized in the duke's territory and imprisoned in Ferrara, where, after a long trial he was condemned to be burned at the stake.

During the period of his incarceration in Ferrara, his case became a *cause célèbre.* The populace flocked to hear him preach through the barred window of his cell. The duchess and the noble ladies who imitated her brought him fruit, wine, and clothing, and hung upon his words. So remarkable was the effect of his preaching, that he was removed to an inner chamber where he would have no audience, but his wardens could not halt the ministrations of the duchess and her servitors. Her solicitations to cardinals, to the duke, to her nephew the king on behalf of "poor Fannio" were added to her dossier in Rome.

Nor was he the only one she helped at this time. Her account book shows money sent to Geneva for Italian refugees, money paid a doctor of Ferrara for treatment of "a poor woman whose feet were burned by the Dominicans to make her confess to being a heretic," and an entry showing money paid for a bed for the same woman. Still there was no open conflict with Rome over her activities.

Pope Paul III died. On 8 February 1550 Julius III ascended the throne of St. Peter. When the duke went to Rome the month following to congratulate his new suzerain, the Holy Father gave him to understand that he was not to be trifled with as his predecessors had been. The Holy See did not appreciate the duchess's attempts to have the sentence of the lapsed heretic Fanino set aside. Her appeals to the cardinals of Ferrara and Mantua were useless, her appeal to Henry II ridiculous. The man had been duly tried, sentenced, and turned over to the civil arm in Ferrara, of which duchy Ercole was ruler. He must see to the carrying out of the sentence, and at once.

Ercole knew enough about the wars of his father and grandfather with the popes to realize his danger. Yet once back in Ferrara he let matters slide, while Renée importuned him daily for "poor Fannio," as though he could defy the pope. She should have remembered how her father's defiance of Leo X had turned out.

Again and again he delayed the date of Fanino's execution, making excuses. He had his ambassador tell the pope that Paul III's condemnation of Fanino must be confirmed in order that the sentence be legal. In mid-May the papal nuncio arrived with a brief ordering the immediate execution of the heretic and the complete suppression of heresy throughout the duchy. Still putting off the inevitable, Ercole replied to the pope in July that if there were still proven Lutherans in his wife's household, "we have given her to understand that it is without our knowledge and against our will. The wisest thing is not to make a demonstration. As a Christian and Catholic prince, we intend to give Fanino the punishment he merits."[8]

Having endured so many months of his wife's reproaches and tears, he gave orders that the criminal be strangled instead of being burned alive and left Ferrara. On 22 August 1550 the sentence was carried out. In Ferrara's Book of Justice is the notation that Camillo Fanino, citizen of Romagna, Lutheran and heretic, was strangled on that date and his body thrown into the Po, as ordered.

In the Estense archives is a letter from Renée written that same day to her husband, in which she complains of the inquisitor's keeping her in Ferrara, and begs him to think of the scandal and shame that will stain his duchy if God does not touch his heart. "As for me," she ends, "I can bear my grief better than the poor fathers and mothers and little children of those [imprisoned?]. I beg you, Monsieur, to have pity, remembering the charity you owe the poor, and rescue them from hands so cruel if I am in your good graces, to which, very humbly, I commend myself. . . ."[9] Early in September the duke's ambassador in Rome wrote that His Holiness was satisfied by the duke's declaration in regard to Madame, now that Fanino was dead.

In May 1551 Ercole was pleased to report to the pope the total extinction of the poisonous weed of heresy throughout his domains. He had just had George of Sicily hanged by one foot from a window of the Palace of Justice, bearing a placard, "Lutheran and Heretic." There is no record that Renée undertook to defend the man or even knew of him. Could she have read Calvin's diatribe against him? At any rate, her husband reported her good behavior: she was now hearing many devout preachers, among them her son-in-law's brother, the pious cardinal of Lorraine, who had lately visited Ferrara.

He did not tell the pope of his wife's correspondence with Cosimo de' Medici, begging him to free Lodovico Domenechi, imprisoned in Florence for translating Calvin's tract, "On the Nicodemites." He knew nothing of that letter and would have ignored it if he had known. It was another of her acts that infuriated him just now: she had helped their oldest son, Alfonso, run away to France.

The flight had been instigated by Henry II, suggested to Renée by Anne's husband, and well planned by mother and son. To Ercole, it was not just a matter of filial disobedience. Alfonso's royal welcome at the French court could not fail to make the emperor think Ercole was deserting his alliance for that of

France. It was, he thought then, the final indignity of his wife. He had just got out of a perilous situation vis-à-vis the Holy See because of her indiscretions, and now he was to be embroiled with the emperor. He poured out his rage and fear in long letters to his brother, Ippolito, cardinal of Ferrara, who had long been in high favor at the French court.

Renée, though proud of her son's welcome and new honors, supported the duke in insisting that Alfonso not be allowed to go to war. The king replied that their son would be kept at court if Ercole would sign a treaty of alliance with France. This the duke refused, and his son went to fight the Spanish in Flanders, whereupon Ercole was forced to write a humiliating letter to Charles V, explaining his son's escapade, washing his own hands of complicity, and sympathizing with the emperor over *his* ignominious flight from Innsbruck.

He had hardly time to draw his breath before his ambassador in France reported that His Majesty was planning a marriage between Alfonso and a French princess. The irate father moved to nip that plan in the bud—there would not be another Este prince saddled with a French wife. He agreed to forgive his son if the boy would come home and promise to be guided by his father. And since Alfonso had exhausted the money supplied him by his sister and mother and what he had acquired by selling wood from the forest of Montargis without his mother's permission, he came home. He arrived in Ferrara on 25 September to find his parents at sword points.

During his son's absence, Ercole had felt himself more and more beleaguered: again the duchess was under constant surveillance by the Jesuits. In August of the year before, letters from Rome again warned him of rumors about his wife. This, added to his worries about Alfonso, and his negotiations with Cosimo de' Medici in regard to a marriage between Alfonso and his daughter, was almost more than he could cope with.

To the pope he expressed his pain at the Holy See's suspicion of him, seeing that he had always governed his state well, never countenancing anything that would detract from the honor of God. In December he thanked the Holy Father for his good opinion, flattered and happy that His Holiness had named fifteen-year-old Luigi bishop of Ferrara. He also congratulated the pope on the success Mary of England was having in exterminating heresy, asserting that he was determined to copy her.

He would begin with his own wife. He knew that she was again writing to the arch-heretic, Calvin. One of his agents had intercepted a letter she had written the man in July, asking Calvin to send her a counselor. He was turning over in his mind what procedure he should follow with her when two episodes in January forced him to act, as usual obliquely.

On 16 January Renée refused to obey the duke when he ordered the last rites of the church to be administered to Ippolito Putti, one of her longtime servitors, whose daughter was one of her favorite maids of honor. Publicly and loudly Renée ordered the priest to take the sacrament out of the room where her old friend lay dying, even charging that Putti had been poisoned by the duke's physician at his orders—an accusation that the Florentine ambassador would repeat later as common knowledge.

This open declaration of heresy she followed up at Easter by refusing to permit Lucrezia and Leonora to make confession or take communion. The confrontation between duke and duchess, the violent quarrel when the duke's sister-in-law arrived to take the girls to a convent, became public knowledge. On 18 March Ercole issued an order banishing every person suspected of favoring the Reformation from his state. This time the duchess's court was decimated. A week later, as a last resort, he sat down and poured out his griefs to the king.

IX

"J'Accuse"

After a long and flattering introduction, in which the duke says that Henry's goodness and prudence lead him to reveal a part of the calamity which he has kept secret until now, reverencing as he does the blood of France, but which he must now tell the king, since it touches Ercole's religion, his conscience, and the honor of his house, he writes the following, much abbreviated:[1]

Sire:

Madame the duchess my consort came to me in Italy twenty-five years ago, observing the Catholic religion and faith, and living and speaking, and her actions indicating, such goodness that everyone knew she was well and truly born of blood royal and had been brought up in a truly Christian court.

Not much time elapsed before she listened to certain bold Lutherans, of whom you may know better than I, since Christian princes have not proceeded severely enough against them, and began to change her opinions, and little by little she put so much confidence in that new and perverse religion that she began to turn away from the sacraments, mass, confession, and communion, commanded by God and the Holy Catholic Church and so necessary to the Christian life.

In witness of which: it happened recently that when Ippolito

Putti, your beloved servitor, sick unto death for a long time, lay dying, I said to my consort three or four times, to make him confess and take communion. She answered that she wished him to die unshriven and was ready and willing to take upon herself the bad opinion she would suffer. There was no way I could change her mind; she would not do it, saying he had made his peace with God and had no need of other confession.

Seeing her so obstinately determined to act against the honor of God and bringing constant infamy upon my house, I begged her thousands and thousands of times that for the love of God and for the reputation of our posterity, she would renounce her fantastic heresy, not bothering her head any more with what she heard from her ribald preachers, whose word she should not believe since they were already slated for the Inquisition and would abjure publicly in the cathedral; that she ought to follow the religion of her father and mother, and that of her sister, Your Majesty's mother, which she herself had formerly observed, as well as all other Christian princes, following this advice by all the other reasons I could think of to induce her to rid her mind of these perverse opinions.

Already for many years to my infinite displeasure and the opprobrium of my house and the dissatisfaction of my servants and subjects, I have been forced to dissimulate and suffer, with the hope that she might come to her senses without making the scandal public, desiring, rather, to hide it for the honor of the blood of France as well as for my own, yet knowing the matter was going from bad to worse, that mass was never heard in the house of my said consort even on Christmas Day, nor feeling it right that my daughters should be brought up in that false religion which, if it were accepted, would make them heretics and Lutherans after the example of their mother, offending God, making it difficult for me to marry them to Christian princes—so much the more since gossip of their mother's heresy is already spread throughout Italy.

I resolved to say to Madame in all kindness that I wished absolutely for my daughters to hear mass regularly, confess and communicate at Easter; in short, to live in the future as I should order, and as she herself lived when she came here from France, telling her not to oppose my just and holy wishes.

The upshot of that was that she said the mass is idolatry, with other words I am too ashamed to repeat, exhorting my daughters *in my presence* not to obey me but to continue in the way they had begun, trying to persuade them that my religion and that of most other princes is not true, with so much fervor and arrogance that anyone hearing her speak would have judged me more patient than Job. I suffered her words solely out of reverence for Your Majesty.

That was not all. The following day I ordered one of my chaplains to go and say mass for my daughters. She sent him back, not permitting him to celebrate the said mass (for which I had paid!). I told her I wanted to be obeyed in that at any rate and if she opposed me I would make her sorry.

Seeing that this situation must be remedied in one way or another and desiring to use peaceful rather than rigorous means, I begged Your Majesty's ambassador, Monseigneur the bishop of Lodi, to persuade her to leave her fancies; and that whether or not she did, it would not matter, since I was resolved that my said daughters should live as I do. . . .

Not knowing what more to do honorably, and since she has refused to listen to three of your French lords in addition to Monseigneur de Lodi and Brasavola my physician, I sent my sister-in-law Madonna Giulia Gonzaga [1513–66] to persuade her on Holy Week to hear mass and confess and communicate; and failing, on my order she took my daughters, for the time being, to the convent where my sister is, where they will live until I make other provisions if necessary. [He says nothing about Renée's rage at Madonna Giulia.]

Now, seeing that my consort has lost her daughters, has persisted in opposing my honest and holy wishes, has shown that she will not confess, communicate, nor attend mass—all this coming after so many tears and words that I am unable to tell— and refusing to hear that priest I sent her, of so exemplary life and doctrine, selected because he was French and I thought he might be better able than anyone else to bring her back to the right way! [He loses his train of thought.]

All this has happened because she would not allow my daughters to confess, nor listen to the priest, calling him a devil, tormenting those poor girls with her pleas, displeased because they did not wish to continue in the bad religion that she has always preached to them.

I know that any change for the better would only be because she is afraid of losing her daughters permanently, rather than because of any real change of opinions. I know also that my daughters will be unable to be good Catholics if they continue living with their mother. I shall be forced to take them from her and place them in Christian company if she refuses to return to the true and only religion.

I have wished, Sire, to give account of all this to you, as to my lord and master, wishing you to know the calamity in case she denies having brought about this disturbance in the house of one of your most faithful and obedient sons. . . . And because I imagine Monseigneur de Lodi either will not write or will not give the entire story, in order not to displease Madame.

I beg you to find some good Catholic theologian, well-versed in such affairs, to find a remedy and draw the duchess back from her enormous heresy; and when it is done, not to tell the world any more than she has already done. Thus Your Majesty shall judge what is most expedient to make her understand your will.

By your letters, by sending her your theologian, she may understand that if she returns to the true religion, I will be content to leave her daughters with her as in the past. Your Majesty knows well that if she perseveres in her perverse opinions she will be abandoned by all, as being unworthy of being considered offspring of the Christian blood of France.

Do not refrain from using very brusque words in your letter to her. I have found in her such incredible obstinacy and hardness of heart that I doubt if the Lord should put out his holy hand, she would return from her heresy. . . .

> Your humble and obedient servant,
> Ercole d'Este, duke of Ferrara
> From Ferrara, 27 March 1554

Henry II had not the slightest interest in the well-being of his aunt, but he was interested in bringing the duke of Ferrara to heel. He needed Ercole in his support of the Siennese rebels against Spain; he wanted Lucrezia d'Este as wife for Jacques de Savoy, duke of Nemours; and, if his aunt by any unlikely chance would be formally judged heretic, all her property in France would revert to the crown. Nothing would be lost by supporting the little duke.

He wrote to Ercole, assuring him that he could hope for all good will and "perfect friendship" on Henry's part, which he would demonstrate by sending Matthew Ory, inquisitor general of the kingdom, to Ferrara, will full power to "reduce and bring back into the fold of Jesus Christ the said lady, who has permitted herself to fall into the abyss of these evil and damnable opinions contrary and repugnant to our holy faith and religion."[2]

Ory would be given express orders to employ whatever means were necessary, since his aunt "instead of following the example of her progenitors who, by a singular zeal, had always protected our Holy Catholic Faith, chose to live so pertinaciously opinionated; a thing which displeases the king more than anything in the world and would be reason to cause him to forget entirely the duties of a good nephew."[3]

The inquisitor-general's instructions were detailed by the chancellor: he could threaten the duchess with depriving her of her goods, her French servitors, and the education of her daughters. He left Paris early in June.

To Renée the king wrote that it was impossible for him to express his grief upon learning that his only aunt, whom he had always so greatly loved and honored, had strayed from the right way. Nothing in the world would give him greater joy than to learn that she had been purged of her evil, damned, and reprobate errors and restored to true obedience to the church in which case he would rejoice as though she had been brought back from death to life.

She should consider, he went on, all the blessings God had given her, particularly that of being issue of the most pure blood of the very Christian kings of France, among whom no monster ever lived; that her wish to live in opinionate pertinacity displeased him and would make him forget the amity and good relationship a nephew should show, there being nothing more odious to him than the condemned sect, of which he was the mortal enemy. After the remonstrances and persuasions Ory knows so well how to make in order to show her the difference between light and darkness, if he realizes he cannot gain her by gentle means, warned the king, he will confer with the duke as to what may be done by rigor and severity to make her see reason.

Anne of Este was well posted on proceedings at court. Ory had no sooner departed on his mission than she dispatched Lyon Jamet, in France on business for Renée, to Ferrara bearing a letter of warning and advice. For twenty years Jamet had served Renée as secretary and, though he was among those suspected of Reformed opinions, had served the duke on important missions. Jamet, under an assumed name, would travel to Ferrara via Geneva.

X

The Second Letter

Anne of Este, though sympathizing privately with her mother's beliefs, realized what the results of the duchess's trial would be, not only for her but for her children. Should Renée be declared heretic, all of her property in France would revert to the crown, leaving no inheritance for Anne and her siblings, and all of them would be tainted with Renée's crime. She sent Jamet to urge her mother to give up her opinions, or at least pretend to do so.

Jamet, himself a secret Protestant with one foot in each camp, felt the need of alerting Calvin at once as to the duchess's predicament. But his news left Calvin in a quandary. Any letter he wrote might fall into unfriendly hands. One must read between the lines here to realize that Calvin was sending Morel to stiffen Renée's backbone and strengthen her for the glory of martyrdom.

Geneva, 6 August 1554[1]

Madame,

My anxiety has been so great since your old servant [Lyon Jamet] passed this way, that it has at last made me change my plan; for if you have been in perplexity, I assure you that I too have had my full share. Though I had at first thought it best to suspend the journey of the man about whom I had written to you, after reflection it seemed to me that at least he could be of some service to you in your present necessity; for if we let slip this opportunity of helping you, there may be danger of our coming to your assistance too late. Besides, I have been much concerned about you since I have had no word about your condition.

Would to God that I were at liberty to offer you my services in person, but because God keeps me confined here, I have chosen the bearer of this letter [François de Morel, Monsieur de Colonges] as the person best calculated to render you every kind of service, both in what concerns our doctrine and his fitness for the position of your almoner. He is so well qualified that I think you will have occasion to praise God for him.

As he is a gentleman of an honorable house, he can be so much the better employed in his contact with those who would seek to drive away a good man who in the eyes of the world does not have the advantage of birth. No doubt our attention should be fixed on the main point. Nobility of birth is not a thing to be desired if a man values himself on that account, seeing that he would thereby be hindered from serving God.

You will find neither vanity nor pride in this man since he is one who believes that the children of God should be led by a spirit of modesty and humility. Though he is affable and courteous toward his inferiors, humble toward those to whom honor is due, and modest toward all, yet such is his exemplary life, his habitual self-possession, and his becoming manner in teaching that these qualities alone would give him the authority to acquit himself of the duty you desire of him.

Of the zeal and devotion which he is prepared to render you, you may judge by this, Madame: upon my first approaching him in regard to this position with you, he has preferred sharing your cross and suffering with you in this crisis, to waiting until he might come to you without any fear of harassment. This trait spares me from giving him any further recommendation; only I beg you, Madame, to receive him not as one sent by me, but rather as one directed to you by the Lord. Indeed, I do not doubt that you will find that in him your heavenly Father has conferred a blessing upon you.

He will inform you that there is a virtuous lady who has promised him that she will enter your service whenever it pleases you to send for her. I am aware that in such a place a woman of the humble class would not only be exposed to envy, but even to suspicion, and looked upon with an evil eye. For that reason I consider it an advantage that she is of honorable birth. What she seeks is the privilege of serving God through serving you. Though I have never seen her, I have for so long heard her virtues commended by many estimable people, that I hope your house will be blessed in possessing her. I will leave the bearer to inform you of the rest. With him you will be able to discuss that subject and any others more fully.

Wherefore, Madame, humbly commending myself to your kind favor, I beg our Heavenly Father to keep you in his holy protection, to direct you by the Spirit, to increase you in all good, being more and more glorified in you.

Your most humble servant,
Charles d'Espeville

XI

The Trial

When Jamet reached Ferrara in mid-July, he found a formidable group confronting his mistress: the chevalier de Seure, sent by Henry II immediately after receipt of the duke's first letter of complaint to keep the king informed of the situation; the bishop of Lodi, now ambassador to Ferrara; Jesuit Claudio Jaio, the duke's chaplain; Pellatario, rector of the Jesuit college; Girolamo Papino, local inquisitor and secretly receptive to reformed teachings; the cardinal of Ferrara; and Matthew Ory.

Already the duchess had been brought from Consandolo at Ory's orders, and lodged at the cardinal's Palazzo di San Francesco, from which she was brought daily to the Palace of Justice for interrogation. Daily he preached to her and her household—courtiers and children—on her chief errors: she had openly confessed the Calvinist-Lutheran heresies; she had refused to acknowledge the efficacy of the sacraments, holding confession and mass odious and the Real Presence an abomination. Letters supplied by the duke, who did not attend the interrogations, were evidence that she corresponded with heretics. It was indisputable that she had sheltered many heretics and enabled a number to flee the arm of the church, notably Ochino and Curione, perhaps

Peter Martyr. These accusations were made in the duke's name by his chaplain.

The sessions of the tribunal were well underway when Jamet arrived with the letter from Anne and counsel from Calvin. Renée had acquitted herself well, haughtily answering the charges, denying that she was either Calvinist or Lutheran, that her opinions were simply Christian. But by early August the incessant grilling was having its effect, and daily the duke congratulated the tribunal on its progress, sure that the next day would see his wife's surrender. The rumor spread that she had agreed to hear mass; later, that on the day set for celebration of the rite, she had refused.

She appeared to gain new strength, and instead of being confused in her answers, responded calmly or not at all, maintaining a singular detachment from the proceedings, as though she thought the whole affair a farce. Her changed attitude coincided with the arrival in Ferrara of François Morel, Monsieur de Colonges, passing through the city on his way to Rome.

But the process was no farce. Ory's directions from the king were explicit: the lady was to be questioned daily; at the end of a specified time, if she showed determination to continue in her errors, the duke should place her in solitary confinement; any of her servitors suspected of maintaining false doctrine were to be punished as examples; procedures were to be undertaken "even such as touch the person of the lady."[1]

Persuasion and fear having failed to break down her resistance, Ory proceeded to make good his threats. Her courtiers were removed, her daughters again taken to the convent. No one was admitted to her presence. The nightly conferences with Colonges ended.

On 7 September, Francesco Babbi, Florentine ambassador, wrote Cosimo de' Medici that judgment of the duchess had been rendered the day before.[2] She had been declared heretic, but Papino, the lenient inquisitor of Ferrara, not wishing to see her pay the penalty imposed upon heretics of lesser rank, had condemned her to perpetual imprisonment with deprivation of her pension and all her French possessions. Her servitors who had fled were condemned *in absentia*. Her daughters would remain in a convent. She would be given one final opportunity to submit.

On that same day, before dawn, Renée was brought in a closed carriage from San Francesco by the duke's ambassador to Rome, to the palace connected to the castle and lodged in the chamber she had occupied on coming to Ferrara as a bride. Guards were placed at her door, and she was served by servants chosen by her husband.

Her attitude seemed quite inappropriate to observers. Babbi, who reported almost daily to Cosimo de' Medici on the scandal, wrote, "She is a very gentle lady of good spirit, but so plunged within the abyss of error, that she would suffer a hundred deaths rather than be drawn out." The chevalier de Seure wrote that her attitude was the strangest thing he had ever seen.[3] Both men sympathized with the duke.

He was in need of sympathy. He had been confident that Ory, so noted for his ability to instill fear in his victims, would be able to coerce the duchess into behaving herself. He had not foreseen an actual sentence of heresy. Nor had he envisaged the result of His Majesty's assurance of "perfect friendship," of which de Seure had warned him, though in fact the thought had already occurred to him that the king had determined from the first that if his aunt were formally declared a heretic, all her French possessions would revert to the crown.

Did Ercole act on that advice to call off the judgment? Would he have been able to? Early writers on this period of Italian history thought otherwise. Documents concerning the process were turned over to Papino. At his death, a few years after, the duke sent in great haste to have all papers concerning the affair brought to him and burned.

On 13 September, Babbi again wrote his master: rumors circulated that the duchess had asked to be permitted to confess, to the great joy of her husband. It was said she had accepted the Eucharist and had been absolved by the cardinal of Ferrara. Babbi did not believe it. The lady was still in confinement, and the duke did not appear joyful.[4]

A letter written by Ercole three days later to his cousin the cardinal of Mantua says things had not turned out as he had hoped; that "the strangest thing in the world" had happened, a thing he could not write about. He would send a faithful man to carry this letter and *tell* all that had happened.[5] That same day Babbi wrote that on the day before, the duke had had a long, private interview with Madame, to whom he had not before spoken since her imprisonment; that the duke had afterward announced that Madame had agreed to confess and hear mass. Again Babbi said he did not believe it.[6]

The consensus of Italian writers as to the "strange thing" to which the duke referred was that Renée had now produced the brief given her twelve years before by Pope Paul III forbidding anyone to molest her in matters of the faith, ordering that any trial of such a nature be transferred to the Inquisition at Rome, and giving her authority to have any person or persons threatening her on such account to be imprisoned.

Only that brief would account for the court's verdict being abrogated; had it been a matter of record, she would have been taken to Rome. It would also account for Ory's precipitative departure, almost flight, from Ferrara.

Fontana quoted documents to this effect from the archives of the Vatican, and said that Pellatario, to sustain the reputation of the duchess as well as that of Ory, advised the duke to give out the lie of his wife's final submission.

For another week, Renée remained isolated, visited daily by Ercole. There were no witnesses to these meetings, but it is presumed that the duke explained to her fully the danger in which the duchy stood. There was only one thing she could do, for the sake of her children. On 21 September she was said to have made her confession and received the Eucharist, weeping. Pellatario wrote the joyous news to Loyola.[7] Her daughters were restored to her, her old servitors—except known Lutherans—given permission to return. Ercole wrote the pope, happy to be able, he said, to report the success of his undertaking.

But did he believe in her reconversion? Babbi said she was playing on the credulity of the duke; that the priest who was supposed to have said mass before her had not seen her; if she had actually confessed, Babbi thought, it was only for show.[8]

To draw a veil over the late unpleasantness, the duke staged a magnificent reception for his prodigal son. Only Alfonso seemed unwilling to overlook his mother's dereliction, declaring that she should have paid the penalty like any other heretic.

On 28 September Ercole dictated a letter to the emperor, a letter so incoherent that parts must be paraphrased:[9]

For months, he said, his wife had not been quite sane on the subject of religion, influenced by some heretical, ribald confessors and preachers, so that she did not hear mass or do anything else commanded by Holy Mother Church. He had done everything possible by gentle means, considering his responsibility to the blood of which she was born, he having always made public the profession of the devotion he wished observed in his state, living as became a Christian Catholic prince. It did not seem honorable, then, for him to permit the state of affairs to continue, with her bad manner of living being such a scandal to all his subjects, and especially since—because he could not prevent it— it seemed as though Ercole himself were consenting to her heresy.

> Many cardinals and ambassadors exhorted our consort to leave these opinions unsuitable to a Christian and attempted to bring her back to the true religion. They did not move her. She grew worse daily until Easter, when our daughters (who were under the governance of their mother) did not hear ordinary mass, confess, or take communion at the appointed season as we do.
>
> I showed my great displeasure to my consort in every way possible. Our daughters would not consent to obey our wishes, having imbibed too much of their mother's errors. Urging them to live as Christians, considering that the plague would grow worse and increase without any medicine, with much shame to her French blood, I decided to write the king, telling him in what a state that troubled mother was in, asking him to send some learned Catholic person to try, Scriptures in hand, to refute the errors in which the said our consort found herself entangled—that false teaching of diabolical persons—and that if it would content His Majesty, if she remained obstinate we would be able to make whatever provisions were necessary for the honor of God.
>
> His Majesty kindly resolved to effect such a good work by means of a great theologian who is now inquisitor of France, writing him a

long letter by his own hand, in which he clearly made known his infinite sorrow and grief to learn that our said duchess our consort had fallen into such abominable errors to such an extent that the powers of reason were insufficient to bring her out of her wrong opinions by any means seeming good to us, and the theologian spoke to her for three months, exposing her errors with good reasoning, interpreted Scripture to her, and by Monseigneur our brother exhorted her to change her opinions and way of living, and by Don Francesco and by Monseigneur the bishop of Lodi, and adopted an infinite number of ways to reach her but was not able to shake her obstinacy.

Then one day she promised to hear mass the following Sunday, perhaps more to satisfy her hearers than because she had changed her opinions. When the day came, she refused to do as she had promised.

Ercole understood that during that time she had spent hours arguing with a certain Lutheran who had come to speak to her, she deliberating as to whether she should make open demonstration of her beliefs, the position he was urging her to take, and so bring upon Ferrara the infamy she wished.

When we saw where her sinful errors were leading her, we took our daughters to a monastery of our city and at the same time had her [Renée] come and stay at our court, next to us, and in the room she used when she first came from France, and for fifteen days she saw nobody and nobody was allowed to serve her except the master of her house who I know is far removed from such heresy, for he has always disputed with the men and ladies who served her and ridiculed the true religion,

Ercole himself remonstrating with her that if she remained obstinate he would be forced to use restraints and she would lose at one stroke daughters, subjects, and everything in the world that she possessed.

At last it pleased the good God our Savior that she confessed her errors, and with true contrition she heard mass, confessed, and communicated, with such devotion that it was an infinite consolation to us and to our House and subjects, since she gave firm intention of wishing to live as becomes a good and Catholic Christian.

Feeling the great contentment for the honor of God and our House over the outcome of this thing so important to our family, it appeared to me proper to tell all of this to the prince who has the name of "Catholic" [the title *Los Reyes Catolicos* was awarded Ferdinand and Isabella by the pope for their ridding Spain of the Moors and Jews], who, the whole world knows by his noble works, is such a great enemy of heresy.

Ercole ends the letter by again apologizing abjectly for Alfonso's escapade, and signs the paper: "to Sir Antonio Maria Collegni di Savoia, to be told to the emperor."

PART THREE

The Blaze Spreads

XII

Geneva
1555

News of the duchess's capitulation was received by her enemies and friends with varying shades of belief. Calvin
wrote to Farel, "I have received sad news, unfortunately too true,
that the duchess of Ferrara, vanquished by threats and by fear of
opprobrium, has fallen away. Constancy is a rare virtue among
the princes of this world."[1]

Celio Curione sent word of the affair to Olympia Morata,
Renée's one-time protégée, and Olympia, writing to Piero Paolo
Vergerio, added her judgment: "I always said she was frivolous!"[2]
But Olympia had cause to feel bitter.

In spite of recurrent bouts of illness that fall, 1554, Calvin's
work went on. As always, he made time for his voluminous
correspondence, now dictated to his faithful secretary: writing to
Peter Martyr, who had fled England for Strasbourg on the accession of Mary Tudor;[3] to Melanchthon, both striving to work out a
compromise on the Lord's Supper;[4] to the congregation at Wezel,
where French refugees from London were having trouble with
their German hosts over election and the Lord's Supper;[5] to the
church at Poitiers, which dated back twenty years to the time of
his preaching in the cave of St. Benoit, to whom he was sending a

minister;[6] to "a gentleman of Provence," consoling him on the death of his unbaptized child.[7]

In October he sent copies of his refutation of Joachim Westphal's tract against Calvin's interpretations of the Lord's Supper to all the Swiss churches, asking them to go on record that they approved the consensus on the subject, arrived at four years previously.[8]

In November he sent an affectionate letter of sympathy to Lord John Grey, uncle of the unfortunate young Lady Jane;[9] one to Bullinger in regard to the consensus;[10] and to Peter Martyr a copy of that carefully worked out compromise.[11]

In December he was continuing his correspondence with Sigismund Augustus, king of Poland, urging him to call a synod to effect reforms in the church there.[12] That ruler had studied *The Institutes*, but his inclination to be part of the Reformed movement was chilled by the continuing Calvinist-Lutheran controversy and, perhaps, by Calvin's ten-page directive.

The new year had hardly begun when the libertines staged an uproarious demonstration in the street before Calvin's house, masked and carrying torches. They were finally dispersed, but Calvin saw it as a sign of growing animosity against him. He wrote to John Wolf:

> You are right in thinking I am familiar with daily bickering. . . . Believe me, neither from Servetus or Westphal and their associates, have I received so much torment as from domestic enemies, whose forces are numberless and fury implacable. If I had a choice, I would rather be burnt at once by the Papists than be torn to pieces by neighbors devoid of moderation and good faith.[13]

Yet he refused to give up.

On 2 February he wrote to the duchess of Ferrara:[14]

Madame,

As I have had no news of you except by flying rumors, since it has pleased God to make trial of your faith, I am quite at a loss as to how I should write to you. I do not, however, wish to lose the opportunity offered me by this bearer. I was extremely sorry to learn that a short time ago a person passed through here without letting me know, who would certainly have taken charge of my letters to you.

Since the ordeal to which you have been subjected, I do not know to whom to trust them; and however much in doubt I was concerning the outcome of your torment, having no certain information, as I desired, I was deeply grieved at having no means to communicate with you. Even up to this moment, I am far from having satisfactory and sure word of your condition and am only able to send you word that I suspect you have been obliged to swerve from the straight path in order to comply with the world. It is an evil omen when those who have waged such a relentless war to turn you aside from God's service now leave you in peace. Indeed, the devil has so triumphed over us that we have been forced to groan over it, hold down our heads, and make no further inquiries.

Leaving all that aside, Madame, since our heavenly Father is ever ready to grant us mercy and holds out his hand to us when we have fallen so that our fall does not prove mortal, I beg you to take courage. If the enemy on this occasion has won some advantage over you because of your weakness, let him not boast of a complete victory, but know that those whom God has raised up are doubly strong to stand against all assault.

When you reflect, Madame, that God, in humbling his children, has no desire to cover them with shame forever, that thought will make you hope in God, with the result that you may stand more courageously in times to come. I am sure that the same attacks which caused you to relapse will be renewed before long. I pray you to think how much you owe the one who has ransomed you at such cost and daily invites you to a heavenly inheritance.

God is not a master in whose service we should be niggardly, especially when we consider the ultimate consequence of all the opprobrium or affliction we have to suffer for his name. Call upon him, trusting that he is sufficient to strengthen your weakness; meditate on those noble promises which are to exalt us by the hope of glory in the heavens. The foretaste alone should make us forget the world, trampling it under our feet. And to prove that the desire of glorifying God is increased in you, or at least not diminished at all, in God's name, Madame, think not only of how to witness to God in your person, but how to order your household so that the mouths of evil speakers be closed.

I trust you have not forgotten what I wrote to you some time ago (to my great regret, but from the respect I bear you and the zeal I have for your salvation) though at the same time I must remind you I never enjoined anyone to breathe a word about it to you. What is more I took special care not to give any indication of having lent the least credit to the many reports I was obliged to listen to.

That the person who so impertinently vexed you might no longer have opportunity to scatter his firebrands, I must tell you I have taken great pains to moderate his folly, without success. What is more, he broke out into curses against me for wishing to restrain him. The individual I speak of is an Italian named Mark. I entreat you, Madame, to be on guard so as not to give a handle to such lies.

Commending myself to your gracious favor, Madame, I pray our merciful Father to have you in his keeping, upholding you, increasing in you the gifts of the Spirit, causing them to redound to God's honor and glory.

Your most humble servant,
Charles d'Espeville

That same month Calvin was impelled to write a very long letter to the church at Poitiers, for a Monsieur de La Vau had upset the congregation by painting an ugly picture of the church and clergy of Geneva. Calvin's letter was a blistering tirade against the man, whom he had known of old. He expatiated on the man's impudence and conceit, calling him a fool and a braggart, a supporter of "that hair-brained wild beast Bolsec" and an accomplice of Calvin's ancient enemy, Sebastian Castellio.[15]

Speaking of Castellio made him revert to denunciation again of the tract published anonymously after Servetus' execution. Calvin, sure it had been written by Castellio and Curione, who had not remained in Geneva, took it as a personal attack, for, he told his Poitiers friends, those scoundrels had said that some who confess the name of Christ are pitiless murderers of other Christians by fire, water, and sword. Who would not think, they had said, that Christ was a Moloch if he wishes people to be sacrificed to him by being burned alive?

> Castellio says everybody here [in Geneva] must kiss my slipper. . . .
> He reproaches me with procuring for my books such authority that
> not even the most courageous and venturesome dare to speak ill of
> them. . . . It is quite lawful for me to be jealous in maintaining the
> doctrine I profess, since I know it is that of God. . . .[16]

Although he was being attacked within and without Geneva, there were a few hopeful signs. The young people of the city had begun to take his part against the libertines, disgusted with their childish tricks such as the masquerade before Calvin's house and affronted by Ami Perrin's arrogance. The first acts of the new syndics, all Reformed, had been to purge the Petit Council of thirty troublemakers, among them Berthelier and Gaspard Favre. Most encouraging to Calvin, they showed themselves disposed to take up the cudgels in his long standing disagreement with Bern.

Bern had welcomed the libertines banished from Geneva, and the magistracy of Bern saw in Calvin's struggle to win the right for the consistory to excommunicate, danger that Bern might have to follow suit. Finally, the ministers of Bern openly supported the Geneva-banished Bolsec, who was now calling Calvin "heretic" and "antichrist" and spreading accusations of homosexual acts against him.

On 15 February, Calvin wrote the seigneury of Bern, complaining of ministers in the Pays de Vaud who were attacking the doctrine of predestination, asking that they be silenced "for the honor of God, the peace of the church, the salvation of the Bernese people, and the prosperity of the state."[17] At the same time he wrote Bullinger, describing the charges of the Bernese pastors, not only against his doctrine but against the civil-religious government which he was trying to make prevail in Geneva.[18]

In response to his letter to them, the seigneury of Bern freed a number of ministers previously imprisoned for calling Calvin "heretic." The magistracy of Geneva then joined in the battle, officially demanding that Bern curb the ministers who had attacked Geneva as well as Monsieur Calvin, their minister.

As this verbal conflict continued, Bern accused Calvin of inciting the ministers of Lausanne to petition for the establishment of ecclesiastical discipline in their churches. Geneva retaliated by castigating Bern for their scurrilous language, and on 28 March sent a commission to the magistracy of Bern, with Calvin as spokesman, to attempt a solution to the bitter quarrel.

Calvin carried out the seigneury's orders to explain (once more!) the doctrine of predestination, to demand that the lying ministers be punished and muzzled, to discuss regulations for administering the Lord's Supper, and to complain again about the intemperate language of Bern's last communication. But peace was not restored.

Within a short time Bern was complaining to Geneva about a letter written by Calvin fifteen years before to one of their ministers, Andrew Zebedée, saying that Zebedée's position regarding the sacraments was false.

Being the sort of person he was, it was impossible for Calvin to ignore these constant attacks. He wrote to the pastors begging them to preach true doctrine and help maintain liberty of the ministry.[19] This letter resulted in his being forbidden to set foot in the territory of Bern upon pain of excommunication. Rumors reached him that Bern had declared him heretic.

On 4 May he dispatched a long, impassioned letter defending his position, protesting the sentence, defending his *Institutes*, and complaining once more about his defamation by Bernese ministers. If his doctrine was condemned, he said, then Geneva was condemned with him, for all Geneva had voted to uphold that doctrine.[20] The ministers of Bern had declared that it was quite unnecessary to write books inquiring into the secret things of God; such authors blasphemed against the holy and eternal counsels of the Lord. Calvin had to reply. When he had dispatched the letter, he wrote Farel to pray for him.[21] The events of 16 May put the quarrel with Bern out of his mind.

Though the four syndics were all Reformed, their elections had come too late to avoid conflict with the alienated forces of the populace. All respect for law and authority had gone by the board as Ami Perrin, now captain of the city, screened criminals from punishment, appointed prefects and judges. Libertines occupied key positions on the Petit Council. Conditions in the city reached a climax on the night of 16 May, when a plot of the libertines backfired, bringing their domination of the city to an inglorious end.

The influx of foreigners had alarmed the older conservative

Genevans, who saw in Calvin's friends and supporters proof of the charge that he was inducing the French to come to Geneva for his own ulterior motives. The city of 13,000 souls absorbed more than 5,000 refugees between 1549 and 1559. In the past month the seigneury had enfranchised sixty new citizens, and leaders of the libertines and nationalists determined to use the resentment engendered by this policy as a means of ridding Geneva of all foreigners and destroying Calvin.

Ami Perrin and his clique led a crowd of several hundred protestors to the hôtel de ville on the evening of 8 May, demanding that enfranchisements cease. Demonstration was not the approved method of petitioning the seigneury, and the answer of the magistrates was an emphatic "No!"

Most of the crowd dispersed, but the nucleus separated into two groups, Perrin and Vandel, with other gentlemen, going to a tavern on St. Gervais to discuss their next move, the lesser fry to the pâtisserie Thomas to drink and grumble.

Apparently no other plan had been devised for that night, but Calvin, writing to Bullinger,[22] said that Perrin inflamed the head of the city boatmen, who left the tavern to go to the pâtisserie Thomas to confer with the "worthless scum" there. At nine o'clock Perrin and Vandel left the tavern to go home. But at the pâtisserie tempers among the commoners were at fever pitch. All the troubles of the city were laid at the doors of Monsieur Calvin and his tools. Someone said Monsieur Baudichon de La Maison Neuve was hiding a company of armed Frenchmen in his house. Someone else suggested burning Maison Neuve's house, and the rabble started out.

Had the French been warned to stay off the streets that night? Calvin said rioters streamed out shouting, "Kill the French," but fortunately met only one, a servant of a newly elected council member. A boatman threw a stone at the fellow, wounding him in the neck. By the time the mob reached Maison Neuve's house, the crowd had doubled, carrying torches, milling about, its leaders trying to generate courage enough to break down doors.

Next door was the house of syndic Aubert, who, hearing the commotion, came forth bearing his baton, symbol of authority, to disperse the breakers of the peace. But Aubert was a short, stout man and was swallowed up by the crowd, ignored by the rude fellows he sought to subdue.

At this critical moment Ami Perrin appeared on muleback. "I have come to help you appease this tumult," he is quoted as saying. "You are too short. Give me the baton to inspire this people with respect." When Aubert refused to relinquish the baton, Perrin wrested it from his grasp and held it aloft, shouting, "Messieurs, the syndic's baton is ours, for I hold it!"

At that the crowd grew silent. This was lèse-majesté. No one was prepared for this turn of events. Before the decision was made to follow Perrin, another syndic living nearby, aroused from sleep, rushed out with his baton and ordered Perrin to follow him to the hôtel de ville.

Meanwhile, in another district of the city, Vandel had sent his wife and her friends to arouse that quarter, crying out that the French were killing everybody, begging sleepers to come out and defend the city. When Vandel was told that the plot had gone awry, he called his wife home and locked his doors. By midnight the city was quiet.

The magistracy began its investigation on the following day, Perrin and Vandel taking their customary seats as council members, as though they had had no share in the tumult. For almost a week they thought themselves safe because of their official positions. When, a week later, marshalls were ordered to arrest them, they escaped, with a number of their followers, and the seigneury announced that they would have until 8 August to repent, return, and stand trial for sedition.

Under torture, two of the boatmen who had precipitated the riot confessed that the plot was to massacre all the French in Geneva. Eight of the ringleaders, including Perrin and Vandel, were condemned to death by default; ten were banished for life and two for ten years. The young man who threw the stone was executed, as well as his brother.

The council, purged of opposition, granted citizenship to sixty-five more French newcomers during the next five months. The consistory was given the right to excommunicate, i.e., the right to pass judgment on evildoers before turning them over to the council for punishment. Calvin does not refer to his triumph when writing the duchess on 10 June.

The remaining months of 1555 were more peaceful, yet sufficiently stressful to increase the severity of his constant headaches and indigestion. He involved himself in troubles beyond the boundaries of Geneva. In June there was a great deal of dissension in the English church at Frankfurt where his friend John Knox was now minister. The Anglicans given sanctuary there, who made up his parish, did not approve of the simplicity of the worship service Knox had instituted, and Knox could not tolerate their ceremonies, which he considered still "papist." His session (or the vestrymen, as they preferred to be called) denounced him to the magistrates for introducing "dangerous innovations," and Calvin felt called upon to act as conciliator.

He had rejoiced too soon at the libertines' downfall. In the cantons to which the banished fled they stirred up suspicion and distrust of both Calvin and Geneva with their lies. The duke of Savoy put Perrin in charge of two thousand troops, and Geneva was put on alert for fear of attack.

Amicable relationships with Bern were greatly to be desired since the alliance between Bern and Geneva was slated to expire the next February. Negotiations in regard to the alliance continued throughout the year, with Calvin advising the magistrates on legal matters.

In August there was the matter of the French church in Strasbourg, which Calvin had organized seventeen years before, and whose minister the Strasbourg magistrates had dismissed because of conflict with the Lutheran clergy over the Lord's Supper.

There was also the matter of the arrest of five Protestant gentlemen in Chambéry—three students, a lawyer of Nîmes, and a former royal judge from Quercy, for whom Calvin induced the council to intercede with the duke of Savoy, all to no avail.

He was incessantly consulted by churches in France. On 9 September he advised the church at Angers, to which he had sent a minister in 1547, and which had already seen five of its members suffer martyrdom.

Early in October he welcomed Count Celso Martinengo, a convert of Peter Martyr, appointing him minister of the Italian church in Geneva. Later that month he was provoked by the publication of yet another tirade against his doctrines by the German, Westphal. He immediately began composing a fitting rebuttal which would be published the following January under the title of *The Second Defense of the Pious and Holy Doctrine Concerning the Sacraments, against the Calumnies of Joachim Westphal.*

In spite of the banishment of the leading libertines, a residue of dissatisfaction with enforced religion and morals remained. On 10 October in a letter to Farel, he said: "I would gladly hide myself away in some retreat if their fury would be softened which my presence seems to inflame. I do not speak of the rabble whom I learned long ago to despise . . . but what without reason gives me pain is that now, from hatred of me, the heavens are continually warred on by these giants . . . . Westphal has published a savage pamphlet against me, to which I do not know whether or not it would be wise to make answer."[23]

In November he was writing the minister of the French church at Frankfurt, consoling him on the death of his wife, who had died of plague.[24] Her husband would soon follow her. In December he worried over the dissension in that church with its new minister, a dissension which would continue and take much effort on Calvin's part to straighten out.[25]

And so the year drew to its close, with a letter to King Sigismund, who had written to inquire if Calvin thought he would be wise in asking the pope to help him with his projected reforms of the church of Poland.

XIII

Ferrara
1555

Whether or not the duchess was hypocritical in her recantation or decided to conceal her beliefs as a matter of expediency, regarding the rites of the Catholic church as "matters of indifference," is a moot question. She had done the only thing possible under the circumstances. In October she wrote the king, thanking him humbly for the "good and holy advice" he had written her in the spring, for which she "did not know how to thank him sufficiently."[1]

Ercole, of course, did not trust her sincerity. At the insistence of the pope he surrounded her with spies. He withheld her pension, refused to return the jewels he had confiscated, and informed her he was pretending to believe her only to save her. At the order of the pope, he imprisoned her friend, Emilia Pia, a Ferrarese gentlewoman, in a convent for life, a convent in which she had taken refuge, forbidding that she have visitors. He ordered all the books of Renée's library burned.

He bombarded Alvarotti, his ambassador to the French court, with letters directing him to explain his acts to the king, to whom Renée had appealed to make Ercole return her jewels and her money. Alvarotti was to make His Majesty understand that for twenty years the duke had not seen one scudo of his wife's money. And when he had her brought to the castle (to imprison her) he saw in her papers something *he* had not written, and some other things that he would be ashamed to put in writing. She was furious when she found his "prying;" but he was her husband, an Italian prince, and not afraid of the king. Then she left the room because of her "headache" (the duchess's headaches were not feigned; her account books show that for the first three months of 1555, she paid Thomas de La Licorne 2,872 livres for drugs and medicines).

In March he was still complaining. Alvarotti was to tell the king that he intended to give back her jewels, a few at a time, if she behaved herself and acted toward him as she should. He had learned that she had put a large sum of money out at interest with a merchant in order to have money for the marriage of Ippolito Putti's daughter, a female of the lowest condition, not even certainly his daughter. It was beyond reason, said Ercole, that she dower her girls extravagantly without spending any of her money on her own daughters. She seemed more interested in marrying daughters of other women than in looking after her own.

Surely it would be more than reasonable to turn her dowry over to her husband for family expenses. "We will not enjoy the income from her money, but at least our children may, at the time of their marriages, if she has not spent it all on daughters of others."[2] He felt it impious and dishonorable of her not to show her bounty toward those of her own family.

God, he said, was pleased to have him born a free prince, not wishing to be a slave to his wife nor be deprived of that liberty and authority which it had pleased God to give him. He had put in more time than he wished in serving His Majesty, and though he would always remember with gratitude the king's good services in recalling the duchess from her enormous heresy, that obligation should not make the king favor her above him. He is still worried by her past in various matters, which (if His Majesty knew all) would make him have compassion and judge him as patient as Job.

He swore that everything she did was for revenge because he did not leave her in her evil way of life. She spent her dowry—

and more than her dowry—as she pleased, and always had, ever since coming from France. "I can not see what cause she has for grief—not that I am too indulgent and overlook her grave errors and perpetual infamy toward our house.

"I swear to you on our honor that the cardinal inquisitor of Rome has had her admonished lovingly by a prelate of authority" without effect. Ercole praised God who knew his good intentions in honor of his divine majesty in all this affair, and he hoped to justify his actions so that His Majesty will hold him his faithful and devoted servitor to the end of his life.[3]

Three days later, Renée wrote her nephew thanking him for his good offices on her behalf. Nevertheless, Ercole gave her to understand that she had not gotten anything and would not be able to, except by prayers and submission to him as a loving, obedient wife. If she acted contrary to his will, she would have no one to blame but herself.

The letter Henry II sent in reply to Ercole's long complaint was impatient and brusque, advising him that he had better treat a daughter of France well and ending with a warning that someday Ercole might come up against a prince not as patient as himself.

All that took place in March. In May Ercole went to Rome for the funeral of Pope Marcellus II. While there he continued to pour out his complaints to Alvarotti, these to be carried to Francis, duke of Guise since 1552, his son-in-law and Henry's favorite, and to Diane de Poitiers, Henry's mistress, with the hope that they would curry favor for him with the king. Alvarotti was to go over all his grievances about Renée, for, he said, if she had not quarreled with him, none of the terrible things that had made such a bad impression on the king would have happened. He had been more long suffering than one should be with people sunk in such error—as his daughter Anne should know. Pope Marcellus before his death had demanded he use rigor to bring her to her senses, and cardinals had told him (again) that every Lutheran brought before the Inquisition at Rome had named the duchess as heretic.

Perhaps by his constant lamentations, he had gotten the bitterness out of his system. At any rate, on his return to Ferrara he attempted reconciliation. On 9 May he ate dinner with Renée, promising not to speak again of her errors. His peacemaking attempt was not entirely successful. She chose to remain in the Palazzo di San Francesco. "She would not live again in that apartment in which we lived together for fifteen years, and made such beautiful children," he wrote Alvarotti, "alleging that she suffered from headaches."[4]

The duchess showed herself most circumspect. In the drive to rid the duchy of heresy, ordered this time by Pope Paul IV, she played no overt part, remaining secluded in her palace. The chief Lutherans in the city and in Modena were arrested, examined by the local inquisitor, and remanded to Rome. Torture was used as needed, and everyone suspected of favoring the Reformed opinions was questioned—except Renée.

From the safety of Heidelberg Olympia Morata wrote Chilian Sinapius news from her mother in Ferrara: ". . . the Christians are treated with great cruelty. Persecution spares no rank. Some are imprisoned, some exiled, and others flee from a sentence still more cruel." Possession of a New Testament was proof of heresy, she said.[5]

Under Paul IV the Inquisition spread throughout Italy. The inhabitants of Locarno crossed the Alps to Switzerland en masse. From Lucca, Naples, Venice, Siena, people disappeared: all who did not flee submitted or expressed their convictions only in the intimate circle of the like-minded, preferring like Calcagnini, Vittoria Colonna, and Cardinal Pole "to remain in the safety of the Ark."[6]

Early in September a young Italian nobleman arrived in Ferrara on his way to Venice. Ercole knew little about the man, except that he had been, or still was, in the service of the emperor; that he was the son and heir of the noble marquis de Vico of Naples, kin to Paul IV. Ercole, therefore, gave him a warm welcome, as did the duchess. The visitor was Galeazzo Caracciolo. He came from Geneva bringing the duchess a letter from her friend Charles d'Espeville, a short letter but gladly and tearfully received by Renée, for it proved that Monsieur Calvin did not consider her submission a mortal sin.[7]

Madame,

Though I could have wished to have better news of you, that is, that in tranquillity of mind you were serving God in peace, nevertheless I rejoice to learn that you are not weary of groaning and being in pain, seeking for the means of fulfilling your duty. Thus it becomes us to do battle, to follow the Son of God. It is certain that Satan never permits us to honor God fully without laying obstacles in our way.

You have encountered many more of them than others; but our heavenly Father knows well why he so tests you, for the anguish you are experiencing is a trial of your faith, to make you realize the value of that inestimable treasure, the gospel, which the world so much despises. It remains for you to take courage for the future and, however long you have yet to languish, always to hope for a favorable outcome to your perplexities, for it is certain that God will at last listen to your groans if you continue to beg him to hold out his hand to you.

Only let it grieve you that you are prevented from striving in every way to glorify his name. Such sorrow is a hundred times more to be desired than the rejoicing of those who flatter themselves in their lukewarmness. Nevertheless, you should be on the watch for every opportunity that God shall give you for making further progress.

It is truly the province of God to lead us on like poor, blind persons when we are brought to a halt in spite of all our human efforts, and to devise expedients which we should never have thought of, enabling us to surmount every obstacle when we cannot see our way. At the same time it is our place to pray that God will open our eyes so that as soon as God gives us a sign, we may immediately follow it.

Do not fail, then, to put into practice day by day all the means in your power to advance on the right path. Doing so, though you may still be far from the mark, it will not be in vain that you stretch toward it; our progress is certain, provided we keep following, however faintly, and such an assurance should fortify us against all temptations. If worldlings labor at random with so much ardor for some hope of which they are often frustrated, how much more should we strive, who have the promise of God to assure us of our salvation.

Nevertheless, Madame, do not let this consideration lull you into feeling so secure that you cease to regret continually the miserable bondage in which you are held. Indeed, we may expect deliverance from God when we feel keenly the wretchedness of our prison-house. On the contrary, the one who takes delight in an unhappy state, shuts the door on the compassion of God.

Now I trust in God that just as God has imprinted on your heart a singular desire to do him honor, so God will at the same time open up the means of putting in practice the good will with which he has endowed you, since it is in his province both to begin and to perfect the good work. Thus I have confident hope in God's power to save, and that in that work will show his might. On my part, I will also pray that God may always have you in his holy keeping, increasing you in knowledge, zeal, and constancy and in all good, so that you may contribute more and more to the glory of God.

Charles d'Espeville

The duchess enjoyed a number of interviews with Calvin's messenger Galeazzo Caracciolo, who had become a disciple of Juan de Valdés when he was eighteen. Converted by the preaching of Peter Martyr, he was ostracized by family and friends and went through a long period of doubt and indecision. On visits to Germany for the emperor, he became more familiar with Reformed opinions, and at Strasbourg in 1550 renewed his friendship with Peter Martyr.

Finally in May of the following year he took the decisive step, leaving everything for the sake of his convictions, and settled in Geneva (after preaching in Flanders and elsewhere). He was kindly received by Calvin, who dedicated to him his *Commentary on First Corinthians* and sent him on numerous important missions.

Upon the accession of Paul IV, the marquis prevailed upon his son to meet him at Mantua, where he detailed the advantages that would accrue to the family if Galeazzo would give up his depraved ideas. When Galeazzo remained inflexible, the marquis loaded him with reproaches and hastened to Rome to divest himself of responsibility in the eyes of his kinsman Paul IV.

Caracciolo had numerous meetings with various members of his family after that, each trying to convert the other. Letters from his wife induced him to come to see her, holding out the incentive that she might go with him to Geneva. When he arrived, after making a dangerous journey, she refused to accompany him. This tour in northern Italy was one of those futile attempts to make peace with his family. On his return from Venice, the duchess entrusted him with letters for Calvin and sent him as far as the border in her own coach.

In late September the duke received a communication from Rome, inquiring about a certain person who had recently visited the duchess. On 2 October Ercole replied, asking that the inquisitor-general question a certain Lutheran prisoner of Ferrara whose process was under way, torturing him if necessary, to learn if the duchess had indeed returned to the Catholic faith, if she had corresponded or held conversation or had sent money to any heretics as she used to do, and if any person had come to Ferrara to see her. In the latter case, he requested a full description, and the date of his coming. The only one Ercole himself was aware of, was Galeazzo Caracciolo, His Holiness's kinsman, and of course he was above suspicion.

The prisoner at Rome was probably Girolamo Caballi, who informed against thirty persons in Ferrara, commoners as well as gentlefolk. Many of them were servitors of the duchess. Questioned as to what opinions he had heard discussed, the prisoner was most explicit. Lutheran opinions, he said: that nuns and priests should be allowed to marry, that one may eat meat on any day without sin, that the mass is not a sacrifice, that prayers for the dead are without value, that there is no purgatory, that the pope's indulgences help neither the living nor the dead, that the pope is no more than any other bishop, that there is no merit in good works, the only merit being in Christ.

The few remaining French courtiers of the duchess were banished, the others questioned, released, or transferred to Rome.

Was it because His Holiness and His Majesty had political

plans for Ferrara that Renée was left in peace? The Holy See was not deceived by Ercole's assurance that she had returned to the faith. When Paul IV sent Antonio Agostino on a mission to England, the ambassador was directed to go through Florence and salute the wife of Cosimo de' Medici, but when he passed through Ferrara, he was not to speak to the Duchess Renée.

XIV

Geneva
1556–58

Calvin was now in his midforties. His poor health should have slowed him down, but the burning passion to spread the truth spurred him on. In the spring of 1556 he suffered a tertian ague, so severe that reports of his death spread through Switzerland and France and were received with great joy in some circles. In Noyon, his birthplace, church bells were rung and Te Deums sung. His health was not improved by the calls made upon him beyond his preaching and teaching, both within Geneva and elsewhere.

The situation in the French church at Frankfurt disturbed him. The congregation had divided over the choice of a minister to replace Vanville, dead of the plague, some supporting Poulain, a refugee minister, others refusing him because he had not been elected by the Frankfurt church. Calvin's attempts at peacemaking were not appreciated by some of the congregation, as his letters to a magistrate of Frankfurt regarding the dissension show.

In one he wrote: ". . . and how vile the calumny about my tyranny is, I leave to the judgment of my colleagues and brethren, who certainly have never complained that they were oppressed by my authority. On the contrary, they have often expostulated with me because I am too timid."[1] He wished his accusers could see him in his teaching, he arrogates nothing to himself. Then he goes into a discussion of infant baptism and baptism by women; the first he defends, the latter he absolutely forbids.[2]

Within Geneva other issues had to be dealt with. The Italian church was in a state of confusion because of the antitrinitarian views of Matteo Gribaldi, who advocated liberty of conscience. In Geneva? After Bolsec and Servetus? The man sought an interview with Calvin, who refused to speak to him without witnesses, refused to shake hands with him, and cited him to appear before the council to give an account of his beliefs. The man could not be allowed to stay in the city, spreading his detestable impiety, saying that Christ differs from the Father and is of a different essence. Gribaldi was banished.

It was, however, the discord between Geneva and Bern that occupied most of Calvin's "free" time. Negotiations for renewal of the alliance slated to expire in February 1556 failed to bring matters to a successful conclusion, primarily because of Bern's support of the banished libertines.

On the heels of the breakdown in negotiations, Perrin and his friends demanded safe conduct to appear before the Geneva magistracy and defend themselves. Geneva denied the petition, since the men had been sentenced to death and at the time of that sentence had been given two full months to return and justify their conduct.

Now, supported by Bern, the fugitives appealed to the Swiss League sitting at Baden to order Geneva to reopen their case. The delegates were about to grant their petition when deputies from Geneva arrived to set the record straight. But the matter was still in limbo when Calvin wrote Bullinger in July, begging him to urge the Zurich magistrates to be on their guard against the intrigues of Perrin, Vandel, and Berthelier.[3]

In August, at the direction of the magistracy, Calvin wrote a true account of the whole affair, copies of which were sent to every ambassador of the League, about "the demands made by them [the ambassadors] for the condemned criminals of this city," explaining why the men were banished; reminding them that Geneva had sent deputies to the assembly to inform the cantons of the truth; that the ambassadors, "good and prudent men" though they were, had determined that Geneva should give passports to those condemned criminals; that when the Genevan deputies had refused to accept that decision, the League had accepted *their* refusal. But now the fugitives had returned to Bern and continued to be a cause of enmity between the two cities.[4]

The alliance not being in effect, Geneva felt itself exposed to concerted invasion by the Catholic powers. In an effort to clear the matter up once for all, the magistracy reversed itself and ordered the libertines to return and stand a new trial. Perrin and his friends refused.

When a libertine-sympathizer died, leaving five hundred crowns for the fugitives, the Geneva magistracy confiscated that money as well as all the decedent's property. This act prompted a letter from the Bern seigneury, accusing Geneva of inhumanity in depriving the decedent's unborn child of his inheritance. Again, Calvin was called upon to reply, pointing out that Perrin had for twenty years been treasurer of the city and had avoided making any accounting of finances.[5]

The stalemate continued. In February 1557 the matter was turned over to Basel, Schaffhausen, and Zurich for arbitration. But in June, the Bernese bailiff of Ternier, without notifying the attorney general of Geneva, called the fugitives before his tribunal to reconsider their sentence and declared them liberated. The whole thing was a flagrant infringement of Geneva's rights, but the Bernese court of appeals upheld the judgment and ordered Geneva to pay the libertines 200,000 crowns and reinstate them.

The Geneva council called an extraordinary session, "praying Monsieur Calvin to resist this oppression by all legal means." Again it was necessary to have recourse to the League, protesting these "acts of extortion and violence."[6] Deputies were sent first to Bern, then on to Baden, to demand that Bern annul the order of the bailiff of Ternier.

In September the cantons exhorted Bern to moderation and

offered to mediate the matter. Their efforts resulted in a compromise, and the libertines found themselves reduced to the status of nuisance. But it was the imminent danger of an attack by France, Spain, and Savoy that finally brought about the signing of the alliance on 9 January 1558.

There was also, in 1556, the unpleasant matter of Calvin's brother's divorce. Antoine's wife was caught *flagrante delicto* in bed with Peter Daguet, Calvin's humpbacked servant (who, it was discovered, had been cheating Calvin for several years of money from his household expenses). The wife was banished, threatened with being whipped publicly if she returned to Geneva, and Daguet was imprisoned. Of course, his enemies derided Calvin that such a scandal had occurred in his home.

But these trials were nothing in the scales with his mental and emotional turmoil over events in France. As fountainhead of French Protestantism, how could he be divorced from the beginning of the Wars of Religion? He remembered only too well the fires in Paris after the placard affair. He remembered his friend Étienne de La Forge burned in the cemetery of St. Jean. In 1553 he had exerted himself passionately when the five young students from Switzerland were arrested in Lyon and condemned to be burned by Matthew Ory. Now violent persecution had broken out against the Waldensians. Henry II was stepping up his campaign to eradicate heresy throughout his kingdom, and others, near and dear to Calvin, were among the increasing number of martyrs.

Two ministers of the Angers church were burned that spring. When the elders wrote, inquiring of Calvin if they might use violence against their enemies, he replied that they would never obtain the blessings of God by such means; that "God has not armed you to resist those whom he has established to govern."[7]

Fifty-six refugees arrived in Geneva from Artois and Picardy in December. In March Calvin sent two ministers to the church at Paris (organized two years before), which was meeting in the house of Monsieur de La Ferrière, near the Près-aux-Clercs, where members prayed together, read the Scriptures, sang songs. Already a consistory had been set up to visit the poor and to watch over the purity of doctrine and morals.

In July Nicholas Des Gallardes was sent to Paris, accompanied by Nicolas de Rousseau, carrying books and letters to various French correspondents from Calvin. Rousseau was arrested on the way and starved in a dungeon of Dijon before his body was consigned to the flames.

To try to stop the persecution, Calvin dispatched Beza to the German princes, asking for a conference of German Protestants to meet with their Swiss and French counterparts, thus proclaiming their unity of Reformed belief, and so placing the French Protestants under the protection of the German princes whom Henry II was wooing to join him in his fight with Spain.

That was in May. On 8 August the Battle of Saint-Quentin was fought, disastrous to France. While negotiations were carried on for a peace treaty between Henry II and his enemies Spain and Savoy, scaffolds and stakes for French Protestants sprang up throughout the kingdom.

On 14 September, Jacquelin de Rohan, marchioness of Rothelin, passed through Geneva on the way to Bern to borrow gold to pay the ransom of her son taken at the Battle of Saint-Quentin. The marchioness was the widow of Francis of Orléans and had promoted the Reformation in her domain for some time, corresponding with both Calvin and Farel. She brought Calvin distressing news of the church at Paris.

Ten days before, a conventicle held in a house on the rue St. Jacques had been raided. The populace vented their fury on the Huguenots (as they were now being called), tearing the robes of the women, showering them with the contents of the gutters, following them with jeers as they were being conducted to the châtelet. There the prisoners were remanded without trial, thrown into cells vacated for the purpose by criminals, where they remained, without food or water.

What could Calvin do, other than write letters to the prisoners, trying to give them courage. His letter "To the Women Detained in Prison in Paris" reveals his grief and solicitude.[8] The

women were Phillippe de Lunz, widow of the seigneur de Gra-
veron and the Mesdames de Rentigny, d'Ouartes, de Longemeau, and de Champagne.

He wrote the churches of Lausanne, Moudon, and Payerne
asking them to take up offerings for the church at Paris. He sent
John Budé, Farel, and Beza to the cantons and to the German
princes, urging intervention with Henry II. Then, though remembering his letter to Francis I years before, and how little it accomplished, and having no hope that this one would be read, he wrote
a long dissertation on the faith of the Reformed, addressing it
"To the King: the Confession of the Churches of France."[9]

Persecutions in the south of France, especially around Grenoble, were increasing, with the authorities offering fifty gold
crowns for information leading to the arrest of every Reformed
minister or schoolmaster.

In December he wrote Madame de Rentigny, daughter of the
seigneur de Rambouillet, who was still in prison.[10] She was wife
of the standard-bearer of the duke of Guise, himself the acknowledged leader of the burgeoning Catholic party and the idol of the
Parisian commoners.

Madame de Rentigny had steadfastly refused to be swayed by
her father or her husband. In his letter Calvin praised her constancy and told her of the prayers of the church. A few days later,
he wrote to Mademoiselle de Longemeau, encouraging her, as
best he could. "Whatever deliverance men may promise you," he
wrote, "God will not let you off. If you pretend to make any
compromise in order to save your life even for three days, it will
mean selling your heavenly inheritance for three days' purchase
of the world. . . ."[11]

That same day he wrote an impassioned appeal to Antoine de
Bourbon, king of Navarre.[12] Already the religious struggle was
entering the political phase. Antoine, duke of Bourbon, first
prince of the blood, had married Jeanne d'Albret (1528–72),
daughter of Margaret, queen of Navarre. By his marriage, Bourbon became ruler of a quasi-independent kingdom fought over
by France and Spain. Only protection by France could prevent
his kingdom's being taken over by Spain.

Feeble and irresolute though he was, he had allowed Reformed doctrine to be preached at his court two years before, and in April 1557 the minister sent by Calvin had reported Navarre's "favorable disposition." Surely if any man would take in hand the cause of the French Protestantism, it would be the king of Navarre.

If only Calvin could have made his requests short and to the point instead of encasing them in sermons of many pages! But that was not Calvin's way. He *had* to preach the word in season and out of season. And though he tactfully suggested that the weak ruler simply bring the matter up at the coming meeting of the States-General, Antoine of Navarre did not even attend that meeting on 6 January. Knowing Henry II, he could be sure that any suggestion of clemency or justice would have been rejected.

By the new year, seven members of the Paris church had suffered martyrdom: three women in September; two men on 2 October; two young students the last of that month. For a while there was a lull, owing to the intervention of the German princes. The thirty members of the church in Paris arrested but not yet executed or dead from natural causes (such as exposure and starvation) were sent to monasteries to be reconverted. Calvin sent two new ministers to the church at Paris: John Macar and a nobleman, Antoine de La Roche-Chandieu.

Five January 1558 was a full day for Calvin. On that day he dictated letters to the church at Paris;[13] to the church at Meaux,[14] which had early supplied fuel for the fires in France; to the church at Dieppe, one of the first in Normandy, to whom he sent exhortations and a minister;[15] and to the marchioness of Rothelin, exhorting her to serve God faithfully in prosperity as well as in affliction.[16]

He had already begun planning for the erection of his college, but he took time in February to write his longtime correspondent, the duke of Württemberg, a zealous supporter of the Reformation and one of the princes who had intervened with Henry II. The letter told the duke of conditions in France: the burnings of the seven prisoners in Paris; the cardinal of Lorraines's rebuke of the king for his apathy in ferreting out heresy, and the cardinal's castigation of French judges for their leniency.

The king, Calvin said, had petitioned the pope to appoint three cardinals of France to judge heresy cases without appeal. The cardinal of Lorraine now had full power to act, since the only remedy for the disease was complete extermination of the carriers of the plague. The king had issued a new edict from Compiègne, giving bishops plenary jurisdiction, judges of the civil arm ordered to execute all heretics handed over to them.[17]

In April a letter from John Macar, pastor of the church at Paris, told Calvin that Madame de Rentigny, harassed by judges and family, had agreed to hear mass in her prison, after which she was freed. Immediately she had asked pardon of the church, and had already bought horses to transport her to Geneva when her husband became seriously ill, his life despaired of, and she returned to him under assurance that he would not interfere with her faith. In July the report came that her husband was no better; she begged for Calvin's prayers.[18]

Calvin was not unduly severe toward her. He reproached her for her weakness but urged her to be courageous, saying she would not be justified in alienating herself from her husband, yet it would be better for her to die than to choose her husband over God.[19]

There was another prisoner of Henry II about whom Calvin was more seriously concerned. In the spring of 1558 the king became suddenly aware that the heretics were more than simply rebels against his divine authority. There was, first, the great crowd congregated on the rue St. Jacques, as many as four hundred it was reported to him, though only a tenth of them had been caught and imprisoned.

The next sign of rebellion, of insurrection, the cardinal of Lorraine had persuaded him, was word that hundreds of believers in the "pretended reformed religion" had gathered for several nights in the Près-aux-Clercs, walking about arm in arm, singing Lutheran hymns and Psalms, a great outburst. The uproar could be heard all over the quarter and even across the Seine, and officers of the guard had to be called out to disperse the crowd. The king was more than alarmed: he was badly frightened, seeing in this disturbance of the peace open political and religious revolt.

A few days later, when it was reported to him by the cardinal of Lorraine that François de Châtillon, seigneur d'Andelot and colonel general of French infantry, had been so bold as to permit Reformed preaching in his domain in Brittany, he acted immediately, calling Andelot before him to give an account of his actions.

Andelot freely admitted the charge. His eloquent and spirited response need not be quoted; two sentences suffice: "Your Majesty will hardly think it strange that after doing my duty in your service, I study to seek my own salvation" and "I pray you, Sire, to leave my conscience alone; let me serve you with my body and my worldly goods, which are wholly yours."[20] Henry II heard the words as offense rather than defense. Andelot was immediately imprisoned in the tower of Melun.

When Calvin heard of Andelot's imprisonment early in May, he wrote at once, congratulating him on his constancy and urging him to persevere.[21] At the same time he wrote again to Navarre, who, following the disturbance at the Près-aux-Clercs had gone to the châtelet and demanded the release of La Roche-Chandieu, the minister taken at the rue St. Jacques riot, claiming him as part of his household. Calvin took heart from his act. The Reform was no longer simply a matter of preaching and secret meetings. Coming into the open, it had become political, and the party must have a leader. The hopes of all French Protestants were now centered on Navarre. Calvin begged the king to profess his faith publicly, before the court, "even though it may disquiet you in your person, your royal dignity, your state, your honors and property."[22]

On 12 July, Calvin wrote again to Andelot.[23] After the young lord's arrival in Melun, his brother Odet, cardinal of Châtillon, and Andelot's pregnant wife begged him to make an act of submission to the king. Andelot refused. The first of July he wrote to the Paris church that he was to be interrogated the following day and prayed that God would put into his mouth words that would redound to God's glory. But a week later he did petition the king for forgiveness, saying, "Except for the obedience I owe God and my conscience, you will never command me to do anything wherein I shall not promptly and faithfully expose my body, my wealth, and my life."[24]

Calvin assured Andelot that God had set him up for an example; that he had been imprisoned in order to do the task to which God called him. He reminded him of Hosea's message: that God reproved Israel for obeying the edicts of the king.

The letter did not reach Andelot in time to shore up his strength. Macar wrote Calvin on 14 July that the prisoner had fully explained his beliefs to the theologian sent to interrogate him, who had agreed with him on many points. Then Andelot had written the king, begging him to give the churchman a hearing, "for after hearing his report, you will not be disappointed with me. . . . I will obey you as God commands me."[25]

But His Majesty was not noted for listening to tedious reports or reading anything. Andelot consented to hear mass in his prison, was released—and condemned his weakness to the day of his death. Calvin, too, blamed him for his weakness, pointing to the courage of martyrs, urging him to repair the scandal caused by his fall, declaring that God had sent the affliction on him to lead him to salvation.[26]

As for Andelot, he had his newborn daughter baptized in the church at Paris, praying "our heavenly Father that first of all he will bless this creature of his of which he has made me father, that her beginning and end may be dedicated to his glory; and grant us the grace and strength constantly to resist his enemies and my own, while I shall fight for the coming of the reign of his Son Jesus Christ."[27] He knew quite well that the king was considering imprisoning him for life as an example to all others of the "pretended reformed religion."

On 19 July, Calvin wrote a long letter to Galeazzo Caracciolo, again on a fruitless trip to Italy, begging him to take care and to hasten his return to Geneva, where he was needed to help straighten out more antitrinitarian trouble in the Italian church.[28] The day after, he wrote to his friend, the duchess of Ferrara.

XV

Ferrara
1555–58

Gradually connubial peace was restored; and though the duchess had not been imprisoned for life, she had come near enough to total disaster to make her realize her danger and that of her children and the duchy. Protestantism in Ferrara had been crushed. She refused to return to the ducal palace however, dwelling sometimes at the Palazzo San Francesco, sometimes at Consandolo.

Throughout 1555 negotiations between the duke and king went forward, French ambassadors spending months in Ferrara for the purpose of drawing Ercole into a proposed league with Henry II and Pope Paul IV against Spain. The old emperor had retired, worn out with fighting, leaving the Spanish throne to his son Philip, an unknown quantity except for his passionate Catholic zeal. It seemed to pope and king a propitious time to push their ambitious projects, Henry to attempt—like Charles VIII, Louis XII, and Francis I—to make himself lord of Naples and assert his dominance over all Italy; Paul IV, to rid the peninsula of Spanish hegemony and then to push the French back beyond the mountains.

As in every Italian invasion, France needed Ferrara as banker and as supplier of arms and ammunition, as well as rearguard. The king's inducements to Ercole were enticing: if he joined the proposed league, he would be awarded great estates in Naples, Tuscany, and Milan, with Cremona thrown in as a bonus— if and when these places were taken. The duke would be named lieutenant general of all the French forces. His Majesty would deposit 300,000 crowns to the duke's account with Venetian bankers. (If it should chance that the king did not have that much ready money, he would pay what he could, borrowing the remainder from Ercole with the promise to pay it back when he could.)

Charles, cardinal of Lorraine, was Henry's chief negotiator. Because he was her son-in-law's brother as well as her nephew's chief advisor, Renée exerted herself to make his stay in Ferrara pleasant and to do all she could to bring about a rapprochement between her husband and the king. She sent a servitor to Ravenna in charge of two coaches and with an escort of eight horsemen to bring His Reverence to Ferrara, and he spent much time with her, discussing strategy.

In spite of the excuses Ercole made in putting off the unavoidable, he signed the treaty of alliance with France and the Papal States on 15 November. Paul IV signed it on 10 December. Ercole recalled his ambassador from the Spanish court, fortified his chief cities, called up his troops. In February he was notified that Henry had signed a truce with the emperor. The war was off, and Ercole was naked to his enemies, Correggio, Parma, and Florence, all allies of Spain.

The duke sent letter after letter to the king, demanding compensation, begging for help if he should be attacked. He was informed that the treaty was predicated on the existence of a league which had never been announced; since the league had not gone into effect, neither had the treaty; His Majesty therefore owed the duke nothing.

After much bitter recrimination by the duke, he was awarded a pension of 12,000 crowns with a "gift" of 100,000 crowns provided he would maintain a certain number of French troops.

All this was accompanied by the soothing assurance that if hostilities between France and Spain were resumed, the duke would still be Henry's lieutenant general in Italy.

Renée took it upon herself to be peacemaker. She knew how greatly disappointed the king already was that Ercole had not leaped at the opportunity of marrying Alfonso to any of the French wives he had suggested—the last two his daughter Elizabeth and his sister Margaret—and how outraged he was that Ercole had not responded eagerly to the proposition of marrying Lucrezia to Jacques de Savoy, duke of Nemours.

Now Renée wrote her nephew: "Monseigneur, it will please you to learn from my husband's ambassador, the great pains he has taken to obey and satisfy you."[1]

Matters were smoothed over. In spite of the duke's resentment, he allowed Alfonso to return to the French court with his blessings as well as Renée's. A little later, when the father discovered, and nipped in the bud, a malicious trick of Cosimo de' Medici to spirit away to Spain Luigi, avid for military glory like Alfonso's, he permitted that son too to depart for Paris, to the tearful joy of the boy's mother.

The Franco-Spanish truce was of short duration. When, at the close of 1556, Spanish troops under Alba invaded the states of the church, the defunct league was reactivated. Henry, though beleaguered in the north by Spain and Savoy, sent Guise to rescue the pope.

Guise came first to Ferrara, to borrow money and to secure arms before setting out for Rome and beyond. But Ercole refused to leave his duchy unprotected while two thousand Spanish troops occupied nearby Correggio. He tried to persuade his son-in-law to join forces with him in seizing Cremona and Parma, both promised him by the king if and when they were taken. Guise, however, was not to be deterred from the glory his brother had held before him of taking Naples and carving out a kingdom for himself.

Guise was besieged by Alba's forces at Civitella; when he was able, he retreated to Rome, where the Colonna were almost at the walls and the pope was crying for help. Meanwhile Ercole was happily occupied with a lengthy trial of one Osimo, a Spanish agent who had smuggled arms into Ferrara with the aim of fomenting a revolt and assassinating the ducal family—"happily," since it prevented his going to the assistance of his son-in-law and the pope.

Osimo's trial was still in progress when Guise, with a part of his army, arrived in Ferrara on his way back to France, responding to the king's urgent call for help. The French in the north, besieged at Saint-Quentin by Savoy and Spain, had been overwhelmed, Montmorency and Coligny with other officers taken captive. There was nothing—and no one—to prevent the Spanish from marching straight on to Paris. Guise was the only hope of saving France.

For the remainder of 1557 and most of the following year soldiers straggled back from Naples—the viable ones Guise had left behind to find their way home as best they could—the crippled, wounded, sick, and starving, who had heard of the benevolence of the lady duchess of Ferrara who dispensed food, clothing, and alms so generously to the men she regarded as her rightful subjects except for the "hateful Salic law." Brantôme said these transients cost Renée more than 10,000 crowns. Her account books for 1559 show that the interest on loans she had incurred for this purpose amounted to more than 700 gold crowns.

Back in France Guise restored confidence and pride to the French people by taking Calais from the English garrison (with strategy devised years before by Gaspard de Coligny, said the admiral's friends). Throughout the kingdom bells were rung and prayers of thanksgiving made to God and all the saints. "Le Balafré"—so-called because of the scar across his face won in the Battle of Boulogne—already a hero, now became the idol of the Paris mob. Rejoicing was not confined to France. Renée rewarded the courier who brought the news of the great victory to Ferrara in January, the king's officer who confirmed it, and the trumpeters whom the duke sent to serenade her in honor of their son-in-law's triumph.

Ercole himself was not in a joyful frame of mind: in order to free Montmorency and Montmorency's nephew Gaspard de Coligny, Henry II was ready again to negotiate peace with Spain, to Guise's infinite disgust. The pope had already signed a truce. Again without allies, Ercole found himself in a dangerous situation: since he was not included in the treaties with king and pope, he would be regarded with a less than friendly eye by Philip II for his earlier defection. Parma and Correggio were poised for attack. It was probably because of the betrothal about to be announced of Alfonso and a daughter of Cosimo de' Medici, that the duke of Tuscany came to Ercole's assistance, securing a treaty between Ercole and Philip II on most humiliating terms for Ferrara.

Negotiations relative to the Florentine marriage continued for so long that the intended bride died, to be replaced by her thirteen-year-old sister. Instead of surrendering to the pressure of Henry II, of the duke and duchess of Guise, and of Renée herself to marry Alfonso to 35-year-old Margaret of France, the duke had his way. The marriage took place in Florence with great magnificence, and Alfonso left his bride there, the marriage unconsummated, to return to France.

Aside from her alarm over the aborted wars of the league, the distress she had felt in the spring when word came that Alfonso had been thrown from a horse and was lying in a coma, his life in the balance, and her worries about the possible recklessness of Luigi at the French court, the duchess enjoyed a time of comparative peace during these last few years in Ferrara. The duke's adherence to the ill-fated league had not been entirely without benefit: it had been tacitly understood that Renée would be left in peace if she preserved the appearance of being a good Catholic.

Her account books show she was often entertained by musicians, dancers, even acrobats. She had her daughters' portraits painted. She supervised the renovation and decoration of a part of the ducal palace for Lucrezia and Leonora, with paintings of glass panels made by Bastianino and artfully-made columns against a background of gold. She employed a goldsmith who designed and made gold chains and buttons for her and a statuette of the Virgin in enamel and gold. She petted her dwarfs, Agnès and André. When little André died, she had a tomb made for him, beautifully sculptured, and a coffin; she gave him a Christian burial and truly grieved for him. She gave dowries to the girls who served her and distributed alms to the poor. She paid monks who came to preach before her. There is only one instance of her pleading for a person accused of heresy. When Giambattista Visconti of Genoa was sent to Ferrara as local inquisitor after the death of Papino, he began a process against a Dominican whom Ercole himself had invited to Ferrara and who became a great friend of Renée. Neither duke nor duchess could prevent the man's being taken to Rome to be tried for heresy.

She spent much time in writing letters. Most of them are found today in the Bibliothèque Nationale. After Alfonso's marriage, she wrote letters of the warmest friendship to Cosimo de' Medici; she wrote to Guise, with whom she had a cordial relation. Anne kept her informed of her own affairs—the birth of her first son Henry in 1550; Charles two years after; gossip of the court, where Anne had an exalted position, enjoying the companionship of her husband's young niece Mary Stuart, who sneered, with Anne, at His Majesty's rather plebeian and quite unattractive wife Catherine de' Medici.

Several times she wrote to Cardinal Caraffa, begging favors for those who appealed to her for help; once for a poor student who wanted to find employment; once to beg Caraffa to remit the punishment of a native of Ravenna condemned to the galleys.

She was rather well-informed of growing tensions in France. She wrote to François d'Andelot, imprisoned in Melun, sending him tracts of John Calvin's, which Andelot sent on to his brother Coligny.

Undoubtedly she continued her correspondence with Calvin, as the duke suspected, confiding her grief at having to appear to conform to a religion she felt wrong. It was to one of these letters that he replied on 20 July 1558.

XVI

The Fifth Letter

Madame,

I thank God that the man I sent you has so well done his duty as to satisfy you.[1] I rejoice to know it, and I trust that his labors may have helped you to advance in the path toward salvation. Now, since God has not seen fit for him to continue serving you any longer, I beg you to continue to be taught daily in the school of Jesus Christ. You are sufficiently aware (without being reminded by others) of the need you have of that, especially when the devil stirs up all the trouble he can to turn you aside from it.

Since you have to resist every plot this mortal enemy of our salvation would hatch against you, remember that God uses such means to test your faith. If the trial seems sharp and bitter to you, consider well what St. Paul said: if a corruptible metal is put into the fire to ascertain whether it be genuine, shall not your faith, which is more precious, also be tried?

If you feel you are weaker than you would like to be, turn to the One who has decreed that those who trust in him shall be like a tree planted by the rivers, having a strong and living root which shall never wither, whatever heats may come. It is certain that God will never permit us to be tempted more than we can bear; and if God allows Satan to assail us, God will at the same time increase our strength sufficiently to overcome every obstacle. It is often useful to probe our wounds deeply, not to make us relax our efforts in despair but to stir us up to seek the remedy.

Wherefore, Madame, while you are confident that the enemy

foaming with rage will accomplish nothing regardless of his efforts without the permission of the sovereign Master, yet do not cease to strive against all temptations; and since you will have need of arms for that purpose in having recourse to the One who will strengthen you for the fight, listen also to holy exhortations. Do not consider it only a slight advantage to have had a man near you to urge you daily to your duty, a resource of which you have already proved the utility.

I hope your friends will not fail you in this, and when you are ready to send me word to procure you a suitable person, I shall most willingly execute your command. Only, Madame, take courage; do not give Satan the advantage he is seeking—of finding you unprovided. And beware when you think you are only making pretenses for avoiding the combat lest this fear give the enemy the very victory he is trying to obtain. We must know his wiles in order to defeat him. Though the condition of God's children should be a hundred times harder, that is no reason to quit the good to which the God of infinite bounty has been pleased to call us.

I have also been informed, Madame, that you are not without torments in your household. This evil you must overcome like the others. There may appear danger that those who refuse to be brought over to the right way but remain obstinate, may if you dismiss them seek vengeance by backbiting and lies; yet it is better to run this risk than to go on thus, irritated continually. The main point is to purge your house, as God commands you to do, for which you have the example of David in Psalm 101. When you have taken pains to dedicate it pure and undefiled to God, you may be sure that God will be its protector. It is true that however much you strive for that end, there will also be imperfections; so much the more it behoves you to bestir yourself that you may at least halfway perform your duty. In the meantime we have the assurance that if we aim at the mark, God will accept the will for the deed.

I have still, Madame, one word to say about your scruples as to the presentation to benefices. Since the property is not yours, if you cannot do better and so as not to burden yourself, entrust the direction of it to the worthy Abbé, who will be delighted to take it off your shoulders. And to the letters of authority which you give him, you may conveniently add the clause that because you do not wish to be mixed up with what concerns the church, and in order to satisfy your conscience, you appoint him to that office. I see no possible way for you to make good use of that trust.

For the rest, Madame, I beg you to make yourself callous to censure while doing good, since these are the wages we are promised from on high. As to threats, which are harder to ignore, strive against succumbing to them; in giving way to them instead of advancing, you will go backward. Do not be astonished if you find contradictions in yourself; however valiant a champion St. Peter was, it was said of him: "They will lead thee whither thou wouldst not go." There we have proof that we can never belong to God without some opposition on our part, because our flesh shrinks from the struggle.

I heard that the excellent lord [Caracciolo, marquis de Vico] of whom you will be glad to have news had crossed the sea at the end of March and before the middle of June had obtained a promise that some galleys should be dispatched to bring his wife, for the passage is not long. He obtained this favor from the captain, who can gratify him in this matter, without trouble or expense. I fancy, however, that he will soon be back if God does not miraculously change the heart of his wife, who loves him in such a way that she would draw him on to perdition if she could. At any rate, it will be enough to excuse him before God and man that he has done his duty.

Madame, I commend myself humbly to your kind favor, supplicating our heavenly Father to direct you always by the Spirit, to fortify you by his strength, to have you in his keeping, and to increase you in all good.

Your most humble servant,
Charles d'Espeville
20 July 1558

XVII

Geneva
1558–60

Calvin's correspondence continued with his oldest friends Guillaume Farel, Pierre Viret, and Heinrich Bullinger, of course, but more and more with those persons directly concerned with the Huguenots, the confederates, of France. For the most part we will follow only these letters from now on and letters telling his friends of conditions in France.

In August 1558 he wrote to James Hamilton, earl of Arran and duke of Châtelherault, who for several years past had been captain of the king's Scots Guards, but was now, through the enmity of the Guises, confined in the castle of Vincennes for permitting Reformed preaching in his domain. The time had arrived, as Andelot had demonstrated, that people could expect no immunity because of their rank.

To John Garnier, a Lutheran preacher in Strasbourg and Frankfurt, he wrote that Andelot had retired now from the court, openly declaring that he had never abandoned the Reformed faith. Andelot asked him to write to his brother Gaspard de Coligny, seriously ill in his prison fortress in Flanders.

Coligny had come to court when he was twenty-five, product of two famous families. His father, the first Gaspard, had been marshall of France, serving in the Italian wars of Charles VIII and Louis XII. His mother was Louise de Montmorency, proudest of all the names of the old French nobility, sister of Francis I's great friend and beloved mentor of Henry II.

At first a friend of Francis of Guise, two years his junior, Coligny soon came to be his military rival. He fought in Italy, Lorraine, and Flanders. He put down a revolt in Rochelle and fought in the battle of Boulogne, where the first open enmity between him and Francis of Guise erupted. Since Coligny was nephew of Montmorency, he became part of the bitter Montmorency-Guise rivalry for favors of the king. He was named admiral of France, received the Order of St. Michael, reformed the army, preserving (according to Brantôme) thousands of lives. In 1556 he was sent to negotiate the short-lived truce of Vaucelles with Philip II, the truce which Henry, advised by the cardinal of Lorraine and the duke of Guise, broke by invading Italy.

But all those honors were his before the disastrous battle at Saint-Quentin, where he held back the enemy for three weeks before his uncle Montmorency brought about the final catastrophe. Now, in his prison at L'Éclus, Coligny had nothing to do but read his Bible and letters and pamphlets sent him by his friends, wait for Henry and Philip to come to terms—again over the protests of Guise—and hope that his family could raise the 50,000 crowns for his ransom.

Calvin wrote him on 4 September. The letter, like those written to other prisoners, was sympathetic and encouraging. He does not need to exhort Coligny, he says, to accept what he already believes—Coligny's mother, as well as his boyhood teacher had been believers of the new opinions—"since God has so strengthened you by the power of his Spirit, I have more need to glorify him for the favor he has wrought in you than to incite you to more." But Calvin could not refrain from warning Coligny of the dangers when "those who hold the highest places in the world are so occupied with it and held captive in its toils that they scarcely give themselves time for the chief of all works— to worship God, to dedicate themselves solely to him, to aspire after the heavenly life. . . ."[1]

The same day he wrote Charlotte de Laval, Coligny's wife, sympathizing with her in her husband's captivity, advising her to serve God in spite of the criticism and hatred of the world. He did not know that Madame de Coligny had already decided on that step and would persuade her husband, when he was released from captivity the following year, to profess his belief publicly. "It is most reasonable," Calvin wrote her, "that we should dedicate ourselves to the One who has bought us at such a price. According to the love God has bestowed upon us, we should esteem divine favor more than the smiles of all the world," He closed his letter with a prayer that God would fill her with divine constancy.[2]

On 10 September he sent a letter to "The Brethren of Metz," rejoicing that the congregation, which had met secretly for fifteen years, had now decided to declare itself openly.[3]

Two weeks later he was writing a long letter to the ministers of Neuchâtel where his old friend Farel, now 69, was planning to marry a young woman from Rouen. This is a letter one must wish Calvin had never written, for it is highly critical of his friend, celibate all these years. To many such a step seemed "strange and unseasonable." Calvin had so sublimated himself in his work that he could not conceive of any reason for such an act. Was it to provide against the infirmities of old age, he hazarded. He blushed, he said, for the man's weakness, but he would not try to break the alliance at this late date. Announcement of the banns had already been made, on 11 September, with two more to follow, on 25 September and 2 October. To break off now would only add to the scandal. But it should have been prevented. "Half a year ago our poor brother would have declared that a person who, at so advanced an age, desired to marry so young a woman should be bound like a madman. . . . I told him it would be better to terminate the affair promptly than, by delaying, occasion a great deal more foolish gossip. . . ."[4]

He was hurt that Farel had invited him to the espousals by letter. He felt that he could have prevented the marriage if his friend had taken him into his confidence earlier. He replied to Farel's invitation, saying that he would be unable to come to either espousals or marriage; that two ministers of Geneva were sick, another in Paris; the city was in so perturbed a state that the magistracy would not permit him to go so far. And anyway, his coming to Neuchâtel for the ceremony would only cause more malicious gossip.[5]

Mid-October saw him suffering with another illness. Acute pain, chills, dyspepsia led to several days of strict fasting, and that to extreme weakness followed by a quartan ague. His doctors, he said in November, had kept him in bed for six weeks, under a double coverlet. His recommended diet was evidently the cause of extreme constipation, for which he had to endure too many painful enemas. He had a burning thirst all the time, for which he was first told, "no strong drink," then ordered to drink malmsey and muscat mixed with spleenwort or wormwood. He was now taking syrup of hyssop to fortify his stomach, elecampane or citrus bark, and using pressure in the attempt to expel the bilious humors from the spleen.[6] Yet he lived for five and half more years!

He was still weak at the beginning of the new year, but his tremendous correspondence continued. He could not rest in his attempts to bring all nations to the Truth. In January he wrote William Cecil (Lord Burghley, 1520–98), hoping for the establishment of the pure gospel in England.[7]

Elizabeth would be greatly incensed with Calvin a few months later, because John Knox's *The First Blast of the Trumpet against the Monstrous Regiment of Women* had been printed in Geneva. The work was, of course, directed at Mary Tudor, but in it Knox inveighed against the right of women to hold the reins of authority, and since Calvin's name was associated with that of Knox, her indignation extended to him. Calvin had sent the queen one of his books, which she refused to accept. Her repulse wounded his dignity. He assured her that Knox's book had been published without his knowing of it, that he disapproved of Knox's inconsiderate vanity, and Holy Scripture approved of government by women, but the queen was not mollified. She might, he said, have just refused his book without repulsing and accusing him falsely.[8]

In February he wrote Martin Miconius, a Protestant reformer who had fled from London, about the Reformation in Sweden and about his concern that the Mennonite heresy was rampant in the Netherlands.[9] Another siege of tertian ague laid him low, and he was told that he could neither read in public nor preach. For a short time he followed instructions, whispering his dictation to his secretary, writing the three prisoners of the church in Paris still in the châtelet, counseling patience, constancy, trust, hope— not hope that their lives would be spared, they were under sentence of death—but hope in the life to come.[10]

The last of the month he wrote again to Madame de Coligny, whose husband had been moved from L'Éclus to the tower of Ghent.[11] To her he said nothing of his ill health, but to Peter Martyr, in a letter written 2 March, he confided that he had stomach cramps, catarrh, and had been coughing for more than a week.[12] But four days later he was at St. Peter's, presiding over the celebration marking the opening of the university for which he had worked so strenuously, bringing outstanding scholars to lecture on theology and philosophy in an institution which would rapidly become world famous, vying with *The Institutes of the Christian Religion* as the crowning glory of his life.

The last of April the Treaty of Cateau-Cambrésis was signed, the cardinals of Lorraine and Granville having come to an agreement in regard to the extermination of heresy in France. At the news, Geneva began girding for the expected three-pronged attack. Philip's army was two days' march distant, Henry's half an hour, Emmanuel Philibert of Savoy right on their doorstep.

In Paris preparations were being made for the magnificent celebration marking the signing of the peace treaty, to be sealed by the marriages of the king's sister Margaret to Emmanuel Philibert of Savoy, and the king's daughter Elizabeth to Philip of Spain. There was another meeting in Paris at the same time, one of more lasting significance than that celebrating the Franco-Spanish pact: representatives from eleven French Huguenot churches gathered, uniting in defense of their rights and their liberty, to set up a church organization similar to that of Geneva and to accept a common confession of faith. The first General

Assembly of the Reformed church met in the shadow of the gibbet. Two years later 2,150 churches would send representatives to the body. This enormous growth was not owing to a remarkable excess of religious feeling. A great number of those who joined the Huguenots were activated by economic and political motives. The Wars of Religion were forerunners of the French Revolution.

Word of this gathering must have reached the king; or perhaps he had resolved to lose no time in showing his resolute piety. With the cardinal of Lorraine he appeared before the Parlement of Paris to hold a bed of justice. He inquired solicitously as to what the judges considered the best way to deal with the Lutheran evil. Three opted for toleration of the doctrines which, they hastily assured the king, they themselves did not profess. Louis de Four and Anne Du Bourg declared their Reformed belief, begging His Majesty to give their leaders a hearing. The two men were immediately imprisoned, questioned, tortured. Du Bourg would be burned in December. When Calvin wrote them, early in June, the outcome was only too sure.

The last of June Pope Paul preached a crusade against Geneva, against the antichrist who reigned there and sent his minions forth to poison souls. Geneva must be destroyed. With that clarion call to all rightful rulers, His Majesty could not be dilatory in punishing those heretics already in his hands.

On the last day of June, the king took part in his last tournament. In the lists before Les Tournelles he showed again and again his virility and prowess against younger men, impatiently brushing aside the queen's protests. When a splintered lance pierced his eye, he fell from his horse into the arms of young Alfonso d'Este, and was carried to his bed, to die ten days later without regaining consciousness. What could the Reformed see in that broken lance but the judgment of God?

Catherine de' Medici retired for her forty days' widow's seclusion. The dauphin-now-king, fifteen-year-old Francis II, married since April to Mary Stuart, turned over all affairs of the kingdom to his wife's uncles: the cardinal of Lorraine would look after the treasury and, with the help of Diane de Poitiers, dispense favors;

the duke of Guise would head the army. The Guises were in complete control. The only ray of encouragement for the Reformed was the clause in the Edict of Blois, establishing a *Chambre ardente* for trial of heretics, which made three French bishops judges of that court instead of setting up a true Inquisition like that of Rome, this palliative owing to the chancellor, L'Hôpital.

Not all the French nobility were supporters of the Guise faction. It was evident that Francis was incompetent; but if a regent was necessary, that office by long-established custom belonged to the first prince of the blood, Antoine de Bourbon, king of Navarre. Calvin, watching from his aerie, doubted that Navarre could be of any help in the present situation. He had no confidence in the man, he said. Although he had corresponded with Navarre, had supplied him with ministers and a tutor for his son, he had a very poor opinion of the prince.

But in France, seeing the depredations of the Guises, many nobles awaited Navarre's coming to court to take his rightful place in the privy council, to confront the interlopers, to help bring about domestic peace. But Navarre delayed his coming. Patently the man was afraid. Weak and irresolute, Calvin called him, seeing no help for the Reformed from that quarter. He wrote to the duke of Longueville, urging him to profess publicly the belief of his mother, the Marchioness of Rothelin.[13] But Longueville was related by marriage to Mary of Lorraine and feared to take a stand.

The countess of Roye, mother-in-law of the prince of Condé, Navarre's younger brother, had with difficulty secured an interview for La Roche-Chandieu, minister of the Reformed church at Paris, with the queen mother, in hopes that Catherine would intervene with her son on behalf of the Reformed. Catherine mocked the minister, deriding his "so-called religion," and dismissed him unheard.

It was reported to Calvin that a house-to-house survey was being made in Paris, people being asked if their neighbors attended mass, saluted images of the Virgin at street corners, or sheltered Lutherans. Informers were awarded the property of the guilty. Private feuds swelled the number of those imprisoned.

Calvin could do little but write letters and pray, refusing to countenance force. Others were itching to take direct action. Theodore Beza went to Strasbourg to confer with François Hotman and other impatient men on ways to curb Guise power. Calvin's warnings had no effect.

In November Calvin wrote to John Knox,[14] just returned to Scotland where Mary of Guise, widow of James V, was acting as regent for her daughter Mary Stuart, now queen of France. Already, Knox had reported, French cannon had been brought into Scotland and the regent had sworn to suppress the growing Reformation by force. It was said she had entered into an agreement with her brothers to help them in their designs against Elizabeth of England, since in the eyes of Catholic Europe the English throne belong of right to Mary of Guise's daughter.

On Christmas Day the seigneury of Geneva conferred citizenship on the man whom they had consulted for the past eighteen years "on legal matters, the economy, trade, police, manufacturing. To him the city owed her trade in cloths and velvets . . . ; sanitary regulations introduced by him made Geneva the admiration of all visitors. . . ."[15] During the ceremony Calvin was overcome by a fit of coughing, spitting blood. His doctors decided an artery had burst and advised complete rest. He continued his lectures and preaching, his oversight of the academy and consistory, his dictation of commentaries and letters.

Calvin's letters to the French churches continued, passed from church to church, while the number of those churches increased in spite of the arrests, imprisonments, massacres, and pillage. In Provence the Reformed were beginning to defend themselves, disregarding Calvin's constant counsel that it was necessary not only to live for Christ but to die for him if need be, pointing to the invincible courage of the hundreds of martyrs, begging them to persevere in that cause for which God had created them, and always to pray.

He did not write to "The Brethren of Metz." Francis II had in October ordered all Protestants to leave his city of Metz, razed the château of the baron de Clervaut and begun a process against him for having allowed sermons to be preached on his estate.

But before the winter was over, the Reformed in Switzerland as well as in France had begun to question Calvin's twenty-five-year advice to submit. On 20 March hundreds of Huguenots were slaughtered at Amboise, when the plot devised at Strasbourg the past October—to seize Francis II and install Navarre as regent—went hopelessly awry. The whole affair can be reconstructed in Calvin's letters.

On 23 March he was still not sure what had happened. "When I was first consulted about the plan," he wrote, "I frankly told them that their whole manner of going about it displeased me, but the plot itself aroused my strongest disapproval because they set about their foolish resolution so childishly."[16] First they set 15 March for the day of their rendezvous, then changed it to the 20th. Everything depended on their securing the support of Navarre and Condé.

On 11 May, Calvin wrote more of the story to Bullinger.[17] Eight months before, soon after the establishment of the *Chambre ardente*, at the time of the meeting in Strasbourg, he had warned Beza, hoping to prevent the plotters from proceeding further. He had believed all ideas of violence were successfully quashed until Godfrey Du Barry, sieur de La Renaudie, came to Geneva boasting that he had been appointed leader of the conspiracy. Immediately Calvin had shown his utter abhorrence of the plan and had tried to put a stop to it. But La Renaudie went about the city, collecting money for horses and arms, telling people that Calvin did not disapprove but to avoid scandal declined to take an active and public part in the enterprise. When he heard that lie, Calvin had called the ministers together and exposed La Renaudie; yet within three days, all Geneva— nobility as well as commoners—was eager to help. Secret meetings were held to raise money and enlist volunteers.

As late as 11 May, Calvin was still sick at heart over the calamity. He went into more detail in his letter of that date to Peter Martyr, in which he said that he was "overcome with sorrow considering the inconsiderate zeal of men of our party"—he recognized that the cause had now become political more than religious—"who thought they could obtain by disorder the liberty which is to be sought by other means." Eight months ago, he said, he had been asked for his opinion. Some time afterward he asked just what was going on when he discovered that some sixty volunteers were going with La Renaudie to France, among them the seigneurs of Castelnau and Villemongis. The men excused themselves, hiding behind the alleged promise "of one of the princes who. . . claimed highest rank in the king's council, his brother being absent, . . . to present the Reformed Confession to His Majesty. If Guise henchmen offered violence, only then would they defend themselves."[18] He had warned them again that from a single drop of blood shed in this affair, streams would flow, inundating all France. Now he could not get their impudence and poor management out of his mind. La Renaudie had ruined everything. . . .

How could they have expected a conspiracy on such a scale to remain secret? Of course the plotters did not arrive at their meeting point at the same time; of course the plot was revealed to the Guises and the conspirators ambushed. Executions below the balcony of the castle went on for days, ladies of the court watching the gory proceedings. Her husband Francis of Guise and Catherine de' Medici both reprimanded Anne of Este for her tears.

The Tumult of Amboise became a signal to the Reformed. In Valence, the church (organized only the year before) protested violently: students of the university and nobles, in spite of pleas by the consistory, seized the church of the Cordeliers, installed their minister, and set armed guards before the church doors.

The church at Montélimar read Calvin's advice to make no innovations in the church in which they worshipped, simply to refrain from praying before images, offering candles, and the like; better, he said, to continue meeting in private homes, thus avoiding superstition.[19] But the church at Montélimar imitated that at Valence. The greater part of Dauphiné supported the Reformation.

Protests against the Guises were made in a number of cities openly. In one Paris suburb people set fire to a gibbet with an effigy of the cardinal of Lorraine. In another town, part of Guise's domain, his lieutenant beheaded two ministers and three leading citizens as an example.

Calvin, still writing to Peter Martyr, looked with foreboding on the time of tribulation he saw approaching.[20] He questioned Catherine de' Medici's sincerity in convoking a council to end the troubles. If the German princes advised her to purge the Roman church of its corruption and set it on a better foundation, would their counsel do any more good than that of L'Hôpital and others of good will? He would continue attempting to rouse Navarre from his apathy but felt his efforts would prove futile. The kingdom was in jeopardy, every day on the brink of ruin from the perfidy of the Guises who were actuated by pride, arrogance, and greed. The queen mother would do whatever she considered best for her children and herself.[21]

In June he laid aside the sorrows of France long enough to answer some of his ever-increasing letters. Among others, he wrote to the ministers of the Reformed church in London;[22] to the Earl of Bedford, telling of the tumult in Scotland:[23] the Lords of the Congregation had seized Edinburgh, and the English fleet lay off Leith in support of the Protestants; to the Waldensians of Bohemia in regard to their uniting with the Reformed.[24]

On 5 July, in answer to a letter brought him from Ferrara, he wrote the duchess, warning her of what might be in store for her if she returned to France.

XVIII

Ferrara
1559–60

In April, after the signing of the Treaty of Cateau-Cambrésis, Renée graciously wrote to Emmanuel Philibert, congratulating him on his coming marriage to her niece Margaret. The double marriage ceremony—of Margaret and the duke of Savoy and of Elizabeth and Philip II—had been performed before the day of the tournament in which Henry II was fatally wounded. How was the news of his injury and death received in Ferrara?

The duke did not disguise his feelings. In a rather injudicious letter to the cardinal of Lorraine, he felicitated His Reverence on the high position and good fortune the death of the king would undoubtedly bring to the Guises. He knew that since the coming to France of the first prince of Lorraine in the early days of Louis XII's reign, they had claimed a better right to the throne than the Valois, since their family traced its origin back to an earlier French king. Never openly claiming the crown, they fought valiantly in the Italian wars, three of them being killed on fields of battle. On his death bed, Francis I had warned Henry against the Guises. He and others, wrote the duke of Ferrara, desired the success of the Guise family's hopes.

The accession of Francis II could only mean an increase in honor to the family of which Ercole's daughter was now part.

With Guise's niece queen of France and her uncles in control of the young king, Ercole saw a bright future for himself as Guise's father-in-law. Anne already occupied a favored position at court, her sons being playmates of the children of the late king.

But in September Ercole became quite sick, his doctors unable to diagnose the malady. He worsened rapidly, and on the 25th made his will, calling Renée to his bedside and forcing her to swear (in the presence of his chaplain, his physician, his secretary, and a lawyer) that henceforth she would have no relationship whatsoever, personal or written, with any promulgator of heretical opinions. How could she do otherwise than take the oath demanded of her?

"Our lord Ercole," wrote Paolo di Signano, "having fallen seriously ill on 25 September, and the most efficacious remedies of the wisest physicians having proved ineffective, died in his palace on 3 October at 3 o'clock in the afternoon, leaving his wife and daughters in the deepest despair."[1]

The duchess took charge, first sending couriers to Paris to inform Alfonso, then ordering the city gates locked, the municipal guard strengthened, and sentinels to man the walls day and night. The duke's body was fittingly and quickly interred. She dispatched his half-brother to Modena, ordering the inhabitants of that rebellious city to swear allegiance to the new duke without delay, a necessary move since the Holy See and Spain had coveted Modena for a long while, and Spanish troops were stationed in nearby princedoms.

Carrying on her late husband's correspondence, she sent letters to many of the cardinals gathered in Rome to elect a new pope—Paul IV having just died—urging them to keep cardinals Farnese and Caraffa from the papal throne and asking that the local inquisitor of Ferrara be appointed master of the apostolic palace. She received a deputation from Modena bearing gifts and condolences, letting it be known that she accepted both but considered them somewhat late in arriving.

Alfonso, after many delays, arrived in Ferrara 25 November, going directly to the Palazzo San Francesco to hold undisturbed conferences with his mother for several days, after which, following long-established custom, the magistracy of Ferrara confirmed his powers. After making the required round of the city streets hung with tapestries, flags, and garlands to show himself to his supposedly deliriously joyous subjects, he received the ducal sceptre.

The day after, a magnificent funeral was conducted for the late duke, a plaster figure complete with death-mask and dressed in ducal robes on a catafalque covered with cloth of gold. At least one person profited by Alfonso's accession: as a favor to his mother, Alfonso released his grandfather's half-brother, Giulio d'Este, who had been imprisoned for almost fifty-four years in the Tower of Lions of the castle.

The new duke took over the reins of government with great pleasure. His mother retired to the Palazzo San Francesco, seldom being seen at her son's court. In February of the following year, Lucrezia de' Medici, Alfonso's bride (now a year older than when she was married, and so potentially able to bear children) made her formal entrance into Ferrara accompanied by a tremendous suite. Renée became the dowager duchess, "the old duchess" ambassadors called her, meaning that term in two ways, for her trouble had aged her prematurely.

By terms of her husband's will, she was left the use of Belreguardo, a beautiful palace on the outskirts of the city surrounded by parks and gardens, provided that she remained in Ferrara, living as a good and faithful Catholic.

Alfonso, in the same instrument, was advised always to live as a faithful Catholic like his father, never allowing anyone to persuade him to accept the new religious beliefs, never to depart from the interpretation of Scripture given by Holy Mother Church unless so determined by a general council of the church. Ercole counseled his son to mitigate the wrath of God by works of mercy, particularly with charity, and to see that he did not offend Divine Majesty. Ercole himself had always been an example to his son: during every Passion Week he had washed the feet of twelve poor men brought to the castle for that purpose.

Renée was in a quandary as to her future. She was now almost fifty years old. Should she continue to live in Ferrara *as a good Catholic?* That was impossible. Should she retire to France where as daughter of the Father of His People she should (but *would* she?) be in a position to help the persecuted, make peace between her beloved daughter's family and her friends, such as Coligny and Andelot, friends whose religious beliefs she shared? In June she wrote to Calvin, asking his advice as to what she should do, asking him also whether she must obey the oath she had made when her husband was dying—a question which greatly troubled her.

There was another solution to her problem. Had she considered the possibility of going to Geneva? Calvin had recommended such a course to other women: to Madame de Cany (Peronne de Pisseleu), sister of Madame d'Étampes, Francis I's longtime mistress who was considered tinged with Lutheranism;[2] to the widow of Guillaume Budé;[3] to Madame de Rentigny;[4] to an unnamed Italian lady, one "Agnese" of Ferrara.[5] And there were others. Why did he not suggest such a solution to Renée? He certainly hinted at it in the last paragraph of the letter she received from him in late July:[6]

Madame:
   Though you have often requested and solicited me, I have never been able to decide upon sending you a man such as you demanded, being afraid that those who brought me your request might have overzealously gone further than you intended. For I had no letter from you to verify if what they told me was exact. Even now, Madame, I very much wish I might have been better assured in order that I might write you more fully. I distrust this bearer, who has given me pretty good proofs to convince me that he came from you; but you know, Madame, how many persons may be bribed to elicit from me things that might bring much trouble and regret upon you.
   As to that oath which you have been forced to take, you are not to treat it as anything more than a superstitious vow since you failed in your duty and offended God by making it. You know, Madame, that Herod is blamed not only for having too well observed his oath which he had made in an unguarded moment, but that it is imputed

to him for a two-fold condemnation. I say this to you, not to urge you to write to me but that you may have no scruples about what God leaves you free to do, and of what he absolves you. I have done my duty in letting you know.

As for the journey which you are determined upon, though the captivity in which you have been held so long is hard and you are deserving of all compassion, nevertheless, I must tell you that you will not have gained much by having escaped from one fire only to be plunged into another worse. I do not see how this move can better your condition. The government with which they intend to embroil you is now in such chaos that everyone is alarmed. If you should take some share in its proceedings—and should your opinions even be listened to—I am fairly well satisfied that things will not continue quite so badly.

But that is not what they are intending. They want to screen themselves behind your name, to foster the evil people can endure no longer. To go and thrust yourself into the midst of these disorders is manifestly tempting God. I desire your prosperity, Madame, as much as possible; but if the grandeur of the world should prevent your approaching God, I should be a traitor to your interests in convincing you that black is white.

If you were completely resolved to act straightforwardly and with greater devotion than you have hitherto done, I should beg you immediately to take a greater share in the management of affairs than what they will offer you; but if your share is only to say Amen to all that is condemned by both God and humanity, I have nothing to say except that you are falling from a bad situation into a worse.

I do not intend, however, to advise you to continue in your present state of bondage, nor to go to sleep in it; there has been too much of that in the past. Only I beseech you to make such a change as may lead you to serve God unfeignedly and press toward the mark, not entangling yourself in snares that might be difficult for you to break and which might fetter you as much as, or ever more so than the former ones.

However that may be, you are continuing too long, Madame, in an inactive state. If you do not take some compassion upon yourself, it is to be feared that you may seek a remedy for your malady when it is too late. Beside what God has so long taught you by his word, your age should admonish you to remember that our heritage and eternal rest is not here below. Jesus Christ certainly deserves that you should forget both France and Ferrara for him. By your widowhood, God has rendered you disencumbered and free in order that he may draw you entirely to himself. I wish I had the opportunity of demonstrating more fully these things to you by word of mouth, and that not just once, but from day to day. I leave you to meditate upon them in your prudence, more fully than what I have written could suggest.

Madame, having commended myself to your gracious favor, I entreat our heavenly Father to have you in his protection, to govern you by the Spirit, and to increase in you all good.

Charles d'Espeville
5 June 1560

She knew she could not profess her religious beliefs openly in Ferrara. Alfonso had a greater horror of Protestantism than even his father. In France he had declared that he would rather live with the plague than with Huguenots. When he returned from Rome on 3 July, where he had gone to make his necessary obeisance to the new pope, Pius IV, he informed his mother that she must either become truly Catholic or leave his duchy. His firmness was admired by his subjects, for by now Protestantism in Ferrara had been obliterated. Quite openly he showed his disapproval of her.

She had asked advice from Anne as well as from Calvin. On 2 September, after bestowing gifts on her doctor and secretary and paying the dowries of twenty-two young girls who had been among her Italian servitors—her gifts during the month of August amounted to 9,635 livres—she quitted her Babylon.

The court accompanied her as far as Modena. A few hours after Alfonso had left her, she wrote him a note: "My son, I could not say to you what was in my heart for fear of being overcome with tears."[7] She went by little stages, welcomed everywhere as her rank demanded. At Turin she secured from Emmanuel Philibert the liberty of a soldier accused of heresy but had no success in begging toleration for the Vaudois.

A Vaudois pastor with whom she had corresponded and to whom she had sent money for his people, met her at Savigliano. Although she had promised him safety, he was thrown into prison, and it was only after writing several letters to the duke of Savoy and her niece Margaret that she was able to secure the man's release.

She crossed the Alps by way of Mount Geneva; she bought straw for her mattress at Lyon and paid a chaplain to say mass before her, lodging there in the palace of the archbishop. Anne came to meet her in a village near Orléans. They arrived in Orléans on 10 November, king and court coming to meet her outside the city gates.

The day after her arrival she wrote Alfonso: "You will learn by this courier of my arrival here where the king is. The honor he has shown me, the favor and affection, are more than anyone could tell."[8] Her long trip had exhausted her. It was only after resting a few days that she realized that Orléans was an armed camp.

PART FOUR

The World Aflame

XIX

Geneva—France
1560–61

Among the first acts of Francis II were edicts ordering the razing of all houses in which heretic assemblies had been held and the execution of all who had attended such meetings. Measures must be taken to root out the heresy responsible for the attempt to kidnap the king.

Some of the conspirators had implicated the prince of Condé as their unseen leader, though he was with the court at Amboise when the ambushes laid for the conspirators brought them to their deaths there. Condé denied before the king that he had had any knowledge of the plot, challenging to a duel any man who would be so bold as to accuse him to his face. Francis of Guise, not ready yet for a mortal fight with a prince of the blood, offered himself as Condé's second. The gesture was superb: Condé could not challenge him. The crisis passed, and, Condé's reputation cleared, the prince retired from the court.

Yet Calvin could not persuade the Bourbons to confront the usurpers of authority by legal means. He heard rumors of what some of the Protestant nobility were planning, and sent Beza and Hotman to Nérac to dissuade Navarre from any attempt to overthrow the Guises by force, thus indirectly attacking the king, urging him to attend the Assembly of Notables called to meet in August.

While Navarre vacillated, Protestant nobles concocted a plan to overthrow the power of the Guises in Provence. The attempt was a fiasco, and Navarre ostentatiously divorced himself from the affair, hurrying to court, where Catherine de' Medici offered inducements to bring him—"credulous beyond belief," said Calvin[1]—to heel.

Calvin's throat continued to bother him and he suffered from a combination of other ills, but he resumed preaching every morning, lecturing every evening, and carrying on his vast correspondence. On 1 October he wrote to Bullinger, giving an account of the Assembly of Notables, which had opened on 21 August, without Navarre, at Fontainebleau.[2]

There, Coligny had informed the king that fifty thousand persons in Normandy, of which he was governor, were prepared to sign a petition asking His Majesty for freedom of worship. The Guises had greeted his remarks with contempt. Then Coligny spoke with disapproval of the barbarous new custom by which the king was protected—not by a bodyguard but by an army. "A youthful sovereign," he said, "should not be brought up to distrust his subjects but should foster their affection by kindness. . . ."[3]

The duke of Guise replied that the king needed neither tutor nor governor since he had been educated in the practice of every virtue; if he needed any instruction, his mother was competent to give it. The cardinal of Lorraine added that it was idle to demand of the council any innovation in doctrine and impious to make what had proceeded from Holy Scripture the subject of controversy. Bishops were competent to correct all vices and immorality.

Coligny was not the only one who spoke for the Reformed. The bishops of Valence and Vienne declared themselves in favor of relaxation of vigor against the Huguenots, the bishop of Vienne adding that it was a disgraceful sign of dissolution when bishops abandoned their churches and frequented the courts of princes. He begged His Majesty not to deprive the Reformed churches of their pastors. For his presumption, he was sent home.

Nevertheless, Calvin continued, preaching went on in Normandy, Protestants of Poitou and Saintonge enjoyed more liberty than before. All of Gascony, much of Languedoc, Dauphiné, and Provence held for the Reformation although the Guises had set up garrisons in ten cities and the prisons of Lyon were crowded with Huguenots.

The only result of the Assembly of Notables was a decree calling for a meeting of the States-General on 13 December. It would be preceded by meetings held in every province to elect delegates. Only those men holding clearly Catholic opinions would be chosen to attend the January meeting; special care must be taken that no Huguenots were named as deputies. At the States-General, bishops would decide what further steps could be taken to correct the abuses of impious persons.

Meanwhile, agents of the Guises seized a gentleman in Condé's service, bearing letters to him from Montmorency and the vidame de Chartres, letters which detailed a plot to assassinate Francis of Guise and the cardinal of Lorraine. The vidame was imprisoned immediately and later executed; but the Guises, sure that the plot against them was widespread, had the king send a gentleman to Nérac, where Condé had taken refuge with Navarre, inviting the Bourbon princes to come to the meeting of the States-General. The bearer of the invitation was accompanied by the princes' brother, the cardinal of Bourbon, who assured Condé and Navarre of their safety in coming to Orléans.

In Calvin's letter to Bullinger of 14 October, he showed his alarm.[4] After the Assembly of Notables, Catherine de' Medici had warned Coligny that the Bourbon princes were to be put to death. Coligny had passed the warning on to his sister, Condé's mother-in-law, that the prince was to be accused of plotting against the state.

Again Calvin told Bullinger that the greater part of French nobility was for Navarre and had offered their services to him. He could have overturned the Guises if only. . . . It had not been hard for the Guises to lead the king where they wanted to take him. Lorraine had persuaded His Majesty that those who wanted a different religion were rebels; that all those petitions—de Rochefort had also presented one at the Assembly of Notables—

were drawn up by people not satisfied with the established religion who would like to dictate laws to their sovereign. Now, said Calvin, the king had sent soldiers to intercept Condé and Navarre.

Again, on 1 November, Calvin poured out his worry to Bullinger, again reverting to Navarre's weakness, saying that the nobility of Brittany would gladly support the man in a civil war, France having defrauded Brittany of her independence when Francis I announced the "gift" of the duchy from Claude. "The kingdom," he mourned, "will be torn by a deplorable and wretched anarchy. The king and court are now at Orléans where the greater part of the magistrates have been sentenced to be executed."[5] That report was confirmed by a Florentine dispatch dated 24 November: "All the officers of the city—bailiff, lieutenant, and others—are in prison; they have also arrested the leading citizens. . . ."[6]

To Sturm, on 5 November, Calvin continued his tale of woe: Navarre had refused the pleas of the nobility. Both he and his brother had refused to listen to the protests of their wives and had gone on to Orléans, where Condé was immediately thrown into prison to be tried for treason with the certainty of being put to death. Navarre was under house arrest. "I forbear to mention," Calvin ended, "how much the rasher spirits have injured our cause by their silly attempts. Assuredly the effects of their ill-timed activities have given the deathblow to our hopes. . . ."[7]

He wrote the news to Sulzer on 5 December, retelling the events leading to Condé's fate and Navarre's situation. "Our plans had been so well laid that without violence or tumult Navarre could have triumphed over all his adversaries, weak and pusillanimous man deceived by false promises, never seeing what was clear to everyone else—that the Guises would lay violent hands on his brother."[8]

When Renée stepped out of the lodgings assigned her in Orléans (which she later discovered were those of the imprisoned bailiff), she could not believe her eyes. Cannons were set up at every street corner, the king's guards and her son-in-law's armed retainers patrolled the streets. She had not been prepared to find a city under siege. Prepared against what enemy?

Nor had her daughter told her that Condé was on trial and was expected to be sentenced to death. When she learned what had happened, she was enraged. Who was this little duke of the house of Lorraine, her own son-in-law and powerful though he might be, who dared to offer violence to a prince of the house of Valois?

She attacked Guise violently with scathing denunciations; if she had arrived earlier, she would have hindered Condé's imprisonment. She warned the duke of further violence against those of the blood royal, saying that such a wound would bleed a very long time. The duke ignored her protests. Condé's interrogation was conducted in secret with none of his peers present. On 26 November he was sentenced to lose his head on the scaffold.

L'Hôpital managed to delay the execution until 10 December. During the interim, Guise and his brother plotted to arrange a scene in which Navarre would apparently try to assassinate the king, upon which the king would defend himself by stabbing Navarre. The plot failed: Francis could not play his part, to the great disgust of his mentors. On 5 December, an abcess in the young king's ear burst and His Majesty Francis II was suddenly dead. Catherine de' Medici immediately declared herself regent for her nine-year-old son Charles. The power of the Guises was at an end—for a while.

"Behold!" Calvin wrote Sturm, "All of a sudden the hand of God reveals itself! Did you ever hear of anything more opportune than the death of the king? The evil had reached an extremity for which there was no remedy, when all of a sudden God shows himself from heaven! He who pierced the eye of the father has now struck the ear of the son!"[9]

Throughout France there were shouts of joy mingled with grumbling; Calvin, in his letters to the churches, tried to restrain the jubilation. The world was suddenly turned upside down. Now everybody at court (except the Guises, who barricaded themselves in their apartments) wooed the king of Navarre, and the Protestant nobles found themselves in great favor with the queen mother. She compelled the duke of Guise to swear before king and court that he had not instigated the plot against Condé. That prince refused simply to forget the whole matter, insisting that his name be cleared by the Parlement of Paris. Antoine de Bourbon, king of Navarre, was now named lieutenant general of France in Guise's place—at the price of relinquishing his claims to the regency.

Calvin was not swept away by the general rejoicing. It was now time, he declared, that Navarre should act. In his letter to the minister of the church in Paris, he gave his recommendations: Navarre should convoke the States-General, appoint a council of regency, bring Guise to trial, and establish a moderate religion—all this at once before the queen mother and the Guises reorganized.[10] But Navarre had his mess of pottage and left everything to Catherine de' Medici.

She was determined to go on with the States-General which had been called to discuss religion. The meeting was opposed by her new son-in-law, Philip of Spain, as well as by Pius IV. The Spanish ambassador, Don Juan Manrique de Lara, brought his master's warning to Catherine: she should be diligent in the matter of religion; above all, she should not have about her those who were not steadfast in the faith. He was, of course, aiming at Condé and Coligny particularly, though the arrival at court of the notorious duchess of Ferrara made both pope and the king of Spain uneasy as to how much influence she might have.

The queen mother did not take meekly Spain's attempt to mix in French affairs. She wrote her daughter Elizabeth, Philip's wife, "Philip can say to those who advise him to interfere in the choice of counselors for Charles IX that he knows no more how the affairs of this kingdom ought to be governed than I do how to conduct the affairs of Spain; he has no need to meddle in the matter."[11]

The first session of the States-General opened on 13 December, a week and a day after Francis II's death. An old print shows the boy king Charles IX seated in the center of a platform, wide steps leading to the main floor, persons seated on these steps in order of their rank. On Charles' left, on the step below his, sit his younger brother Henry and the king of Navarre. The queen mother sits at his right, on a level with him. On the step below, and to her right, sits seven-year-old Margot, and beyond her the dowager duchess of Ferrara. Prelates and favored nobility sit on lower steps.

The chancellor L'Hôpital opened proceedings with a long and eloquent plea for peace. He called for a reformation of the clergy, reminded nobles and commoners of their duty, and the necessity of bringing back gently those in error. "Let us lay aside those inventions of the devil, the names *Lutheran*, *Papist*, and *Huguenot*. Let us call ourselves only by the name of Christian."[12] Vain delusion. The problem of religion in France was not to be solved by words.

The first real deliberation of the assembly began on 1 January, and with few peaceful speeches. Jean d'Ange, a counselor of the Parlement of Bordeaux, spoke for the Third Estate, thundering against the ignorance, avarice, and luxury of the clergy. He was followed by the count de Rochefort, who declared fearlessly that the Guises were insults to princes of the blood and that in the past, kings of France had successfully resisted the clergy; why not now? He demanded reform of the church and liberty of worship for Protestants.

Jean Quentin spoke for the clergy, defending repression of heresy by the sword and declaring that anyone who presented a petition on behalf of heretics should himself be declared heretical. Upon which, Coligny complained to the queen mother, who forced Quentin to make public apology.

Catherine de' Medici was incensed over Guise's undercover appeal to Spain. She would have been still more furious had she known of Renée's private meetings with Throckmorton, ambassador of Elizabeth of England, sending to and receiving messages from the English queen, suggesting that Elizabeth should try to influence the queen mother who, she was careful to say, was a "wise and judicious lady who was beginning to listen to the word of salvation."[13]

For a moment it seemed that Catherine was more than willing to support the Reformed. It was simply the beginning of her balancing act, her only means of keeping the kingdom out of the hands of the Guises and safe for her sons. She was quite sincere when she wrote Pius IV suggesting a number of ecclesiastical reforms that she thought could very well be made: abolition of private masses, sermons in the language of the people, communion in both kinds. The Venetian ambassador sent alarming reports to the Council of Ten concerning the spread of the new doctrines in France. All classes were affected, he said, except the lowest.

Calvin kept a close watch on proceedings of the States-General. On 16 January 1561 he again wrote Navarre: "The gospel must be restored in France!" Both God and the law of the nation called Navarre to govern. He had it in his power to help the Reformation. He should stand up to the queen mother since she held power only through his favor.[14]

He wrote Jeanne d'Albret that same day, praising her for her open stand for Protestant beliefs at Orléans.[15] A longer letter went to Coligny, who, knowing his own danger before setting out for Orléans, warned his wife that he might not return. Coligny now had the gospel preached openly in his household. In this letter, Calvin begged Coligny to make Catherine de' Medici understand that Geneva's independence was essential to the security of France.[16]

Evidently his message to the queen mother was ill received. A week later the magistrates of Geneva received a threatening communication from Charles IX, saying that the troubles in his kingdom were fomented by preachers from Geneva, and ordering the magistrates to recall those ministers immediately.

After much debate, the council directed Calvin to compose a reply:[17] the magistracy expressed its sorrow at being unjustly blamed; the proper persons had been exhorted to do their duty to advance the knowledge of God in France as the Lord commanded; the preachers were not to blame for the French troubles and were ready to justify themselves fully before His Majesty. The letter was dispatched, and all council members and ministers were warned to keep the king's letter a secret.

Could Renée have actually thought that her influence was in any way responsible for the Edict of Romorantin which Catherine and L'Hôpital secured from the States-General? All subjects were forbidden on pain of severe punishment to use the terms *Huguenot* or *Papist*. Parlements were ordered to release all prisoners incarcerated because of religion. Trials for and punishment of heresy were to be the province of bishops, not secular judges. The edict was hailed with joy by Huguenots, fought to the bitter end by Catholics. The Parlement of Paris refused to register it, but scores of French émigrés, thinking their battle almost won, returned from Switzerland.

At Fontainebleau, where the court had retired on 5 February during the interminable sessions of the States-General, Renée found herself in a difficult position, caught between her love for Anne and the children and her own Protestant inclinations. The situation was made worse by her disagreement with the king and his mother over her rights to Brittany, a quarrel which has no place in this narrative.

An unlooked-for result of the meeting of the States-General was the alliance of Guise, Saint-André, and Montmorency in opposition to the Bourbon-Coligny coterie, not only on religious grounds but also because of the latter's support for the royal order demanding that gifts lavished by Henry II on his favorites should be repaid or given up. This alliance, engineered by the late king's mistress Diane de Poitiers, was to form the nucleus of armed opposition leading to the Wars of Religion. It was also partly responsible for Catherine de' Medici's temporary favor to the Reformed.

In spite of the blandishments of Catherine, it did not take Renée long to discover that she was to have no place in governmental affairs, not even a seat on the council, but was expected to serve by looking after small Margot. She had not returned to France to be a nursemaid. Inwardly furious, she left for her town and castle of Montargis, one of the places given her at the time of her marriage, tactfully assuring the queen mother that she would rejoin the court whenever she was needed.

Montargis was a large city, situated at the confluence of the Loing, the Puiseaux, and the Ouanne, on the highway uniting the basin of the Loire and the Seine, important from a commercial as well as a military standpoint. The inhabitants of the area were violently Catholic, as Renée discovered immediately.

She had barely arrived in Montargis when a riot broke out in the nearby town of Nemours, a dependency of Montargis, where Jean Papillon, minister of Châtillon-sur-Loing, her neighbor Gaspard de Coligny's domain, had preached at a newly organized Reformed church and had even baptized an infant—sacrilege in the eyes of the townspeople. In the tumult the minister was forced to hide in a deacon's house until Renée, roused by a messenger, arrived and ordered him set at liberty.

It was not to be wondered at that her first care was to fortify her castle and the approaches, strengthening the walls, emplacing cannon, deepening the moat.

She was still busy with repairs to the castle when a visitor arrived, Jean Raimond Merlin, Madame Coligny's private minister. The visit was not pleasant for either. Merlin expected the worst from this Valois kinswoman of the Guises who, he had been told, blew now hot now cold for the cause. Renée, having heard him preach at Coligny's lodgings at Fontainebleau, was unimpressed, wanting to hear the word of God rather than diatribes against the papacy.

He accused her to her face of being a coward and showing little zeal for the faith, and reported as much to Calvin. The lady, he said, exhibited a multitude of fears and perplexities hindering her from giving full glory to God. Calvin took it upon himself to caution her, demanding that she give such an example of her faith as God required of her. When she did not immediately declare herself, Merlin was still more severe, threatening her with the wrath of God. Then "with the help of some greatly esteemed personage who had entrée to her house," surely Coligny, he drew from her the promise to break with idolatry and take a personal minister as other noble ladies had done, and to defend her minister if necessary even to endangering herself and her estate.[18]

Merlin wrote Calvin concerning the qualities her minister should have: "not too young, not too old (like me), not seeking the companionship of women or girls, not always talking but capable of defending the Reformed beliefs." He named certain

Genevan ministers who would not do for various reasons, and begged Calvin to act at once before she changed her mind.[19]

That letter was written mid-June. On 3 July the magistracy of Geneva agreed that a minister should be sent to the Lady of Montargis provided it was neither Calvin nor Beza. Calvin chose to send her the man he had sent to advise her in Ferrara at the time of her trial, François Morel, le sieur de Colonges.

In January 1561, while Coligny was still at Orléans, Calvin had written him a long letter, praising his courage, bemoaning the fact that others were not so outspoken, hoping "that the magnanimity which God has caused to shine forth in you, will be a good lesson to draw out the lukewarm."[20]

Calvin's brother Antoine returned in April from France, where he had gone on a mission, bringing a message from Coligny urging Calvin to print a full account of his involvement in the conspiracy of Amboise, since at court ugly tales were circulating that he was the instigator of the whole affair. The answer was an eight-page document, detailing his complete disapproval of the plot from beginning to end. He ended with the reminder of the number of sermons, the number of letters he had made decrying the use of force. "Now excesses have been committed in Provence. . . . Several persons have been killed. . . . It will be found that I have no less condemned all their acts. . . . The origin of all these disturbances lies elsewhere."[21]

The queen mother knew quite well where the origin lay. She wrote her daughter Elizabeth:

> I want you to know that all this trouble has grown out of the hatred which this entire kingdom bears to the cardinal of Lorraine and the duke of Guise. They thought I would hand over to them the government of this kingdom. I have assured them to the contrary, nor am I under any obligation to do so.
>
> You know how they treated me in the time of the king your brother [Francis II] and even now, when they have no one to look to but me. . . . I have resolved to protect them so that they will come to no harm, but for the rest to look after your brother's interests and my own and not to let them mix their quarrel with mine. They would

have made themselves regents if they could and would have left me out as they always have when any greatness or advantage is to be gained, for that is the one thing they have at heart.[22]

The temporary surcease of persecution encouraged Protestants in many areas to acts of violence and reprisal. Mobs in Dauphiné and Languedoc sacked churches, pulling down and breaking images, outraging monks and priests. Calvin expressed his disapproval vehemently: "God never commanded private individuals to cast down images, except each person in his own house; only those in authority should do so in public," he concluded.[23] But at Montpellier two hundred persons were killed in a riot occasioned by the sacking of the cathedral (where two centuries later the enthusiastic crowds would witness the execution of Protestant ministers). On 1 May, Calvin wrote the church at Aix that it was their duty to endure persecution without resistance or murmuring.[24] His advice was disregarded: martyrdom had turned to warfare.

Calvin was not taken in by the seeming favor of the queen mother toward the Reformed. He wrote Ambrose Blaurer in May calling her treacherous and deceitful, Navarre (again) pusillanimous.[25] The Parlement of Paris was kindling animosity there, the Parlement of Toulouse imprisoning and burning heretics throughout the area. Yet he was being importuned from all quarters for ministers and was sweeping the workshops in an attempt to supply enough men of sound doctrine.

He expatiated to Bullinger on the "sluggish and sliding" Navarre, "without constancy or good faith, completely trapped and wholly taken up in amorous intrigues at court." Beza's reproaches to the man fell upon deaf ears. The admiral, Coligny, was the only one the Reformed could count on now.[26]

At Fontainebleau the minister Calvin had sent to Coligny, Jean Raimond Merlin, who would visit Renée in June, was preaching to crowded audiences in the admiral's lodgings, not far from the palace. The admiral's enemies had run screaming to the queen mother, who begged Coligny to discontinue the sermons. Yet many of the most influential nobility seemed eager to bring

Catholics and Protestants together and were talking of a solemn conference between theologians of the two religions. Catherine de' Medici had said that unless John Calvin came to Paris all remedies would prove fruitless, but he had refused adamantly to go.

Again Calvin showed his disappointment at Protestant seizure of Catholic churches in spite of reprisals. They were acting without sense. Huguenots in twenty cities had been massacred without any official notice being taken, except at Beauvais, where Coligny's brother Odet was bishop. Twelve persons were killed and forty severely injured when a mob attacked the house of a Protestant nobleman of Paris.

Throughout the summer Calvin continued his letters to the Reformed: to Coligny;[27] to the churches of Nîmes[28] and Sauve.[29] He had no hope that his excoriations would influence Navarre, yet he wrote him again, censuring his behavior, berating him for the "foolish amours which prevent you from doing your duty.... I beseech you in the name of God to rouse yourself!"[30] But Navarre, seduced by one of Catherine's maids of honor and bloated with his new honors, took no one's advice.

In July the Parlement of Paris issued a decree that religious worship by Protestants would henceforth be punished by death and the confiscation of all property of those arrested. The queen mother had nothing to do with that edict. She was striving for peace.

On advice from the chancellor, L' Hôpital, she had decided to call a council to meet at Poissy in September, to determine if a rapprochement could be worked out between Calvinists and Catholics. The Protestant princes desired Calvin or Beza to come and, with Catholic theologians, expound their beliefs. The minister would be welcomed with all due honor. Catherine asked particularly for Monsieur Calvin and assured him of safe conduct.

Calvin refused to consider going; the whole thing was preposterous. If Swiss and German Protestants could not agree on the Lord's Supper, after all his efforts and those of Melanchthon, how could there be any meeting of minds on that subject with

Catholic theologians? Nevertheless, he wrote Peter Martyr, asking him to go and support Beza who would speak for the Reformed.[31] On 23 August he notified Sulzer that Beza had left Geneva by post horse although Catherine de' Medici, afraid of the pope, had at the last minute refused to assure him safe conduct. Coligny and the Bourbon princes guaranteed his safety.[32]

He had warned Beza to advocate nothing but a remedy for the Huguenots—permission for them to worship; certainly not to say that any wished to secede or that they wanted a change of religion. He warned Beza and Navarre that if Lutheran divines came, as the Guises desired, and with reason, they would only fan the flames of discord by demanding that the French Protestants subscribe to the Augsburg Confession—which Navarre had already announced he was prepared to accept.

XX

Geneva—France
1561–62

When Morel arrived in Montargis, he was appalled to find that the duchess had made no provision for an apartment for his wife and that she intended to change her minister every six months. Not only that, he complained to Calvin on 3 August, she ordered him to make his sermons shorter, without touching on any abuses of the papacy such as images, which she already knew enough about.[1] The man had no conception of the touchy situation in Montargis. He called the citizens "beasts" and immediately set about quarreling with the bailiff and other municipal officers.

Still, he and Renée made their peace, for on 25 August he wrote Calvin: "I want to tell you that Madame the duchess has taken courage by the grace of God, so much so that she would be very loath to let me leave. She has become accustomed to our manner of preaching; she would not at all wish one to speak in circumlocutions like the old-time preachers but takes pleasure in my speaking straight to the point."[2]

Not long after Morel's letter to Calvin, Beza and Peter Martyr stopped briefly at Montargis on the way to the council. Early in September Renée and her retinue, including Morel, arrived in

Saint-Germain-en-Laye, where the court would be in residence during the colloquy at Poissy.

The Holy See was rigidly opposed to any conference at which Protestant theology was considered on a par with Catholic theology, but the queen mother, as we have seen, had already written the pope suggesting certain reforms in the service of the church that might bring the sinners back into the fold. Now she emphasized the importance of this conference since such great numbers of the king's subjects had left France to take up residence in foreign lands, and it was necessary to reduce those who remained to obedience by means of laws and arms.

Before the colloquy began, the king with his whole court gathered in the great hall of the château to listen to the sermons of Jean de Montluc, bishop of Valence, who at that time supported the Reformed. At court the Protestant leaders were jubilant. In spite of an edict forbidding Protestant worship during the conference, Reformed sermons were preached in the lodgings of Coligny, Condé, and Navarre, and in Renée's lodging, a mansion vacated for her use by Odet, cardinal of Châtillon.

There she received the Reformed ministers who had come to take part in the colloquy. She did not compromise herself by doing so, for, as Catholic historian Claude Haton wrote, the Protestant ministers were welcomed at court better than the pope would have been. The queen mother received her compatriot Peter Martyr warmly and listened attentively to Beza, regretful that Calvin himself had not been able to come.

As for the colloquy itself, all of Calvin's prophecies were fulfilled. Letters to and from him during September and October show his deep concern for the proceedings. To Coligny he wrote on 24 September, warning him again about the Lutheran-Guise intrigue, and that same day to Madame de Coligny and the countess de Roye.[3] To Beza he wrote congratulating him on the speech he had made at the first session.[4] At the second session, on 16 September, Beza asked—and was refused—permission to reply to the cardinal of Lorraine. The cardinal of Tournon cut him short, pontificating, "In the very Christian kingdom of

France, there is one faith, one law, one king."[5] Before the closing session, on 9 October, the "conference" had degenerated into violent disputes and the two religions were farther apart than before. The queen mother's colloquy simply laid bare the irreconcilable positions of the two religions.

Unfortunately the colloquy also increased the audacity of the Reformed in many cities. Their ministers were unable to control them, and letters from Beza, Viret, and Calvin had no effect. At Paris and Dijon, Rouen and Toulouse, bloody battles were fought between Reformed and populace. In November the king (Catherine) took notice of the anarchy and issued an edict ordering the Huguenots to obey their pastors and relinquish the churches they had seized. Calvin saw in his coreligionists' illegal acts the ruin of all his attempts to secure any toleration of Protestantism in France.

After the collapse of the colloquy, Renée lost no time in returning to Montargis, which she was determined to make a Protestant city. She began by reducing the powers of the municipal officers and taking over the administration of civic affairs. She imprisoned those who had the temerity to oppose her. She hanged some who resisted.

Remembering the streets that Ercole I had widened in Ferrara, she demolished houses and widened streets in the main part of Montargis, paving many of them. She renovated the city hall, completed the fortifications of the château, and repaired the Church of the Magdelene. The work was still going forward when Calvin wrote Beza, "The Lady Duchess has begged me not to recall Colonges [Morel]. It is also hardly right that her hopes concerning you should be frustrated. She eagerly expects you and Peter Martyr who with Peter Viret, she says, have been promised her" as they returned from Poissy. At the same time he warned Beza to avoid returning through Burgundy.[6]

Renée had by now made Morel her chief steward as well as her chaplain, surrounding herself with Calvinist servitors and ladies of honor (most of whom had been with her in Ferrara) and exchanging frequent visits with Coligny and his wife.

In December she sent a short note to Calvin, one of the few found today in the Bibliothèque Nationale:[7]

To Monsieur d'Espeville by Francesco Porto.

I received your letter and have read the good advice you give me, which I understand and willingly receive. I beg you to continue. As for Porto, I am very glad he is with you to serve the church, but it would be very profitable in furthering religion in this kingdom (as I desire and pray for) if you would send him to me, for I find many places here where he could serve to the glory of God; here, near me, the teachings of holy Scripture could be sown, and here he would be such a good witness by his doctrine and his life. [She recommends Porto again to Calvin, begs him not to deprive Porto of his favor] any more than you would to me who prays our Creator, Monsieur d'Espeville, that he may maintain you in his service and augment his reign with your good health.

Your very good Renée of France

In Geneva, as the year drew to a close, Calvin wrote to both the king and the queen of Navarre: to Jeanne d'Albret, commending her on having taken a public stand for the Reformed;[8] to her husband a much longer letter, berating him again for his vacillation but more especially for the fact that on 3 December at Saint-Germain-en-Laye, while his wife listened to a sermon of Beza's, Navarre attended mass at Sainte Chapelle.[9]

Antoine de Bourbon was now the complete sycophant of the Guises, who were holding out to him the possibility of marriage with their niece Mary Stuart—the pope would certainly annul his marriage to his heretic wife—and the exchange of his kingdom of Navarre for Sardinia. Navarre had already sent his submission to the pope and after an ugly scene with Jeanne d'Albret had broken off relations with her, giving her "permission" to return to Bearn and to live as a Calvinist.

On 10 January 1562, we find Calvin writing a long reply to an inquiry of Morel:[10] Was it permissible for a minister of God to lend money at interest? Yes, Calvin judged, if one did so not for the sole purpose of deriving profit but to assist a merchant of integrity. A fair profit was permissible if God made that industry thrive. Should men be required to make oath before the consistory? No, the consistory had no legal jurisdiction. Should officers of justice and police be permitted to serve on the consistory in the capacity of magistrates? There should be no blending of the functions of church and state. Morel was actively immersing himself in community affairs as well as in the church he was organizing in Montargis.

The queen mother and L'Hôpital had not give up their attempts to achieve peace in France. In January they called an assembly, deputies from the eight provinces, chosen this time by the chancellor himself. The Edict of January passed by this convocation was an attempt at justice for each side: restoration of churches, houses and goods seized by Protestants; Protestants interdicted from destroying crosses and images or otherwise disturbing the public peace; Huguenots forbidden to hold any public or private assemblies to preach, pray, or administer the sacraments within the walls of any city on pain of death with no hope of pardon; there would, however, be no punishment for Protestants who held their assemblies outside cities, and magistrates would be required to protect them and move with all vigor against any who molested them. His Majesty's subjects were forbidden to maltreat each other on the subject of religion or provoke each other by using odious names. A magistrate must be present at all meetings of synods or other Protestant assemblies.

The Parlement of Paris refused to register this decree, as did parlements of Dijon, Aix, Burgundy, and Provence, in all of which places murderous attacks on the Huguenots now took place. Yet the dame of Montargis approved the celebration of the Lord's Supper in the bishop's palace at Chartres, one of her dower cities, an act of complete insubordination.

It was hardly to be wondered at that Renée was viewed with suspicion by extremists of both Reformed and Catholic parties. The Huguenots resented her favors to several convents of the city, her welcome to officers of the king passing through, her graciousness to merchants bearing letters from the queen mother.

Her first serious confrontation was with Catholics of the little city of Nemours, where she had interfered to rescue the Huguenot minister. The sequel to that affair was ludicrous: Catholics kidnapped the infant Papillon had baptized and rebaptized him by Catholic rites. A violent quarrel ensued between father and godfather, ending in a full-scale riot, with the father hiding in a granary from his pursuers, his shop sacked, the infant's mother attacked and left for dead in a ditch, the father's house set afire. It was only then that the bailiff intervened; fearing the spread of the flames, he managed to have the fire extinguished, and restored peace to the city.

The Huguenots addressed a complaint to the king, but Renée did not wait for him to render justice, sending a troop of her gentlemen to Nemours to take depositions and transmit their report to the bailiff of Gien, a city preponderantly Reformed. The settlement of claims was still in abeyance when a tragedy took place which made even Renée forget the affair in the little city of Nemours.

XXI

Vassy and After
1562–63

On 28 February the duke of Guise and the cardinal of Lorraine, with Guise's two young sons and his pregnant wife, accompanied by the duke's armed retainers, set out from the family estate at Joinville, headed for Paris. On the following day, a Sunday, they reached Vassy, a village of some three thousand inhabitants, where a large Huguenot congregation had gathered for worship in a barn outside the city walls.

Guise's mother, Antoinette de Bourbon, aunt of Navarre and the prince of Condé but more Guise than the Guises themselves, had complained loudly of the riffraff heretics in the neighboring village and attempts had been made to disperse them. But since the Edict of January gave Protestants the right to worship beyond the city walls, her protests had been ignored.

Guise's forces, in advance of his family, stormed the barn, their weapons blazing. Guise, coming up, was hit by a stone thrown by a Huguenot. The melee became a massacre. Sixty-four of the worshipers were killed, more than two hundred seriously wounded. It was said later that Anne of Este begged her enraged husband to spare the pregnant women.

There had been worse massacres than this, at Dijon and

Toulouse, in Paris even, but never one so unprovoked, never one so blatantly contemptuous of the king's edicts, never one in which the duke of Guise had been personally involved.

When the queen mother heard reports of Vassy, she sent Guise word that he was not to come to Paris. When he continued on his way, she took the king and hurried off to Monceau, leaving the nobility to meet Guise and escort him in triumph through the streets where the populace acclaimed him a hero.

The massacre was a powder train. Vassy meant open war. Protestants and Catholics alike responded with acts of vengeance. At Sens, Auxerre, Blois, Troyes, and Cahors, Protestants were attacked. In Toulouse and its environs more than two thousand persons, Catholics and Protestants, were slaughtered. At Annonay, Grenoble, Poitiers, and Meaux, Huguenots indulged in an orgy of bloodshed and vandalism. It was in vain that Calvin begged the ministers to restrain their people: passions could not be held in check. In Lyon the Reformed minister armed himself and led a mob that vandalized the cathedral and threw twelve priests into a well.

At Montargis, the duchess ordered the city gates locked, with no person allowed to enter or leave. She doubled the city watch, gauging correctly the effect of the news on the volatile populace.

In Orléans Condé declared that one could no longer hope but in God and one's arms. On 11 April Huguenot leaders signed a manifesto declaring their loyalty to the crown; nevertheless, they were driven to take up arms for liberty of conscience. The civil war had begun.

Opening hostilities took place in the flat country between Orléans and Montargis, and before the end of the month Renée had opened her castle to the hordes of old people, women, and children, Catholic as well as Protestant, who streamed for sanctuary to Montargis, fleeing before soldiers of both armies.

The Ferrarese ambassador wrote Alfonso d'Este that the duchess was in danger of being treated as a heretic. Guise, as grand master, had decreed that the king's household, his servants and officers, must live as good Catholics or leave the kingdom. It was said that the duchess had given all her money to the Huguenots and offered them her castle. The duchess of Guise was being sent to make her mother understand the gravity of the situation.

It was a logical step for Guise to take. As commander of the king's army, it was unthinkable that he should permit his mother-in-law to offer Montargis to the Huguenot army or to succor their families. In His Majesty's name he sent Anne to tell her mother than unless she sent her ministers away immediately and emptied her castle of refugees, promising to live as a good Catholic, she would be removed to a convent.

The duchess received her daughter gladly, inquiring as to the health of her grandsons Henry and Charles and the new baby whom she longed to see. It was only after amenities that Anne, deferential and embarrassed, gave her mother the duke's ultimatum. Renée received the message cheerfully. She had heard that same message in Ferrara, and she made the same response, agreeing to do as she was bid. When Anne had gone, her mother continued living as before.

Her Huguenot subjects took her noncompliance as carte blanche for any outrage against their Catholic neighbors. They forcibly took over the cathedral, an act which the duchess seemed to condone when she attended services there. When her Catholic subjects petitioned her, however, she refused to worship with the Reformed.

Her too-late decision did not cool Catholic tempers. They threatened to defend their church by arms. To prevent fighting in the streets, Renée forbade her subjects to assemble anywhere, by day or night, to commit any violence against each other. Her orders were merely words. The warden of the cathedral and some eighty followers armed themselves, hid in the church, and when the Huguenots arrived for a "preaching," began a battle which spilled out into the streets. Houses of several Protestants were sacked, and Renée was forced to send some of her gentlemen to rescue the besieged and bring them to safety in her castle.

When it became clear that she would be unable to enforce peace in the mutinous town, she sent to Condé in Orléans, begging him for a body of troops to garrison Montargis. Unfortunately, the Huguenot soldiers who came were among the "exalted," fanatics who showed their piety by vandalizing churches, pulling down bells for the lead, stealing chasubles and chalices, and destroying both church and municipal records.

A few weeks later Condé recalled his troops, leaving only a token force in the citadel to help keep a tenuous peace. The duke of Guise, informed of how his mother-in-law was obeying his orders, sent orders again, through his wife. Renée was forced to temporize, commanding her Protestant subjects to cease annoying their neighbors in any way.

Morel added his complaints against the duchess to those of his coreligionists, writing to Calvin that she was much too friendly to Catholics.[1] The two exchanged angry words, Renée accusing the minister of wishing to obey Condé rather than the king; Morel threatening to return to Geneva. Calvin ordered him to remain with the duchess until he could find a minister more to her taste.

In spite of his complaints, Morel sometimes showed a little understanding of Renée's feelings. "The duchess is full of affection and compassion toward our brothers," he wrote Calvin, "but she cannot help wishing her son-in-law well because of her daughter. . . . It is a sad struggle between zeal for the religion of Christ and the affections of the flesh."[2]

From Calvin's letters that summer, we can see his continuing concern for the Huguenots. In June he sent letters to the Swiss cantons urging succor for the Protestants besieged in Lyon.[3] In August, a letter to Francesco Porto, still with the duchess since Ferrara, told him of a minister he was sending to Montargis to replace Morel. The uncertainty of the roads, however, forced this man to return to Geneva, and Morel remained with Renée for some time longer.

In August a letter reported the landing of English soldiers in Normandy and Andelot's mission to Germany to hire foot soldiers. The queen of Navarre was raising troops also.[4]

Huguenot forces in Bourges had held out against Saint-André for months, but Saint-André's troops were experienced, had already sacked Poitiers and the cities of Touraine and the Bourbonnais. The surrender of Bourges was only a matter of days. The queen mother was invited to be present at the capitulation in order to show the world that the Huguenots were rebels in spite of their protests of loyalty to the king.

After the surrender of Bourges, the combined forces of the Catholic armies moved against Rouen. Their road would lead them past Montargis. Renée, warned by the fate of Gien, opened her castle to the Protestants of her city, adding them to the hundreds already within the castle walls. She sent Morel and his assistant to a distant château off the beaten track and braced herself to meet the arrival of Guise and his party.

Anne and the cardinal of Lorraine arrived with the vanguard to convince the duchess of her safety and that of her people. The only ones in danger, she was assured, were rebellious subjects of the king. His Majesty followed with Guise and the main body of the army, greeting his great-aunt with tears and kisses and protestations of affection while the troops set to pillaging Huguenot houses, breaking the tables and chairs in the hall which the duchess had prevailed upon the Huguenots to use as their church. At Renée's protests, Charles ordered a herald to proclaim that His Majesty forbade any further outrages on the part of citizens or soldiers on pain of death, immediately hanging a disobedient soldier to emphasize his words.

Francis of Guise had no more confidence in the promises of his mother-in-law than her husband had had. He had been perfectly informed by Henry II of the Ferrara fiasco and distrusted her not only as a heretic but as a confederate of his political enemies, particularly Gaspard de Coligny. With the king's approval, he appointed an archer of his guard to remain in Montargis as governor of the city and demanded that Renée employ no more ministers and give no more assistance to the rebels.

She had already sent her ministers away, though temporarily. The refugees in her castle were Catholic as well as Protestant, sheltered because of their need. She was in no position now to aid the Huguenot army. She promised with a clear conscience to obey all demands. The army departed to besiege Rouen, and the castle of Montargis remained open.

Calvin, like Renée, disapproved of the taking up of arms. Though she never departed from that position, he was more pragmatic, seeing in this warfare a parallel with the God-approved battles of the children of Israel with the enemies of the Lord. He appealed, now, to the churches of France to raise funds for Condé to carry on the war provoked by Guise's violation of the Edict of January.

On 6 December 1562 he wrote Johann Sulzer a detailed account of the taking of Rouen.[5] The city had been stoutly defended, its fall in late October attributed to the small number of troops sent by the English queen, who was boasting so loudly of her aid to the French Protestants [and who would later extort her pound of flesh]. Lyon was quiet, Switzerland crowded again with penniless refugees. The king of Navarre, seriously wounded before Rouen, had died in November. The queen mother was talking peace but no one was fooled.

Writing to Bullinger later in the month, he told of Condé's sortie to the walls of Paris: "Nobody knows what Condé was planning."[6] When Guise's troops were beaten back, Catherine de' Medici had asked for a conference with Condé, apparently prepared to throw her weight on the side of the victors. But when Breton and Spanish troops came to the aid of Guise's forces, Condé withdrew. Guise followed. By the middle of December the armies faced each other, and on 19 December a bloody battle was fought. In the first skirmish seven hundred Spaniards were slain. At first the Huguenots seemed to be victorious, and Catherine de' Medici, when the news was brought to her, was reported to have said, "Well then, we shall have to pray to God in French!"

That was not required of her. Condé, wounded, was captured. On the other side, Montmorency was captured and hurried off to prison in Orléans. Nevers was seriously wounded; Saint-André killed. The queen mother, with Condé a prisoner in tow, departed for Paris.

Calvin was extremely worried about the situation. Condé was defending himself by saying that the war had been declared in order to free the king. Since Parlement had created him one of the guardians of the king (whom they had declared of age at the same time, hardly a month before) it was unlawful for anyone to set hands on the second person of the kingdom. But what would be the result of the negotiations Condé would now be compelled to hold with the queen mother? Would he allow himself to be deceived by her promises?

Coligny had written a full account of the battle at Dreux to Calvin and was as worried as he. Condé had sent him a letter naming him head of the Protestant army, saying the troops had taken an oath to obey him, but Coligny would put no credence in Condé's letters until the prince was set at liberty.

Francis of Guise, now sole leader of the Catholic party, pursued his next objective: the reduction of Orléans, still in Huguenot hands. His first need was to get rid of the viper's nest his mother-in-law maintained in spite of her promises and the orders of the king (and his own). From His Majesty's council he secured an order that Madame de Ferrara should be removed, willingly or not, from Montargis, offered the choice of one of three of the king's dwellings—to wit, Fontainebleau, Saint-Germain-en-Laye, or Vincennes. He deputed one of his captains, Poulin, to inform the duchess of His Majesty's ultimatum.

When Poulin presented himself at Montargis ordering Renée to accompany him to court, she refused to budge. Word was carried back to Guise in his camp near Orléans. Furious that the old woman—she had just turned 53—should defy him, he dispatched his lieutenant, the sieur de Malincorne, with four companies of cavalry to Montargis to enforce his order, nevermind that she was the daughter of Louis XII and supposedly sacrosanct.

The townspeople of Montargis opened the city gates to Malincorne, whose appearance was signal for a general uprising against the Huguenots of the town. A more able politician than Poulin—after all, he was a gentleman—Malincorne told Renée that he had come to protect her from insurgents infecting the area and had been sent by her son-in-law to take her to a place of safety.

But Renée was also an able politician. She knew she could not protect her Huguenot subjects in the city, but she would not throw her refugees to the soldiers nor leave her castle. She told

Malincorne that her castle would be of no strategic importance to the duke of Guise even if it were repaired from roof to foundation; that her city was already defended by one of her son-in-law's captains and his soldiery. Why then should she be dispossessed of her lawful habitation?

To take her to one of the suggested palaces would be to sentence her to the butcher. Both Vincennes and Saint-Germain were at the very gates of Paris and unable to withstand an attack from a Parisian mob; Fontainebleau was in the midst of a lonely forest where she would be exposed to assassination. What had she done to be ordered away from her château? Apparently the sieur de Malincorne had misunderstood the duke's wishes. She demanded to be more fully informed of *His Majesty's* wishes. She proposed that Malincorne remain in Montargis while Poulin, accompanied by one of her gentlemen, go to court and ask for further instructions from the king. Malincorne was not taken in by her ploy. He sent some of his men to Guise's camp at Orléans to borrow a field piece and informed the duchess that he intended to force the castle.

De Thou reported her answer, so these are his words, not hers, yet the substance must be the same:

> Consider well what you are planning to do. There is no man in this kingdom who can command me except the king himself. Should you be so rash as to open a breach in these walls, I shall be the first to put myself there to see if you will be so audacious as to kill the daughter of a king! Nor is my connection with the royal family so slight nor am I so little loved that I have no means of repaying your audacity to yourself and to your family, even to the infant in the cradle![7]

Malicorne hesitated, then rode off to Orléans to confer with the duke. A few days later he returned to Montargis and without a word to the duchess ordered his troops to evacuate the city with all speed. Renée expected the worst, but she would not be molested again. On 8 February the duke of Guise was seriously wounded by a would-be assassin as he rode from the camp to the house where his wife and children were awaiting him. Six days later he was dead.

XXII

Letters from Geneva
Spring 1563

The assassination of Francis of Guise shocked all Europe. Letters from ambassadors flew from court to court, and rumors flew still faster. Poltrot, the assassin, was hustled off to Paris for torture and interrogation, and implicated all the leaders of the Protestant party, contradicting himself time after time, agreeing to whatever questions were put to him, without a real trial in spite of Coligny's demands, before he was finally drawn and quartered. Rumors spread and were believed that the Huguenots had planned to kill the royal family as well as all the leaders of the Catholic party.

Renée, hurrying to console her daughter, was convinced that Coligny had had no part in the plot, if plot there were; yet few believed his innocence. The admiral admitted that Poltrot had openly discussed his plan to kill Guise, but that it was because the man was a Huguenot spy that he had been given money, a pistol, and a horse. Yet why should anyone have been surprised or horrified? Political assassination was an acceptable gambit in peace as in war. Guise had publicly put a price on the heads of the Coligny brothers and Condé. He had announced that he intended to kill every living thing once he took Orléans, even to the cats. Coligny quite frankly admitted that he had been aware of Poltrot's threats but swore by his life and honor that he had not solicited the man or anyone else to murder Guise.

Rejoicing among Protestants was universal and loud, though Calvin attempted to moderate it. "God alone has the right to deliver his church," he wrote,[1] yet he understood and partook of the relief.

His words were no comfort to Renée, surrounded by members of the formidable Guise clan: the mother, Antoinette de Bourbon; Charles, cardinal of Lorraine in addition to a multitude of lesser titles; Claude, duke of Aumale; Louis, cardinal of Guise, archbishop of Sens, bishop of Metz; Francis, grand prior of France; two sisters, abbesses of great convents. All were dedicated to the advancement of the Guise dynasty. All had dreamed of the elevation of Mary Stuart, daughter of the duke's sister Mary, to the throne of England as well as the thrones of France and Scotland.

Now, added to this ambitious family was Anne of Este with her sons. Anne and young Henry would pursue Coligny to his death on St. Bartholomew's Day nine years later. Henry would almost achieve the crown and bring down the last Valois king before that king, Henry III, had him assassinated. Perhaps it has never been proven that Anne's daughter incited a mad monk to assassinate Henry IV, but there is evidence to that effect. The Guise motto might well have been noli me tangere with a different implication from the original.

Both Renée and the queen mother rushed to the bedside of the dying Francis, duke of Guise, Renée praying for the salvation of his soul, Catherine promising him that all his estates and honors, including that of the post of grand master, would be bestowed immediately upon his thirteen-year-old son Henry.

The Ferrarese ambassador wrote Alfonso d'Este a full account of the duke's magnificent funeral in Notre Dame, the eulogy declaring that no man could live and die more gloriously, happily, and holily than had the duke. His devotion to the church, the life he had lived, and the death he had suffered— all made it certain that his soul had gone straight to Paradise without having to suffer the pangs of purgatory.

He gave Alfonso the details of the crime as Guise's family and friends had reconstructed it:[2] Jean de Parthenay, sieur de Soubise, son of the notorious Madame de Soubise whom Alfonso's father had banished, had suggested the deed to the admiral, who at first declared he would have no part in so dishonorable an act but later changed his mind. Soubise had sent Poltrot to the admiral. Then Coligny and Andelot planned the coup, assuring the assassin that what he was about to do was for the good of the kingdom and pleasing to God.

It was not only the good bishop who felt that Guise's soul had gone to Paradise. Santa Croce, the papal legate, who had for the past ten years expressed his suspicions of Renée, wrote Cardinal Borromeo that the queen had received Coligny's denials of complicity in the plot and that the duchess of Ferrara, though a close friend of the Châtillons, herself suspected (and with reason) of heretical leanings, had declared that her son-in-law had believed differently from what most people thought and that she was sure his soul had gone to eternal life. Renée's attitude aroused the wrath of her coreligionists, who saw in Guise's death a third judgment of God and vindication of their cause, condemning anyone who did not condemn Guise in this world and damn him in the world to come.

Meanwhile Anne of Guise petitioned the king's council to try Coligny for instigating her husband's murder. Coligny, told of the petition, set out from Châtillon with a hundred men-at-arms to go to Saint-Germain and defend himself. Catherine de' Medici, fearing that his appearance with armed followers would precipitate new hostilities, dispatched Condé—with a guard, since he was still nominally a prisoner—to meet the admiral and persuade him to go home. Andelot was permitted to speak for his brother before the council, which tabled Anne's petition in order to keep the uncertain peace.

There were other, more pressing, matters before the Council. The kingdom was in a state of near-anarchy and widespread devastation. Unpaid foreign soldiers were pillaging the countryside. The treasury was empty, with Florentine and Venetian bankers clamoring for repayment of loans. The whole Catholic party was in disarray, and the opportunity to work out a peace treaty could not be let slide. Within a few days after the death of Guise, Catherine began negotiations with Condé as leader of the Protestant party.

Calvin's letters show his estimation of Condé, his lack of either ability or stability, his affinity with his brother, the late king of Navarre. When the treaty, arrived at too quickly between Catherine and Condé, was announced on 17 March, Calvin wrote to Bullinger: "We have been basely betrayed by the other brother also. He had promised by oath to conclude nothing without the consent of his associates while clandestinely negotiating with the queen mother."[3] Condé had sent word to Soubise in Lyon to make no more war until Coligny arrived, and had written his mother-in-law, Madame de Roye, to send her troops away since everything was settled. To regain his freedom as soon as possible, he had agreed to all that the queen mother asked, when he could have gotten everything he pleased. "He has prostituted himself by the most abject obsequiousness," Calvin concluded.[4]

Coligny agreed with Calvin, accusing the prince of sacrificing the cause of God and bringing about the ruin of the churches by the terms of the treaty he had signed in the name of all Huguenots at Amboise. But Condé was free and had been named a knight of the Royal Order.

Calvin, again writing to Bullinger, again lamenting the Peace of Amboise, noted the clauses of the treaty:[5]

All nobles who were barons and who had jurisdiction might worship as they pleased in their own castles, where their own vassals might join them.
Inhabitants of towns and villages might worship in their own houses.
The Reformed religion was not to be practiced in Paris.
All cities were to revert to their ancient customs.
All knights, noblemen, gentlemen, and burgesses were forgiven.
The king would pay all obligations to foreign soldiers.
All prisoners except robbers and assassins would be released, and all injuries forgiven.
All alliances of Protestants with foreign powers or leagues within the kingdom were to be broken.

Protestants were to swear that never again would they levy troops or raise money for such a purpose nor hold any assemblies except for worship.

Calvin could not conceal his disappointment over the measures that would hinder the churches in their organization and worship. He wrote Condé's mother-in-law, Madame de Roye, letting her know that everyone was displeased with Condé, "who had provided better for his own personal safety" than for the church. "I shall always advise our people to abstain from arms," he finished. "All of us should perish rather than have recourse a second time to the disorders we have witnessed."[6]

He wrote the Marchioness of Rothelin who, like Renée, had made her château a sanctuary during the war;[7] to de Crussol, lieutenant governor of Dauphiné, Provence, and Languedoc, begging him to try to pacify the provinces under his control;[8] to Madame de Crussol, one of the queen's ladies-of-honor who had influenced her husband into becoming a Protestant, urging her not to try to swim between two currents.[9]

On 10 May he forced himself to write to the prince of Condé, chiding him, but "hoping for a better future. . . . If you do not make good by your authority what has been concluded to the advantage of our brethren, the peace will be like a body without a soul. Your experience has already proven to you how wantonly the enemies of God seek occasion to do evil."[10] He warned Condé of the enemies around him at court, of men who would try to entangle him into a debate concerning the Augsburg Confession.

After the promulgation of the Peace of Amboise, Renée, back at Montargis, again opened her castle to the needy. To avoid harassment, she wrote Catherine asking that the obligations laid upon her by her late son-in-law might be rescinded, that she desired to serve only the queen, her son, and God; but her poor refugees had lost everything, even their homes, and she felt it would be a great pity to turn them out without the queen's assurance of their safety. The queen mother did not reply; Renée contented herself with having gone on record and kept her refugees.

Since the treaty permitted persons of her rank to have sermons and prayers in their own castles and with their own vassals and families, she considered the refugees her family and recalled Morel, putting her domestic affairs into his hands and assigning him the oversight of the municipality.

In many places the Reformed saw in the treaty leave to revenge themselves on their neighbors, committing unlawful acts even though no physical violence was offered. The Huguenots of Montargis grumbled when Renée adamantly refused to permit them to pillage shops of the papists. Even when she permitted them to have public worship within the town, they complained that she was lukewarm toward the cause.

In April she was thrown from a horse, badly bruised and shaken. Scarcely recovered in May, she moved her court to Choisy to escape an epidemic that had broken out among her crowded refugees. She was at Choisy when Calvin wrote her on 10 May, the same day on which he wrote Condé.

XXIII

The Eighth Letter

Madame:[1]

I have experienced much distress during these troubles arising from the war and the attendant confusion into which everything was plunged in France, and all the more so since I had no means of writing to you at a time when you stood more than ever in need of support. Now I hope that means of communication are more open; though for some time to come there will be robbers and bandits [on the roads], yet at last God will provide a remedy for all disorders. Indeed, if God does not intervene, we shall be in a worse state than before; for if those in authority do not put into execution all the provisions of the peace, advancing the honor of God more than the others oppose it, religion will be like a body without a soul.

I know, Madame, how God has strengthened you during the rudest assaults and how by God's grace you have courageously resisted all temptations, not being ashamed to bear the opprobrium of Jesus Christ, while the pride of his enemies rose above the clouds. I know also that you have been, as it were, a nursing mother to those poor, persecuted brothers and sisters who did not know where to go. I know that a princess, considering only the things of the world, would have been ashamed and taken it almost as an insult that her castle should have been called God's hostelry.[2]

But I cannot pay you a higher compliment than in expressing myself thus, to recognize and commend the humanity you have exercised toward the children of God who found refuge with you. I have often thought, Madame, that God reserved such trials for your old age so that you might have the opportunity of paying the debt due for your timidity in the past. I am speaking in human terms, for even if you had done a hundred—or a thousand!— times more, you could not pay a tenth of each day's debt you are continually contracting for the infinite blessings God continually bestows upon you.

I mean, of course, that God has done you a singular honor by employing you in such a duty and allowing you to carry his banner in order to be glorified in you, while you hospitably entertained his word, the inestimable treasure of salvation, and afforded an asylum to the members of his Son. So much the more then, Madame, is your duty to preserve in the future your house, pure and uncontaminated, that it may be wholly dedicated to God.

On this subject I cannot refrain from mentioning to you a cause of scandal of which I have heard rumors before: there is a young man whom you have brought up and settled in marriage, who has dismissed his wife to keep up intercourse with a strumpet. I inquired of Monsieur Biry the circumstances of the affair, knowing that he was such an affectionate servant to you that you would not feel offended if I told him what people reported to me on the subject. At first he replied that you had taken pains to correct the disorder; later he admitted that though there had been some amendment, people did not think it would last.

I pray you, Madame, in the name of God, to be vigilant, in this and similar cases, to keep your household unsullied from all disgraceful taint in order to shut the mouths of the ungodly who ask for nothing better than to blaspheme the name of God. Nevertheless, rejoice! You have good grounds for joy amid so much sorrow. It is no slight blessing that God has so approved of you to choose you in order to be glorified through you.

I hope you will excuse me, Madame, for not having satisfied immediately your wish for me to send you [another] preacher. I shall not fail to attend to this commission so that you may be provided with one. One cannot find at every moment such ministers as one could wish; we are importuned from so many quarters that we scarcely know where to turn. At any rate, you may count upon being served in preference to all others. If you were here, you would see that it is not without a reason that I beg you to be patient.

There is a private matter about which your old servant, Monsieur Francesco [Porto], has begged me to write to you. Since you were graciously pleased to promise him that you would interest yourself in the future of his daughter, doing something toward procuring her a husband, and since she is now of marriageable age, he would like to know your good pleasure and what he may expect from you.

You know that I am not in the habit of soliciting you for anyone, and I would not venture to do it if it were for myself or for any of mine. But since he is your old servant, whom you were pleased to recommend to me, I did not dare refuse his request, particularly since he faithfully discharges his duty here and conducts himself to the satisfaction of all good people. On the other hand, his salary, like that of the rest of us, is so small that it would be impossible for him to live if he did not derive some support elsewhere to enable him to cover expenses.

Madame, humbly commending myself to your indulgent favor, I shall pray that our heavenly Father may keep you always in his care, strengthening you with invincible courage, and increase you in all good and prosperity.

Charles d'Espeville

XXIV

June 1563—January 1564

Calvin was still concerned about conditions in the south of France where Soubise had delayed surrendering Lyon. Huguenot forces under the counts de Beauvais and de Crussol were encouraging Soubise, disregarding the Peace of Amboise, to continue fighting. Though "ill of a desperate colic," Calvin wrote Soubise on 25 May, "I do not see that God permits you to act in direct opposition to the king."[1] He advised him to lay down his arms and admit the duke of Nemours (now head of the Catholic forces) to take his office as governor of Lyon.

Calvin's correspondence with Jeanne d'Albret continued.[2] He had written her after the death of her husband, encouraging her in her attempts to make her kingdom completely Reformed, urging her to purge her territories of every kind of idolatry; to arm herself with the promises of God, for if she knew what God commanded, and did the divine will, God would never fail her. She had need of courage, for Montluc, governor of Guienne and Gascony, was "pacifying" those provinces by fire and sword. Calvin promised to send Merlin to her from Châtillon.

On 1 June, he wrote her about a loan the magistracy of Geneva had promised her late husband.[3] She had written him of her excommunication, the constant threat of invasion by Spain, her efforts at eradicating Catholicism by abolishing the use of images, forbidding religious processions, suppressing monasteries, turning Catholic churches into Protestant houses of worship. She intended to take over ecclesiastical lands and use the revenue to establish schools and help the poor. Already she had introduced preaching in the tongue of the people. Calvin congratulated her upon her endeavors and promised to send twelve ministers to help her. He had warned them of the seditious populace and the danger from Spain and Montluc, perils that would not prevent their coming.

By the middle of the year Calvin's physical condition had deteriorated to such an extent that many of his activities had to be curtailed. Now he began dictating all of his letters, fewer than ever before, to Charles de Jonvillers.[4] There were no more to Farel. Perhaps the falling out over Farel's wedding had lessened their friendship. During the last two years of his life, it was Heinrich Bullinger to whom he wrote most often, telling not only of affairs in France but, as to no one else, his physical suffering. In his letter of 2 July he gives the gruesome details of his attempt to dislodge and excrete a kidney stone the "size of a kernel of a filbert," resorting to horseback riding, violent exercise, the drinking of quarts of warm water before the painful process met with success.[5]

Other news he gave Bullinger. On 2 July he reported that at Lyon Huguenot outrages continued. At court the queen was loading favors on Condé; many counselors of the Parlement of Paris had resigned, and the chancellor was offended since he had hoped for as many as possible to favor the Reformation. Andelot was at court, Coligny at home. Everyone knew the queen was insincere, but if Condé was prudent he might be able to accomplish something if he would comply with advice. The admiral was urging Condé to publish the Reformed confession. The condition of the churches in France was not too bad just now.[6]

On 19 July the latest gossip from the court was that the king's brother Henry, duke of Orléans and a year younger than Henry of Guise, provoked by young Guise, struck him with an arrow. Guise ran to his mother, who indignantly confronted Catherine. The queen mother, hearing the story, told her son to *forgive* the other Henry. Orléans then burst out that he had never been able to endure the sight of Guise, that he detested him and his whole family, which had been from the beginning so fatal to the kingdom. To make peace, the queen sent her son from the room.[7] (It would be twenty years yet before Henry III had Henry of Guise assassinated.)

In Paris, Calvin continued, Catherine de' Medici was inflaming the passions of the populace. Parlement had no authority over the rabble. Condé remained silent, and Coligny was awaiting the opportunity to throw himself into open danger. The admiral, Beza, and Rochefoucauld had published a common defense against their accusers and had presented it to the king's council, and the admiral had published another to be offered for sale at the coming bookfair in Frankfurt. Lyon was peaceful, most churches still in possession of the Protestants with no one venturing to make any opposition. The same was true of Montpellier and Nîmes. Le Havre-de-Grâce was besieged, Huguenots helping the royal army to wrest it from Elizabeth, to whom the Reformed themselves had bartered it for her help in the war.

On 29 July Calvin reported riots against Huguenots in Rouen, fomented by Catherine. Everything previously decreed by the king's council had been turned upside down. Coligny was still at home, unwilling to be part of the expedition against England since he had been responsible for the deal with Elizabeth.[8]

Others Calvin wrote to in July included Crussol, urging him (unsuccessfully) to stand firm in the faith,[9] and Coligny, giving the admiral his support in the process the Guises were still attempting to bring against him and his brothers, Rochefoucauld, the prince of Marsillac, and other Huguenot leaders.[10]

Odet, cardinal of Châtillon and bishop of Beauvais, had been excommunicated but continued to wear his cardinal's robes on formal occasions, notably his wedding day, a double scandal to faithful Catholics. Calvin thought such levity unseemly. Again Calvin urged Coligny to publish his declaration of innocence in the murder of Guise and to return to court, where he would be in a better position to keep up with the machinations of the queen and the Guises.

Anne of Guise could not have known how close a check Calvin made on her activities. Determined to persuade the king to begin her process against Coligny, she staged a dramatic scene at court. Dressed in deepest mourning, as were all the women in her party, she led a procession into His Majesty's presence: Guise's weeping mother, his children, relatives, and retainers, all the women sobbing and moaning as Anne fell before Charles, calling for justice against the men who had made her a widow and her children fatherless. Charles was moved to tears and promised fervently that he would continue the investigation at a more propitious time.

Surely this dramatic scene is what prompted the undated letter from Calvin to Renée:[11]

Madame:

I am delighted in having the means of writing to you in surety by the bearer; not that I have anything of importance to communicate to you at the moment, but that I may acquit myself of my duty; and also because I fancy my letters, in consequence of your favorable indulgence, are not unwelcome to you. If they can be of any profit to you, I shall make an effort to let you have them more frequently.

But you have in your household, thank God, a man in every way qualified to exhort you and confirm you in all that you have need of.

I have no news to send you that you have not heard from other sources, especially none that can afford you much pleasure, and I dislike to cause you pain, though I am compelled to unburden my mind, regretfully, of a sorrow common to all the children of God.

You know, Madame, what the enemies of the truth are hatching; witness the league of the pope with the king of Spain, the Venetians, and the powers of Italy, in which our neighbor is included. They verily think it their duty to banish all Christianity from the world. Now, in the meantime, Madame de Guise is pursuing a course which can only lead to her confusion if she continues in it; for, though she may not think so, yet it is most certain that she is seeking the ruin of the poor churches in France, of which God will be the protector in order to maintain them.

Again, I protest that I do not tell you this to distress you; on the other hand I wish she might be induced by your authority to moderate her passions, which she cannot obey as she does without making war upon God. I tell you frankly, Madame, what everyone knows, so that you may decide what good measures you may use to divert her from conspiring with those who seek for nothing but to abolish pure religion, and so that you may prevent her from being mixed up with intrigues of which the issue can only be unfortunate since they are directed against God.

Madame, humbly commending myself to your indulgent favor, I pray our heavenly Father to keep you ever under divine protection, fortifying you by divine power and increasing you in all good and prosperity.

Charles d'Espeville

Early in September Calvin wrote Bullinger that the French had retaken Le Havre.[12] He was afraid the civil war was going to break out anew since each party had imprisoned envoys of the other. The queen wanted the Parlement of Paris to proclaim Charles of age, since the Parlement of Rouen had already done so. In which case, Calvin said ironically, Charles would have to obtain the "dispensation of age" from himself. As soon as the Parlement of Paris agreed, Charles could dispense with all advice from the council of regency and Catherine would have everything to herself.

Later in the month he wrote to Condé, lieutenant general of France since his signing of the Peace at Amboise, begging him to protect the cause of Jesus Christ, urging him to "testify by your public life so that your example may edify the good and shut the mouth of malicious gossipers." He had been told he said, of Condé's dalliances with the ladies of the queen—Condé had been involved in a most unsavory affair which had become the talk of the court—which, Calvin said sternly, "derogates from your authority and reputation," and causes the malicious to laugh and the good to mourn.[13]

In late September the duchess, having recovered her health at Choisy, went again to court, this time in Paris, where Protestants were, for the time being, in favor with the queen mother and her son; where, in fact, Catherine seemed to be trying to mediate

between Catholics and Huguenots. It seemed to Renée a propitious time to put Calvin's advice into effect: she would try to
make peace between her daughter and Coligny. She took Catherine into her confidence, and the latter, only too eager to see
peace restored, became stage manager of the drama.

On a day when Renée, the Châtillons, Condé and his brother
the cardinal of Bourbon were in her apartment, Catherine sent
for Anne, and without waiting for the duchess to speak, impe-
riously lectured Anne on her duty.

One must realize the implications of this scene. An unattractive, short, stout, swarthy Italian woman, Catherine was married
at fourteen by her uncle, Pope Clement VII, to a sullen third son
of a king who disliked him. She was so immature physically that
for years she was unable to conceive and was almost sent back to
Italy for that reason. When she finally did bear a child, Francis,
he was weak and sickly from the first. Looked down upon by the
court for her "low" birth, she was now in a position of power onto
which she would hold tenaciously. Here she was, confronting the
aristocratic Italian princess, tall, blond, and regal, her husband's
cousin, his favorite's widow, mother of handsome, healthy children. Catherine relished the moment.

This embarrassing confrontation was not in Renée's plans,
but she could do nothing except to follow the queen's lead,
appealing to Anne to lay her hatred aside for the good of the
kingdom.

Alvarotti reported to Alfonso that "the lady fell on her knees
before the queen mother, saying she had always considered herself a very obedient subject and a very obedient daughter. On her
husband's deathbed he had advised her always to follow their
advice.[14] De Thou and Fontana go on to say that she prayed the
queen not to ask her to pardon the one who was the cause of so
much treachery, to see that justice was done without further
delay. If the queen did not, she ended, it would mean the death of
herself and her children, as it had been for her husband.

The king promised to continue the investigation, putting off a
verdict for three years, and the duchess of Guise appeared ready
to possess her soul in patience. She even attended the sermons

Morel preached daily in her mother's apartment in spite of the Peace of Amboise, bringing with her, at least once, her son Henry—so Calvin wrote Bullinger.[15] There were those who had suspected Anne of Reformed sympathy since her arrival in France, and her pleas for mercy for the plotters executed at Amboise and the poor mothers at Vassy were held against her. It was, perhaps, not the Huguenots as such that she hated, but only Coligny. Like her son, however, when the time came, she would sacrifice all of them to bring about Coligny's death.

It was no wonder that Calvin wrote Bullinger, "The Guises have been bridled!"[16] There was general rejoicing in the Protestant party that the royal family seemed to be inclining toward toleration. Calvin saw more clearly into the future without having to consult Catherine's astrologer, who predicted that she would see all of her sons upon the throne.

On 2 December he wrote Bullinger that no one knew what to expect from the queen mother, her favor shifting from one side to the other daily. Charles had rescinded all acts of the Parlement of Paris. The chancellor was still trying to pour oil on troubled waters, issuing edict after edict which no one obeyed.[17]

Nearly all members of the court were now hostile to the Reformation. Condé, angry at not having been consulted about the king's coming marriage, had left the court. Coligny, however, following Calvin's counsel, had gone to Paris with an escort. His uncle the constable had gone with him to the palace, where he was graciously received by the king.

Upon the arrival of Coligny, the Guises left the court, sending the duke of Nemours to tell the queen mother that the Guises were astonished she would allow Coligny to come into so close contact with her son. To which Catherine replied that the Châtillons were old servants of the Valois kings, and that His Majesty was pleased to receive the admiral, that there was sufficient room at court for everyone. The Guises were not placated, and when they heard of the imminent arrival of two other Protestant lords, they hurried their departure.

Who could put any confidence in the queen, Calvin demanded. Charles was a slave to his mother, not daring to express his own opinion about anything. The pope, Venice, Savoy, and Spain were planning to attack Geneva. A Swiss alliance with France was a necessity, but what would the queen do?[18]

The queen had no policy other than that of balancing Catholics against Huguenots, favoring one side until it became too strong, then elevating the other. Now the Protestants were in the ascendancy. Wives of Reformed nobles brought their ministers to court as Renée did, and their ministers preached openly. But when complaints were made to the queen of Beza's open attacks on the papacy, made in the apartment of the queen of Navarre, Catherine was forced to act. Perhaps if Beza had confined himself to preaching religion, as Renée demanded of her minister, there would not have been so violent a quarrel between the two queens. But Catherine could not afford to antagonize the pope, with Philip II wanting an excuse to interfere in French affairs. It was impossible for her to permit an excommunicant to flaunt her heretical beliefs in the court of the very Christian king of France. The queen of Navarre and her minister left at once for Nérac.

Renée's attempt to reconcile Anne and Coligny was not her only reason for coming to court. Catherine de' Medici was determined that the duchess should sign the document giving up her rights to Brittany, which she had signed at the time of her marriage at Francis I's direction. Since Renée was a minor at that time, her signature meant nothing until it was validated by her husband. But Ercole had neglected to validate it. To make it valid now, Renée must sign, and must do so within ten years of her husband's death. She had no intention of signing away her rights until or unless she received adequate compensation and the rich bequests left her by her father.

Unable to arrive at a satisfactory compromise, Renée left Fontainebleau the last of November, returning to Montargis, where she was immediately embroiled with Morel over his dictatorial treatment of her and her servitors in the church and in her own castle.

On 6 December Morel wrote to Calvin of the deplorable condition of religion in Montargis, the impossibility of enforcing church discipline in either the duchess's household or in the city. Three days later he wrote again, expanding his complaints:[19]

Great danger arises from a woman being the sovereign. The church is in a miserable condition. I was obliged to forego dispensing the sacrament of the Lord's Supper in the bypast month of September, because from other quarters came so many *dogs* and *swine* that I should have been obliged to admit along with the sheep. The festival of Christ's birth is at hand. At that time it is customary to administer the Lord's Supper. I do not know how to act. Do you then, my most worthy father, advise me. . . .

The duchess says she wants to attend meetings of the consistory, since Madame de Coligny and the queen of Navarre do so. . . . If we let females mix in our affairs, we will become the laughing stock of Anabaptists and papists alike!"

Already one of the deacons had resigned, saying he would not submit to the whims of a woman.

At the same time Renée wrote her side of the dispute to Calvin, pouring out her complaints against Morel and some of the other ministers she had heard preach, telling him of the malicious rumors being spread about the late duke of Guise, the libels linking Anne's name with the cardinal of Lorraine.[20]

Yet Calvin delayed sending a replacement for Morel. Late in December he was still with her when she returned to the court at Fontainebleau, offering prayers in her apartment with the doors wide open. With an eye to the future, Renée had bought a house on the outskirts of the village, beyond the walls, suitable for Reformed assemblies should she be forbidden to hear sermons at court.

But on 28 December Catherine, furious because her "aunt" refused to sign the Brittany papers, informed her that there were to be no more prayers or sermons in the duchess's rooms and demanded that she dismiss Morel. One word led to another. Renée asked why *she* was singled out for such treatment. Being the daughter of a king, she said, it seemed to her she should be treated as well as the princess of Condé, who was permitted to enjoy the preaching of her minister.

Catherine had, of course, known what was going on and had chosen to wink at the open defiance of the Peace of Amboise on the part of the Condés and others. But now that she discovered Renée's adamant stand on her claim to Brittany, she would no longer tolerate insubordination.

As for her aunt being the daughter of a king, the queen mother remarked, and so close in blood to His Majesty, for that very reason Renée had done a great wrong in not informing her of the princess of Condé's acts. She would be reprimanded. Meanwhile, if Renée did not send her minister away immediately, he would be hanged. And if the duchess wished to remain at court, she should be careful to live as the king ordered.

There was no alternative. Renée returned to Montargis where, by the Peace of Amboise, she could have prayers said by her own minister, to which none might be admitted except her servitors and household. Her troubles with Morel continued and could not have been made any easier by the letter she received from Calvin, written on 8 January.

XXV

The Ninth Letter

Madame:[1]

I believe you have received my last letters, to which I expect an answer in order to acquit myself of my duty respecting the subject you were pleased to inquire of me. Meanwhile I am unwilling to neglect the opportunity of recommending the present bearer to you so that you may learn from him how things are going here. It is better that he inform you by word of mouth than for me to write such matters, since he is one of my most intimate friends, one in whom I have the most absolute trust. He is [Jean Budé] the son of the late Monsieur Budé, the king's master of the rolls, noted for his great erudition.

Well, Madame, you have shown by your decision [to return to Montargis] that residence at Paris was very little to your taste. It is true that it would have been from my point of view highly desirable for you to remain at court all the time, for the relief you might have secured for the poor churches, but I am not surprised that you prefer a quieter manner of living.

Now, since God has brought you back to your own place, it behooves you to redouble your care to administer properly both your subjects and your household. I know, Madame, how obstinate the people are and how you have worked, without much success, to bring them into subjection. Be that as it may, I beg you to follow completely St. Paul's teaching on this head: never to be weary of welldoing, whatever malice you may encounter to dampen your ardor. Above all, let your household be a mirror to set an example to those who show themselves obstinate and to confound those who are incorrigible and completely hardened. To accomplish this, I urge you to keep a firm hand, as much as you possibly can, to establish good discipline in order to repress vice and occasion for scandal.

I do not mean simply that you should police your household and subjects in matters political, but you should also do so in regard to the consistory of the church. Let those who have been chosen for the office of having an eye over the conduct of others be God-fearing men, of holy life, with such sincerity and straightforwardness that nothing will prevent them from doing their duty, being zealous in maintaining the honor of God in its integrity.

Now let no one, whatever may be his rank or condition or however much you may esteem him, be ashamed to submit to the order which the Son of God himself has established, bending his neck to receive the yoke. I assure you, Madame, that without this remedy there will be unbridled licentiousness, which will only engender confusion.

Those who make a perfunctory profession of Christianity will be, for the most part, dissolute. In one word, there will be a compliant and many-faceted gospel, everyone flattering himself and disposed to follow his own appetites.

It is wonderful to see how those who have voluntarily subjected themselves to the tyranny of the pope, cannot endure that Jesus Christ should bear gentle rule over them for their salvation. But it is true that the devil uses this device to bring the truth of God into opprobrium, to cause pure religion to be condemned and the sacred name of our Redeemer blasphemed.

Thus, Madame, to have a church duly Reformed, it is requisite to have people charged with the duty of superintendence, to watch over the morals of each member. So that no one may feel himself aggrieved at having to give an account of his life to the elders, see to it that the elders themselves be selected by the congregation. Nothing can be more reasonable than to preserve to the church this prerogative; this privilege will call forth greater discretion in the choice of fitting men, men approved by the consistory.

I am sure, Madame, that you have assisted our brother de Colonges with your authority in establishing such order, but knowing how much corruption the court of princes is subject to, I have thought it not superfluous to exhort you to maintain order in your own. It is only proper that you should be reminded of one thing: that always the devil strives by sinister tales and defamation to paint the ministers of God as contemptible in order to make them the objects of aversion or disgust.

For that reason all the faithful should be on their guard against such wiles. To quarrel with one's spiritual pasture is worse than finding fault with one's bodily food, since the matter at risk here is the life of the soul.

Be that as it may, if there are any who aim, even indirectly, to discourage you in pursuing what you have begun so well, you should shun them as deadly plagues. Truly, the devil stirs them up to alienate people by indirect means from God whose will it is that he should be recognized in the person of his servants.

Above all, Madame, let no one persuade you to change anything in the state of the church, such as God has consecrated it by his blood. It is the Lord before whom every knee should bend. If they attempt to wheedle you by saying that members of your household should be honored above others [in the church], reflect that they cannot do you more dishonor than by seeking to cut you off from the body of the church. You cannot be more highly honored than by having your household purged of all pollutions.

Where, I ask you, Madame, should we apply medicines sooner than in cases from which the disease is most likely to spread? Are not courts more likely to break out into all kinds of licentiousness than private households, unless precautions against the evil are taken? I am not implying that if there is any scandal among the members of your household, you (as chief member of the church) should be reminded of it in order to deliberate in perfect agreement [with the elders] how the scandal may be corrected. What I recommend is that your authority should not interfere to interrupt church discipline. If your domestics are spared, all respect for the consistory will disappear like water from a leaky vessel.

Now let us speak of something else. Madame, I have wished for a long time to make you a present of a gold piece.[2] (Imagine my boldness!) But because I supposed you had a similar one, I have not ventured to send it to you until now, for it is only its rarity that can make it of any value in your eyes. Finally, I made up my mind and have delivered it to the bearer of this letter to show it to you. If it is something you have not seen before, will you be pleased to keep it? It is the finest present I have in my power to give you.

Madame, very humbly commending myself to your indulgent favor, I pray our heavenly Father to have you in his holy keeping, increasing you in all good and prosperity.

Charles d'Espeville
8 January 1564

XXVI

January—February 1564

The Catholic powers viewed the apparent French tolerance toward Protestantism as threatening to all Christendom. Early in February ambassadors of the pope, the emperor, and Philip of Spain met with Catherine de' Medici at Fontainebleau to urge the king to revoke pardons granted to rebels by the Peace of Amboise, condemn the perpetrators of the Guise murder, and cease alienating the goods of the French clergy. Their sovereigns would support His Majesty with all force necessary for achieving these objectives.

The queen listened attentively to these and other suggestions without committing herself. Later she dictated a letter, signed of course by Charles, reiterating His Majesty's attachment to the Catholic faith but promising nothing. She did not appreciate interference in the affairs of her kingdom.

Renée had returned to court by this time for further talks concerning her claims to Brittany. She found preaching still going on at Fontainebleau, but of a sort she did not like. A letter of Cardinal Santa Croce, dated 25 February 1564, shows the temper of her relationship with the queen:[1]

> Last Sunday His eminence the cardinal of Lorraine preached in the apartment of Her Majesty where not only the king and queen

with all their court had gathered, but also the prince and princess of Condé with the duchess of Ferrara. The cardinal revealed much erudition of piety in his sermon concerning the cult of images, the sacrament of the Eucharist, and the mass. . . .

He went on to say that when the cardinal had concluded his sermon, Catherine asked Renée what she thought of his remarks. The duchess answered frankly that she had just heard great blasphemies against God, adding that if Her Majesty would do her the favor of hearing one of the duchess's ministers, she would hear other things which would please her. To which the queen replied heatedly that she would rather die than listen to such things.

Catherine was ready to show the Huguenots the dark side of royal favor, beginning little by little to make the Peace of Amboise a dead letter. All fortifications built by Huguenots during the war were razed, in order "that the Reformed, reposing on the good faith and sincerity of the king, of which he had given great testimony, might dwell in perfect rest."[2]

A new declaration was issued, an "interpretation" of the Peace. The Reformed could no longer have schools, colleges, nor academies. Their ministers must live in the localities reserved for their assemblies. Protestants might not have their assemblies in places where the king might pass through, nor within any royal palace.

Seeing what was happening, hearing of the great number of Huguenots killed since the beginning of the year because of hatred of the Reformed religion, with no resultant punishment of the criminals, Renée returned to Montargis, where Calvin's letter of 24 January reached her.[3]

Madame:
   When in your last letter you said you had intimated to Monsieur Francesco [Porto] that it would be expedient that I exhort to charity those who profess to be Christians, I understood you to be referring to some ministers that you have found not very charitable, according to your judgment. I gather you alluded to the harshness with which they have condemned the late duke of Guise.

Now, Madame, before I proceed to examine that accusation more closely, I pray you in God's name to reflect seriously that on your part too it is necessary to observe moderation. It is only the person who is unable to reflect that will fancy that we can ever have too much of it. And without taking into account the report of others, I have perceived in your letter that your affection has made you forget what otherwise you would have certainly known.

In respect to what I said to you about David's teaching us by his example to hate the enemies of God, you replied that it was only during those times when the Israelites lived under the rigor of the law that it was permitted to hate enemies. Now, Madame, this interpretation would lead us to overthrowing the whole of Scripture; so we should shun it as a deadly plague.

David surpassed in kindness of character the best of those who can be found in our times. When he protests that he has wept and has shed tears in secret for those who were plotting his death, we see that his hatred consisted in mourning for their death, that he was meek spirited as could possibly be desired. But when he says he holds the reprobate in mortal aversion, it cannot be doubted that he glories in an upright, pure, and well-regulated zeal, for which three things are requisite: first, that we should have no regard for ourselves or our private interests; next, that we should possess prudence and discretion not to judge at random; and finally, that we observe moderation not to exceed the bounds of our calling.

All of this you will see, Madame, more in detail in several passages of my commentaries on the Psalms when you shall be pleased to take the trouble to read them. Indeed, the Holy Spirit has given us David as a model, that in this respect we might follow his example. In fact, we are told that in this ardor he was the type of our Lord Jesus Christ. If we pretend that we surpass in meekness and humanity the One who is the fountain of pity and compassion, woe to us.

But to cut short all disputes, let it satisfy us that St. Paul applies to all believers this passage: "The zeal of thy house hath eaten me up." Wherefore, our Lord Jesus, reproving his disciples because they desired him to cause fire to come down from heaven as Elias had done and consume those who had rejected him, does not allege that we are no longer under a law of rigor, but simply shows them that they are not led by the same spirit as the prophet. Nay, St. John, of whom you have retained nothing but the word *love*, clearly shows that we ought not, under show of affection for humanity, become indifferent to the duty we owe to the honor of God and the preservation of the church. That is shown when he forbids us even to salute those who, as much as they can, turn us from the pure doctrine.

On that subject, I pray you to pardon me if I tell you frankly that in my opinion you have taken in a wrong sense the comparison of the bow which we bend in the opposite direction when it has been bent too much on one side. He who employed that figure of speech doubt-less only meant to say that in seeing you carried to excess, he had been constrained to be even more vehement, not that he intended to falsify the Scriptures or disguise the truth.

I come now to a fact which, not to annoy you with my long-windedness, I shall only touch upon briefly. You are not the only one who has suffered much anguish and bitterness during these horrible troubles that have befallen. Perhaps the evil has stung you more poignantly, seeing the throne with which you are connected by your royal descent has been subjected to such disorder. But certainly the sorrow was common to all the children of God, and though all of us might have said "Woe to him by whom this scandal is come!" never-theless there was special reason for mourning and lamenting, seeing that a good cause had been very ill-conducted.

Now, if the evil distressed all good people, the duke of Guise, who kindled the conflagration, could not be spared.

For my own part, though I often prayed that God would show him mercy, yet it is certain that I often desired God to lay his hand upon him in order to deliver the poor church out of his [Guise's] hands unless it pleased God to convert him. I can affirm that before the war I had only to give my consent to have had him exterminated by men of prompt and ready execution who were bent on that objec-tive and were restrained only by my exhortations. To pronounce him damned, however, is going too far unless one had certain and infal-lible proof of his reprobation. There we must guard against presump-tion and temerity, for no one can know that but the Judge before whose tribunal all of us have to render an account.

Your second point seems to me too much, that some pronounce the king of Navarre in paradise and the duke of Guise in hell. If we institute a comparison between these two men, we find that the former was an apostate, the latter always an avowed enemy of the gospel. I would wish in this matter a great deal more moderation and sobriety.

Meanwhile, Madame, I beg you not to show so much displeasure at the expression *not to pray for anyone,* without making due distinc-tion between the form and the reality of the subject in question. For though I pray for the salvation of anyone, that does not imply that in all respects and everywhere, I recommend him as if he were a mem-ber of the church. We ask God to bring back into the right path those who are on the way to perdition, but that does not mean that we are placing them in the same category as our brothers and sisters in order to pray for them all kinds of prosperity.

Let me tell you a tale of the queen of Navarre that is a case in point. When her husband the king had fallen away from us, her minister ceased to make mention of him in the public prayers. Irritated with him, she remonstrated that he should not omit the king, if for no other reason than out of consideration for his subjects. He defended himself by saying that he had altogether abstained from doing so, it was to conceal the dishonor of the king her husband. He could not pray to God for him with a clear conscience unless he prayed for his conversion, which would be revealing his fall. If he asked God to maintain him in prosperity, it would be a mockery and a profanation of prayer. Having heard that answer, she did not say a word until she had asked advice of others, and finding that they all agreed, she had to acquiesce.

As I know, Madame, that this virtuous princess would be disposed to take advice from you as a thing due to your age and your virtues, I entreat you not to be ashamed to imitate her conduct in this matter. Her husband was a closer connection to her than your son-in-law to you; nevertheless, she mastered her affection in order not to be the cause of having God's name profaned, which it would have been assuredly if our prayers had been feigned or militated against the repose of the church.

To have done with this pretext of charity, judge, I beseech you, Madame, if it is reasonable that at the capricious desire of a single person, we are not to consider a hundred thousand; that charity should be confined to one who had endeavored to throw everything into confusion, that the children of God should be kept completely in the background. Now the remedy for all this is to hate evil, without taking persons into account but leaving everyone to the Judge. If God should grant me the favor of speaking with you, I trust I would quickly satisfy you. In the meantime, I entreat you to weigh well what I have handled slightly, that you may not let yourself be upset by a little idle talk, which you can afford to treat with the utmost contempt.

You say you are solicited to permit the shops of the papists to be robbed and pillaged. I certainly do not approve of such acts, no matter who has countenanced it. On the contrary I commend your virtue and greatness of mind in having been unwilling to acquiesce in so unjust a demand. I say the same thing in regard to the other excesses you mention.

As to the quarrel which has arisen in your household between the two persons you named, I do not know what reason there may be for speaking against the women. I have no doubt as to the truth of what you tell me, Madame, but I do not know whether there have been any bad symptoms that might have forced Monsieur de Colonges [Morel] to give such an admonition as a kind of preventive remedy, or whether he has gone too far, with lack of due reflection on his part.

One thing is certain: the husband reacted too violently when they offered to satisfy him; and the answer and refusal of Monsieur de Colonges savors more of his ambition and of worldly vanity than of the modesty expected of a man of his calling, for which I am very sorry. He must have forgotten himself to go so far. If the parties agree to lay before us an account of this affair, I will do all in my power to remedy the evil on whichever side it may lie.

On this point, Madame, I am afraid it is much to be feared that God is not going to leave us much time to enjoy the blessings he had granted us, since everyone is so taken up with his self-interest that we do not know how to support our neighbor in a spirit of meekness and humility. And so far are we from loving our enemies, striving to overcome evil with good, that there is no gentleness among us to keep up filial love between those who boast that they are Christians.

Nevertheless, I pray you again, Madame, not to dwell any longer on that distinction which deceives you, while you imagine that under the law it was permitted to avenge oneself because it is there said "an eye for an eye." For vengeance was as much forbidden then as it is under the gospel, seeing that we are commanded to do good even to the beast of our enemy. What was addressed to the judges, each individual applied to himself.

There remains the abuse of the precept which our Lord Jesus Christ corrects. Be that as it may, we are all agreed that in order to be recognized as children of God, it becomes us to conform ourselves to his example, striving to do good to those who are unworthy of it, just as God causes the sun to shine on the evil and the good. Thus hatred and Christianity are incompatible. I mean hatred toward persons in opposition to the love we owe them. On the contrary, we are to wish and even procure their good; and to labor, as much as is within our power, to maintain peace and concord with all people.

Now if those who are commissioned to dissipate all enmity and rancor, to reconcile enemies, to exhort to patience and repress all lust of vengeance, are themselves brands of discord—so much the worse, and so much the less are they to be excused. At any rate, Madame, the faults which displease you ought not to cool your zeal or prevent you from continuing as you have so well begun.

I know that God has fortified you with such courage that it is unnecessary to solicit you yet more. Wherefore, I am confident that you will set an example of charity to those who do not know what charity is, and your integrity and plain dealing cover with confusion those who practice toward you hypocrisy and dissimulation. On the other hand, I praise God for having made known unto you the real character of the admiral, to inspire you with a taste of his probity When it pleases him, God will find the rest. . . .[4]

XXVII

March 1564

Calvin's physician Sarrazin had treated him with medicines prescribed by doctors of Montpellier. On 8 February Calvin drew up a list of his complaints for his secretary to send to the medical faculty in Montpellier, asking for their help.

Twenty years before powders had helped him, he said, but that was before he had experienced arthritis, gravel, colics, hemorrhoids, expectoration of blood, quartan agues, acute pain in the calves of his legs. Circulation from his feet to his knees was affected; his hemorrhoidal veins had ulcerated; the movement of intestinal worms caused him constant pain, the vermicular disease was followed by an attack of nephritis.

He had been carried in a litter into the country and had been too weak to walk a mile. Instead of urine, he had voided blood, then had passed a large stone and several smaller ones of uric calculus and was still emitting small ones, all this in addition to gout, hemorrhoids, indigestion, and a throat never free of phlegm.

To his friends it was evident that Calvin was dying. On 6 February he preached his last sermon at St. Peter's, then went home to bed. His suffering continued without respite. On 10 March the magistrates ordered citywide prayers to be made for him, knowing there was no *earthly* hope. In that letter written to Renée in late January, he had said no word of his own condition, being, even then, occupied only with making clear to her the duty God requires. And Renée had no inkling that she was writing to a dying man when, on 21 March, she answered his January letters, pouring out to him her distress, her willingness to be guided by him, and yet showing clearly her continued independence in matters spiritual.

This letter and that written to Antoine de Pons twenty-five years before reveal two entirely different women. Portions of this one are indecipherable. Evidently she was writing under great stress. This is a paraphrase, rather than a literal translation, reconstructed from a number of sources.[1]

Monsieur Calvin,

I was not able to answer your letters of 8 and 24 January immediately because I was preparing to return to the court at Fontainebleau to finish some necessary business and remained there a full month.

The reason I left there before the king was my being forbidden to have preaching there, as I had for several days. It was refused me not only in the house of the king but also in one I had bought in the village and had lent to be used for assemblies when I was not at court. What particularly hurt me was that this happened at the solicitation of a husband and wife who are communicants and who have ministers.

Monsieur the admiral and his wife arrived the day I left and were no more able than I to have preaching. They stayed at court for a week, then came here [to Montargis] with the cardinal their brother to acquaint me with the facts.

As to the present and New Year's gift you sent me, I received it with much pleasure. I had never seen one like it, and praise God that the late king my father adopted such a device. If God did not give to him the privilege of executing his purpose, perhaps he reserves its accomplishment for some one of his descendants.

Now I must tell you, first, that I read your advice in regard to my subjects and my household. As to my subjects, I began the work long ago and am striving to complete it, if it pleases God. As to the matter of administering justice and to the daily subsistence to the poor, whether inhabitants of Montargis, transients, or members of my own household, and the providing against vice and scandals generally, you will hear all about this from Soutenix, who will be with you soon, and from Monsieur de Colonges, whom I have instructed to write you. Those matters will be settled by whatever means you advise and by a good arrangement which you will suggest for the future.

I hope that the interests of the church in this place will thrive, on which point I am unable to inform you since de Colonges has always had entire charge of it. Before God, I have assisted him in whatever he has required. At first he told me not to come to meetings of the consistory. He chose the elders he wanted. Then he told me it was unnecessary for women to attend, not even me (although I knew that the queen of Navarre, Madame the admiral's wife, and Madame de Roye took their places in the consistories in their own houses, and I felt that the prerogatives of my house should be observed).

I did not insist. Whenever he asked me to send any of my household there (to the consistory) or when they informed me that he had summoned them, I always told them to obey him and serve God as Monsieur de Colonges bade them. There was one exception: a young man who was in charge of the kitchen expenditures. I did not want him to go because of his youth and his mental capacity for fear he would commit some outrageous act. I was right in my estimation of his character, for afterward he struck an old man in poor health who worked in the kitchen because he would not become one of the religion.

De Colonges has put in and out whatever persons he has thought proper, in the city and in my own household (as you will learn from Soutenix, one of those in my household who was put out). I do not know that any of my subjects in the city has molested anyone.

I receive help constantly from Monsieur the admiral, next to the help and counsel of God, for repression of vice and scandal. Among the admiral's subjects the religion thrives, although some are as much opposed as those in this place. . . . As to the members of my household, most of them are of the religion and are communicants. Some few are not yet Reformed, but I hope God will draw them to himself.

As for my thinking that I or anyone in my household should be considered privileged, I assure you that I have never required or wished for special treatment, and that I have had so few privileges among the faithful that whatever affects me is ignored or disregarded. My ladies and attendants have been put in the worst places or even driven away at banquets and festivals. [There follows an incomprehensible passage concerning the lack of courtesy of the faithful toward her and her ladies of honor.]

I wish you could be here to see and understand what goes on better than I can describe it. I realize that the remonstrances you send me are necessary in order to maintain the church, and I wish that my judgment and intelligence were greater; but according to the qualities God has given me and the advice you have sent me through messengers and letters, it seems to me that so many ministers and people coming here, each one shouting his opinion, are unnecessary. May God grant me the grace to employ myself in serving him purely and sincerely, as you desire. I assure you that is my desire too, and I hope he will accomplish it and will continue to make you know, as he has in the past, those by whom the religion is *not* extended.

Monsieur Calvin, I will not try to reply to everything in your last letter in order not to delay writing to you as long as that would require. As briefly as possible I will try to make clear what I did not succeed in doing in my last letter. Or perhaps some other person has "explained" what I meant.

I wrote you about two ministers, one of whom argued with me by a process of falsehood which I consider unlawful; the other on the ground of a judgment of God of election and reprobation caused by human prayers. The second one would have incited me to hate what God has not commanded me to hate.

I had not forgotten the point which you had brought out— that David hated the enemies of God with a mortal hatred. I do not mean to contest that for if I *knew* that the king my father, the queen my mother, my late husband the duke, and all my children were judged reprobate *by God*, I would be willing to hate them with a mortal hatred and desire them to have their portion in hell, thus conforming myself entirely to the will of God if God were pleased to grant me the grace to do so. . . .

As to my late son-in-law, it seems to me that there is more than enough evidence to judge whether I gave up my beliefs on his account in any way. It was he who yielded, to protect those of the religion here, even (with his brother the cardinal) to be answerable for them to the queen. Did God not use them to protect his own? And it should be recognized that not only here but at Châtillon he used his influence that the admiral's property should not be confiscated, sacked, and his people oppressed. There are other extenuating facts which other people do not want known and which I say before God that I know to be the truth.

I am not attempting to excuse his faults, nor his failure to have the knowledge of God. But as to what the Huguenots are saying— that he alone lighted the flame of war—everyone knows he had returned to his own house; everyone knows of the letters and messages he received urging him to come forth. But even though he is dead, the venom of hatred continues to spread all the falsehoods that can be invented or imagined.

I must tell you that I do not consider it possible that such lies proceed from God. I know that my son-in-law did persecute, but I do not *know* nor do I believe (to express myself freely to you) that he was a reprobate by divine judgment. For he gave signs to the contrary before he died, but people do not want that to be spoken of. They wish to hush and lock the mouths of those who know of it.

I know I have been hated and held in abomination by many because he was my son-in-law, on whom they wish to place all the blame. They cannot rest satisfied even after he is dead. Even if he had been the greatest reprobate who ever lived, is it right that they never cease talking of his wickedness?

A secretary of Monsieur d'Arsay was talking with me and the queen of Navarre [Jeanne d'Albret] saying everything evil possible about my son-in-law and some others. When I commanded him to say if what he was saying were true, he confessed there was no truth in the story and told us who had put him up to repeating it, saying such malicious things put upon the duke could help the religion. He thought it perfectly right to imply all sorts of defenses for the cause and that a lie used so was good and holy. The lady approved of this, but I insisted—and still do—that God is not the father of lies but the devil is, and that God is the God of truth and his word powerful enough to defend his own without our taking up arms of the devil and his children.

Nevertheless, the lady is so zealous and has such sound judgment on most things that I admire her. As the late queen of Navarre [Margaret] her mother was the first princess of the kingdom to favor the gospel, it may be that the present queen of Navarre will complete the work by establishing it in her kingdom. She is well equal to that task. I love her with a mother's love and praise the graces God has bestowed upon her.

Monsieur Calvin, I must tell you that I have heard words such as it would take too long to repeat. Of a good and holy cause—the defending and supporting of the children of God—some people have made a diabolical one. They say that on account of the enmities that existed between the king of Navarre, Monsieur the constable, and my son-in-law, we ought to put a mask on the word of God. It seems that even after he is dead, no one but God can vex those of the religion, that there was no other than he who favored the papists. Human bodies, when the souls are out of them, do not work such miracles; not even when they are alive can one person destroy so many as he is charged with destroying.

Some have tried to prove that the king of Navarre was a veritable

King David and the prince of Condé after him. They would make David their model and not Jesus Christ. They have taught such things to the simple people. . . . If there are reprobates, I think they are those who twist the truth of God, which they know well, into insolent lies.

Monsieur Calvin, I am surprised that you do not seem to know how half the people in this kingdom conduct themselves nor the adulation and ill will rampant in it, even to the exhorting simple young women to say they would like to strangle and kill. That is certainly not what Christ and the Apostles taught us. I say it with all the regret in my heart, for the love I hold the religion and to those who bear the name of Christian. I do not speak of the whole church but of a great number among them.

If they say that my outlook is distorted because of my affection for my late son-in-law, I can answer that I was never so passionately devoted to him or to my own children. Perhaps my accusers have not considered that I left my children to follow the path on which God has led me. Nevertheless, there are some who take up the passion and side of others without considering whether or not they proceed from God, to twist and pull Holy Scripture to the string of their bow which they themselves have fashioned. I know that they will continue to lie and slander, taking delight in it, and that such people give you to understand that things are different from what they are.

I beg you, Monsieur Calvin, to ask God to show you the truth of all things, since by you I pray that God will expose the hidden works of malice prevailing in this world and in this age. Our present state makes me fear that the chastisement of God will inevitably fall upon those of the church.

I have never requested from ministers whom I have heard suggest it, that they should pray for me or for any other person. I leave to the consciences of others their own prayers. And I never asked prayers of those to whom I have given alms; it would seem that I was asking some recompense if I asked them to pray for me. We should all pray for each other and should all pray the prayer our Lord taught us to pray.

Nevertheless, I pray constantly for those for whom it seems to me that God would have me pray, especially for those of the household of faith, for those who preach the word of God, for the king whom God has given us, for princes, lords, and judges of the earth (because God has commanded it), and that everyone may live a quiet and peaceful life, not only in the peace which this world gives but in that which our Lord has left to us.

I am not one of those who pray or cause prayers to be made for those who are no longer in the world. I know there are those who say that everyone who is against the religion is bad. I grant that that may be so, but I do not know whether or not God may call them so. It is not my business to complain of them. I know before God that there are too many defects and sins in me for me to judge them, but God commands us to give testimony before God's creatures by our manner of living, and I am ready to do so if it please God.

As to what I have heard charged upon the ministers and children of God, I have not remained silent but have taken it upon myself to defend them with more care than I have taken to defend myself. I know there are those who threaten to banish them from the kingdom. Therefore we ought not to do or say things that will make it possible for them to accomplish their designs.

Monsieur Calvin, all these concerns have caused me to be prolix in this letter and in others which I have written you from time to time, and which I have begged you to burn, as I now do with this one.[2] And I beg you to continue to write to me freely whatever seems good to you, which I shall always receive gladly. With this I shall conclude, praying to God, Monsieur Calvin, to keep you in his holy and worthy care.

Renée of France

XXVIII

Geneva
April—May 1564

Calvin dictated his last letter to Renée two weeks after hers was written, the last French letter he would write as he lay dying.[1] Yet, except for the first few lines, he makes no allusion to himself, concerned only for her spiritual and emotional welfare, urging her to continue a life of faith shown by her works. As it had been from the beginning of his ministry, he felt himself only a conduit for the knowledge of God, and his doctrine the veritable word of God.

Madame,

I pray you to pardon me if I employ the hand of my brother in writing to you because of my weakness and the pains I suffer from various diseases—difficulty in breathing, the stone, the gout, an ulcer in the hemorrhoidal veins which prevents my taking any exercise, the only thing from which I might hope to derive some relief.

I must ask you also to excuse me if this letter is short in comparison to yours [of March 21] since I am still waiting for the return of Monsieur de Budé, through whom you promised to let me have news of you. Also, I have not yet received any letters from Monsieur de Colonges to tell me what means should be adopted to reconcile the differences in your household and to remedy for the future everything that might breed troubles and misunderstandings or keep up animosities and rancor.

Concerning other matters, however, if my advice has any weight with you, I beg you not to torment yourself any more about them. Whatever may happen, too violent and impulsive a response makes matters worse and shuts the door on reason and truth.

As I told you, I distinctly separated the person of the duke of Guise from my remarks [about reprobates] and insisted that those who damn people according to their fancy are presumptuous. You have taken my remarks in quite a contrary sense. I am astonished that you did so and for that cause refrain from saying anything more, either good or bad, on that subject.

I must refer to one remark of yours, however. As for virtuous people entertaining feelings of horror or hatred of you because you were the mother-in-law of Monsieur de Guise, they only love and respect you the more since that connection did not deter you from making a pure and forthright confession of Christianity, and that not only by words but by deeds so remarkable that nothing could exceed them. As for myself, I protest to you that this has caused me to hold your virtues in so much the greater admiration.

There is one more thing on my mind: I understand that your niece the duchess of Savoy [Margaret of France, wife of Emmanuel Philibert] is thinking about making an open declaration for the religion, in fact is almost persuaded. But you know how many meddlesome intriguers there are to restrain her or cool her ardor. You know how timid she has always been, and I am afraid that her good disposition of mind will proceed no further unless it is stimulated.

Now, Madame, I believe that there is no one in the world with more influence with her than you. For that reason, I beg you in God's name to give her a good and earnest exhortation in order that she may have the courage to make a decided resolution. I am confident that you will do your whole duty according to your zeal for having God served and honored more.

Madame, very humbly commending myself to your indulgent favor, I beg our heavenly Father to keep you under divine protection, to lead you continually by the Spirit, and to maintain you in all prosperity.

Charles d'Espeville
4 April 1564

Two days after writing to the duchess of Ferrara, Calvin wrote his friend Bullinger for the last time.[2] Later Beza, who remained almost constantly with the sick man during his last two months, wrote Bullinger a longer letter describing the patient's condition: constant pain in his legs, so much phlegm in his throat he could hardly breathe. For the past twelve days he had suffered from a stone in his bladder, for which his doctor could find no remedy. The ulcer in his stomach was so painful he could neither sit nor lie in comfort. Now he refused food, saying he had no appetite, and the sweetest wine was bitter. He coughed constantly [being in the last stages of tuberculosis], yet—incredibly—not complaining.

On Easter Sunday he was carried to St. Peter's to celebrate Holy Communion. Many wept openly at the singing of "Lord, now lettest thou thy servant depart in peace," knowing that Calvin would not be with them again.

On 2 May, the news spread that Calvin was dying, and again the whole city prayed for him. But he was not ready to die. He had one thing more to do: he dictated a farewell letter to Guillaume Farel, seeking to make amends for their estrangement.[3] When he received the letter, 75-year-old Farel walked to Geneva from Neuchâtel to pray with him, assure him of his love, and returned to Neuchâtel overcome with grief.

After 6 February when he had barely breath to finish his last sermon and realized he could not preach again, Calvin had refused all remuneration from the city. Now, on 25 April, he dictated his last will and testament.[4] The will was shorter than the testament, which was a concise confession of faith.

As for his will, he had only one thing of value—a silver cup given him by the sieur de Varennes, and this he left to his brother Antoine as sole heir. Antoine was to see to the distribution of his other bequests, all dependent on the sale of his books and meager furnishings: ten crowns to the poor refugees; ten crowns to the academy; ten crowns to his half-sister Antoinette; forty crowns each to Antoine's sons Samuel and John, twenty-five crowns to Antoine's disinherited son David; thirty crowns to each niece; whatever remained, to de Trie's children.

Two days later he was visited by the Petit Council in a body, to express their appreciation of what he had done for the city, and to offer Antoine a good sum for his brother's books. The day after, ministers of the city came to pray with him and tell him good-bye.

He died on 27 May, quietly and peacefully, having been unable to speak for a week but regaining his voice shortly before evening. He was buried without pomp or ceremony the day after. That no stone marks the spot where he was interred would have pleased him; he would have wanted no epitaph. After his death, in its official pronouncement the Petit Council said, "God gave him a great majesty," but it was the majesty of God alone that Calvin sought to show.

Epilogue

Since the thrust of this work is to show the influence of Calvin, through his letters, on the spiritual development of the duchess of Ferrara, his death should be the stopping point; yet his influence continued through the remaining years of her life.

One must resist the temptation of going into detail concerning those tempestuous years during which she was so intimately associated with the royal family, with Coligny, and above all with that star-crossed Guise clan, and confine oneself to a brief running account of the ten years remaining to this woman who, within a short time after her cry to Calvin that she was hated by the Reformed, came to be regarded by them and their enemies as the help and stay of the Huguenots, symbol of their independence.

This feeling of the Huguenots may have been stimulated in part by the long journey the duchess undertook in 1565–66, traveling sometimes with the court on the itinerary Catherine de' Medici devised in order to show the boy-king to his subjects (and to meet the duke of Alva in Bayonne to lay plans for the extermination of French heretics); more often paralleling the court's route, (since no Reformed worship was permitted in towns through which the king might pass), visiting Protestant congregations throughout the Midi, in Languedoc, Provence, and

Dauphiné, continuing her pilgrimage while the court was snow-bound in Carcassone, on up to Poitiers and beyond, encouraging Huguenot assemblies, having her minister preach in their pulpits, aiding them financially.

During the ongoing war punctuated by disastrous battles in which Huguenot leaders were assassinated after surrender (Condé), died of wounds and fever (Andelot), or were executed (Montgomery), and uneasy truces and "peaces" which brought no peace, Renée maintained her sanctuary at Montargis in the face of threats by Catherine and her sons. Only once during the years of open warfare did she send away the hundreds of refugees crowding her castle—in the fall of 1569 after a massacre in Orléans—when she was forced to obey a definite royal ultimatum. One other time, threatened by the garrisoning of companies of the royal army in Montargis, she sent her ministers to a place of safety.

The duchess was not at the court at St. Maur when her daughter Anne married Jacques de Savoy, duke of Nemours. The wedding had, of course, been arranged by Catherine de' Medici, and the union was a cause of anxiety to Renée. Nemours was now leader of the Catholic party and so an enemy of the Reformed. But as she had done with the duke of Guise, Renée developed a warm friendship with her son-in-law. A second cause of anxiety brought her more grief.

Nemours had for seven years been defendant in a suit brought against him by Françoise de Rohan, niece of the now defunct king of Navarre, whose cause had been taken up by her aunt, Jeanne d'Albret. Nemours had seduced the young girl with promises to marry her and had abandoned her. Now, released by the pope from any obligation, since Françoise was Protestant, his marriage to Anne was celebrated with much éclat.

On Calvin's death, the duchess had taken Coligny for her counselor in religious matters, and their friendship grew with the years. She was delighted when Catherine effected a reconciliation between the admiral and the cardinal of Lorraine as spokesman for the Guises, saddened that her grandson Henry refused to be a part of the love feast.

When, finally, lack of money on both sides forced Catholics and Huguenots to negotiate for peace, Renée's coach and favorite coachman transported Coligny to court to sign the pact of Saint-Germain-en-Laye in August 1571.

In September Renée herself traveled to Paris to attend the wedding of her grandson and Catherine of Cleves, widow of the young Protestant prince of Porcien, a casualty of the wars. The wedding was a surprise to the grandmother, for rumors of Henry's love affair with the Princess Margot had reached her. But Charles IX had been informed of his sister's meetings with Guise and had ordered Guise assassinated. It was necessary for the Lorraine prince to prove, quickly, that he was not involved with Margot.

The month following, when Henry came with some seven hundred armed retainers to Montargis to thank his grandmother for her attendance at his wedding, the admiral at nearby Châtillon-sur-Loing prepared to defend himself, being well aware of young Guise's hatred. That hatred was increased the year following when Coligny, having become a great favorite of the king, persuaded His Majesty that a union between Princess Margot and Jeanne d'Albret's son Henry, now king of Navarre, would help to bring about peace between Huguenots and Catholics.

In spite of her visibly failing health, Renée made several journeys to Paris during the spring of 1572. She visited Catherine's new Tuileries palace and gardens under construction, giving alms to the workmen. She was in Paris again in June for Anne's accouchement, and received a personal invitation from the king to attend his sister's wedding in August.

On 23 July she set out from Montargis with her gentlemen and ladies-of-honor in order to attend various celebrations before the wedding. She lodged at the house of Monsieur de Chemynon, with her ladies in houses nearby, close to the Palace of Justice on the Île.

With the court she witnessed the elaborate wedding ceremony outside the cathedral of Notre Dame, then attended the nuptial mass inside while the Protestant bridegroom walked in the ca-

thedral garden. She was in Paris when Coligny was shot by
Guise's servitor. She may have visited him with Catherine and
Charles on the day before the massacre. Coligny's minister,
Merlin, was with him, and his son-in-law Teligny. Only Merlin
escaped.

There have been enough graphic accounts of that St. Bartholomew's night of horror without its being retold here. The
Saint-Germain-des-Prés quarter and the Île were spared during
the early morning hours, when Coligny was thrown out of the
window and his body mutilated. Shouts and screams reached the
Île, however, and the duchess's ladies came to join her behind
locked doors guarded by men whom Anne had sent to protect
them. They remained with doors closed and with no visitors
during the following week. When the city gates were finally
opened they silently and fearfully boarded the carriages Henry of
Guise had sent with outriders to take them as rapidly as possible
back to Montargis.

Once behind the locked doors of her own castle, Renée went
to bed. She had been told of Coligny's death, of the arrest of his
wife and children. She did not ask the details. Perhaps she did
not need to, for among the gentlemen who escaped with her from
Paris was Merlin.

For several months she remained very quietly in her castle,
learning from Anne of matters at court. His Majesty was going to
issue an edict requiring everyone in the kingdom to attend mass.
Anne was afraid the king was going to send all of her mother's
servitors away. She hoped her mother had sent her ministers
away; they would certainly suffer. She begged her mother to
attend mass. Henry of Navarre and the young prince of Condé
had done so.

Rumors spread that the old duchess had attended mass in
Montargis, that she had agreed to come to Paris and recant
before Notre Dame. Catherine was sure that her "aunt" had been
frightened sufficiently to cause her to abjure and wrote her an
affectionate letter telling of the benefits she would receive at
returning to Holy Mother Church.

Renée was not tempted, nor, after the first shock, was she

frightened. At La Rochelle, in Dauphiné and Languedoc, Huguenots were arming themselves to fight for their lives now, not their religion. at Sancerre peasants and townspeople chased the garrison from their town and locked the gates. Taking courage, the duchess again opened her castle to refugees from Orléans, where a massacre as bloody as that in Paris occurred in September.

Though fighting went on, the Reformed knew it was a last-ditch business. After La Rochelle gave up, another edict of pacification was signed in July 1573, a bad peace, badly observed by each side but at least a cessation of organized battles.

In March 1574 the duchess's son Luigi, cardinal of Ferrara, fell seriously ill in Paris. After sending her favorite physician to attend him, his mother followed, though she herself was not well. No sooner had she reached Paris than she collapsed with a high fever and was put to bed in her daughter's house, her life in danger. Nevertheless, in April she demanded to be taken back to Montargis. She was still too weak in June to attend the funeral for Charles IX, who died on 30 May.

The last year of her life was sad. At court she was all but forgotten, Henry III rude and insolent. She had not gone to his royal entry into Paris when he finally returned from playing at being king of Poland.

The death of her niece, Margaret of Savoy, the last of her sister Claude's children, whom she had cared for when Margaret was a child, grieved her profoundly. Her world had become inhabited by strangers. Except for Anne, she was disappointed in her children. (How could she have borne it had she known the part Anne played in planning the massacre in Paris?)

It was not harassment or persecution that finally overcame this woman of until-now indomitable spirit, but sickness of body, grief, and depression. When one of the stewards of her household to whom she was deeply attached died suddenly, the autopsy showed he had been poisoned. Investigation proved the murderer was a young servitor who had hoped to be promoted to the steward's place. Her world was falling apart.

In February 1575 she was bled again and again to cure her of recurrent fevers, but she did not recover her strength. Early in

June she became ill of pneumonia and dysentery. On 15 June 1575 she died.

At the time of her illness in Paris she had made her will. There are, in fact, three different ones: the first written ostensibly by her minister and laid aside; the second, revised, with the duchess's corrections in the margins; a third and shorter one, containing the same bequests but not so lengthy a confession of faith. There is no doubt that Anne knew the contents of the will—one of them was preserved in the archives at Turin—for as soon as she was notified of her mother's death, she hurried to Montargis to carry out the duchess's instructions for her funeral, which were incorporated in her will.

Her body, in a closed and locked wooden coffin, was interred in the chapel of her castle, without pomp, ceremony, or witnesses except for those of her gentlemen, ladies, and servants who chose to attend. The coffin was carried by six poor workmen of the castle who were paid twenty-five livres apiece.

Anne carried out her mother's wishes before the ambassador of Ferrara appeared to transform the chapel into a proper *Chambre ardente* with a cloth-of-gold-covered catafalque— though no body was there—and a mass said for the repose of her soul by a Montargis priest. The ambassador's desire was that the world should believe the duchess had made profession of the Catholic faith on her deathbed.

In Paris, Henry III had a brief memorial service for the late duchess, his great-aunt performed in the Bourbon chapel. He wrote Anne that she need not expect her mother to be interred at Saint-Denis (where the kings and queens of France and their children were buried) because of her erroneous opinions. Catherine de' Medici wrote that she hoped Anne's grief for her mother's death would not make her sick.

It was Alfonso who suffered the most embarrassment at his mother's death. When word reached him, he wrote his sister that news of Her Excellency's death displeased him but since everything comes from the hand of God, "it is necessary for us to conform to his supreme will." And with an edged side-remark, "I am sure Your Excellency will know how to do so with your habitual prudence."

Alfonso could not decide whether or not he should have bells tolled and a mass said for the repose of his mother's soul. After all she was a heretic. He was relieved when the pope advised him to forbid any public displays of mourning; it would be sufficient for the court to retire for a week to Belreguardo.

The very long confession of faith found in her will is what one would expect from a disciple of Calvin, reading much like *The Institutes of the Christian Religion* in simplified form. But at the end of her list of bequests is a characteristic note to her children: to Luigi, indolent cardinal of Ferrara; to Alfonso, with whom the legitimate line of the Estensi would end in spite of his three political marriages; to her unhappy, spendthrift daughters Leonora and Lucrezia; to Anne, who alone of her children, mourned their mother's death.

She ended,

> ... praying ... Messieurs and Mesdames her children, in the name of God, to read and listen to the word of God, in which they will find all manner of consolation and the true rule by which they ought to conduct their lives in order to gain that eternal life promised to us in that word, praying in the name of the Father, the Son, and the Holy Spirit that he may be gracious to all.[1]

Was the duchess of Ferrara a true Calvinist? Did she return to the Catholic church before her death? Later each faith would claim her. In Ferrara today they call her Calvinist and show her chapel in the castle, faced with marble, with no place for shrine or crucifix.

Perhaps she was truly Christian, Protestant but ecumenical, beyond Calvinism and Catholicism alike. Though she took John Calvin as her spiritual guide, he was not her director. She refused to follow blindly, refused to hate in the name of religion. She questioned doctrine and dogma, leaving surmise and supposition to theologians, responding to human need, attempting always to be one of those peacemakers called the children of God.

Notes

PREFACE

1. Émile Doumergue, *Jean Calvin, les hommes et les choses de son temps*, 5 vols. (Geneva: Slatkine, 1969), 2:3–94.
2. Williston Walker, *John Calvin, the Organizer of Reformed Protestantism* (New York: Shocken Books, 1969).
3. A. L. Herminjard, *Correspondance des Réformateurs dans les pays de langue Française*, 9 vols. (Geneva: H. Georg, 1864–97).
4. Henry Beveridge and Jules Bonnet, eds., *Selected Works of John Calvin: Tracts and Letters*, trans. David Constable (Philadelphia: Presbyterian Board of Publication, 1858; reprint edition: Grand Rapids, Michigan: Baker Book House, 1983), 4:295–306.
5. Emanuel Stickelberger, *Calvin, a Life* (Richmond: John Knox Press, 1954). It seems that one of Renée's legs was considerably shorter than the other and the misalignment of her body caused one shoulder to protrude.

I. ALIAS CHARLES D'ESPEVILLE

1. Theodore Beza, *The Life of John Calvin*, trans. by Henry Beveridge (Philadelphia: Westminster Press, 1909), 15.
2. Stickelberger, *Calvin*.
3. Bartolommeo Fontana, *Renata di Francia, duchessa di Ferrara, sui documenti dell' Archivio estense, de' medíceo, del Gonzaga e dell' Archivio secreto Vaticano*, 3 vols. (Rome: Forzani, 1887–93).

4. Beza, *Life of John Calvin*, 12.
5. C. A. Mayer, *La Religion de Marot* (Geneva: Droz, 1960).
6. Beza, *Life of John Calvin*, 15.
7. E. Rodocanachi, *Renée de France, Duchesse de Ferrara, une protectrice de la Reforme en Italie et en France* (Paris: Paul Allendorf, 1896), 120.
8. Ibid, 119.
9. Fontana, *Renata di Francia*, 2.
10. Lodovico Muratori, *Annali d'Italia* (Florence: 1840), 10:275.
11. Girolamo Tiraboschi, *Storia della Literatura Italiana*, 16 vols. (Florence: 1812), 3:chap. 33, cited by Stickelberger.

II. RENÉE OF FRANCE

1. Pierre de Brantôme, *Oeuvres complètes* (Paris: Société de l'histoire de France, 1894–96).
2. Rodocanachi, *Renée de France*, 100.

III. TRIAL AND ERROR

1. Karl Barth and Charles Gagnebin, eds., *Calvin* (Paris, 1948), 32–39.
2. Sovereign power in Geneva was vested in three councils: the Great Council, composed of all (male) citizens 25 years or older; the Council of 200, citizens of 30 years or over, who held office for life unless expelled at the annual meeting; and the Petit Council, men chosen from the Council of 200. Four syndics elected annually for one-year terms were elected from the Petit Council.

IV. TO STRASBOURG AND BACK

1. Calvin to Louis Du Tillet, Strasbourg, 10 July 1538, *Works*, ed. Bonnet, 4:72.
2. Calvin to James Bernard, Ulm, 1 March 1541, ibid., 235.
3. Calvin to the Church of Geneva, Strasbourg, 1 October 1538, ibid., 82–88.
4. Calvin to Guillaume Farel, Strasbourg, 19 May 1539, ibid., 141.
5. Calvin to Farel, Strasbourg, 21 June 1540, ibid., 191.
6. Calvin to Farel, Strasbourg, 29 March 1540, ibid., 175.
7. Calvin to Pierre Viret, Strasbourg, 19 May 1540, ibid., 187.
8. Calvin to Farel, 27 October 1540, ibid., 211, 212, 213. Bonnet incorrectly labels this as written in Strasbourg rather than in Worms.
9. Calvin to Farel, Worms, 13 November 1540, ibid., 218.

10. Calvin to Nicholas Parent, Worms, 14 December 1540, ibid., 224.
11. Calvin to the Seigneury of Geneva, Strasbourg, 19 February 1541, ibid., 225.
12. Calvin to Viret, Ulm, 1 March 1541, ibid., 231, 233, translated by the author.
13. Calvin to Farel, Ulm, 1 March 1541, ibid., 233, 239.
14. Calvin to the pastors of the Church of Zurich, Ratisbon, 31 May 1541, ibid., 265–71.
15. Calvin to Farel, Strasbourg, August 1541, ibid., 280–81.
16. Calvin to Farel, Geneva, 16 September 1541, ibid., 284.
17. Ibid.
18. Calvin to Martin Bucer, Geneva, 15 October 1541, ibid., 294.

V. FERRARA 1536–41

1. Pietro Giannone, *Istoria civile del regno di Napoli*, 34:84, as quoted in John Harford, *The Life of Michael Angelo Buonarroti* (London: Longman, Brown, Green, Longmans and Roberts, 1857), 2:261–64.
2. Rodocanachi, *Renée de France*, 146.
3. Ibid., 152.
4. Ibid., 147–51; Archives of State, Modena; Fontana, *Renata di Francia* 2:127–33.
5. Archives de Turin (Papiers de Genevois et de Nemours), cited in Rodocanachi, *Renée de France*, 155n.

VI. THE FIRST LETTER

1. Calvin to Madame the Duchess of Ferrara, Geneva, [October] 1541, *Works*, ed. Bonnet, 4:295–306. All letters edited by the author for the modern reader.

VII. GENEVA 1541–54

1. Calvin to Oswald Myconius, Geneva, 27 March 1545, ibid., 452.
2. Calvin to John Frellon, [Geneva], 13 February 1546, ibid., 5:30n.
3. Calvin to Farel, Geneva, 13 Feburary 1546, ibid., 33.
4. Calvin to Farel, Geneva, 4 July 1546, ibid., 61–63.
5. S. E. Herrick, *Some Heretics of Yesterday* (Boston: Houghton, Mifflin and Co., 1884), 229.
6. Calvin to Farel, Geneva, 21 August 1547, ibid., 138.
7. Calvin to Viret, Geneva, 26 December 1547, ibid., 151.
8. Calvin to Viret, Geneva, 12 February 1545, ibid., 4:450, see 449n.; Calvin to Viret, [Geneva], 20 September 1548, ibid., 5:176–79.
9. Calvin to Viret, [Geneva], 7 April 1549, ibid., 216–17; Calvin to Farel, Geneva, 11 April 1549, ibid., 217–19.

10. Ibid., 256n.
11. F. Whitfield Barton, *The Sage and the Olive* (Philadelphia: Muhlenberg Press, 1953).
12. Calvin to Farel, Geneva, 10 November 1550, *Works*, ed. Bonnet, 5:284–85.
13. F. Whitfield Barton, *Olympia* (Philadelphia: Fortress Press, 1965), 142.
14. Bonnet, ed., *Works*, 5:335n.
15. Calvin to Farel, Geneva, 8 December 1551, ibid., 328– 29; Calvin to Heinrich Bullinger, Geneva, January 1552, ibid., 331–34; Calvin to Farel, Geneva, 27 January 1552, ibid., 335–38.
16. Calvin to Monsieur de La Falaise, [Geneva, 1552], ibid., 381–83.
17. Calvin to Edward VI, Geneva, 4 July 1552, ibid., 354–55.
18. Calvin to Cranmer, [July 1552], ibid., 356–58.
19. Calvin to the French Church in London, Geneva, 27 September 1552, ibid., 360–63.
20. Registers of the Council of Geneva, 9 November 1551, as cited by ibid., 5.
21. Paolo Gaddi to Calvin, cited in Rodocanachi, *Renée de France*, 233. *Corpus Reformatorum* 14:516.
22. Calvin to Bullinger, Bonnet, ed., *Works*, 5:414, 425.
23. Archives of State, Modena, as cited by Rodocanachi, *Renée de France*, 233–34.
24. T. H. L. Parker, *John Calvin, a Biography* (London: J. M. Dent & Sons, 1973), 120.
25. Calvin to Viret, Geneva, 4 September 1553, *Works*, ed. Bonnet, 5:424.
26. Calvin to Farel, Geneva, 20 August 1553, ibid., 417.
27. Ibid.
28. Ibid., 428n; Calvin to Bullinger, Geneva, 7 September 1553, ibid., 425–27; Calvin to Sulzer, Geneva, 8 September 1553, ibid., 427–30.
29. Ibid., 435n.
30. Registers of the Council of Geneva, ibid., 424n.
31. Stickelberger, *Calvin*, 2:7.
32. Calvin to Bullinger, Geneva, 30 December 1553, ibid., 448.
33. Ibid., 442n, 440–41n.
34. Calvin to Bullinger, Geneva, 23 February 1554, ibid. 6:20.

VIII. FERRARA 1541–54

1. Rodocanachi, *Renée de France*, 164; Fontana, *Renata di Francia* 2:183.
2. Rodocanachi, *Renée de France*, 168
3. Archives of State, Modena, ibid., 210.
4. Rodocanachi, *Renée de France*, 176.

5. Archives of State, Modena, Fontana, *Renata di Francia* 2:.
6. Rodocanachi, *Renée de France*, 213.
7. Ibid., 216n.
8. Archives of State, Modena, Fontana, *Renata di Francia* 2:.
9. Rodocanachi, *Renée de France*, 217–18.

IX. "J'ACCUSE"

1. *Archivo storico italiano* 13:417–20. Bibliothèque Nationale, fonds française 3126, fols. 56–60.
2. Rodocanachi, *Renée de France*, 231–32. F. Le Laboureur, *Additions aux mémoires de Michel de Castelnau*, 1:3:717–18.
3. Rodocanachi, *Renée de France*, ibid.

X. THE SECOND LETTER

1. Calvin to the Duchess of Ferrara, Geneva, 6 August 1554, *Works*, ed. Bonnet, ibid., 6:50–52.

XI. THE TRIAL

1. Fontana, *Renata di Francia* 2:370.
2. Ibid., 2:372n.
3. Rodocanachi, *Renée de France*, 250.
4. Ludovico Antonio Muratori, *Delle Antichità Estensi ed Italiane* (Milan, 1744–49), 2:321.
5. Fontana, *Renata di Francia* 2:374.
6. Ibid., 2:375.
7. Rodocanachi, *Renée de France*, 253.
8. Fontana, *Renata di Francia* 2:375.
9. Archives of State, Modena; *Minuta di dispaccio ducale per Germania*.

XII. GENEVA 1555

1. Calvin to Farel, Geneva, 1 November 1554, *Works*, ed. Bonnet, 6:88.
2. Olympia Morata to Vergerio, *Corpus Reformatorum* 18.
3. Calvin to Peter Martyr, Geneva, 27 August 1554, *Works*, ed. Bonnet, 6:59–60.
4. Calvin to Melanchthon, Geneva, 27 August 1554, ibid., 61–63.
5. Calvin to the Brethren of Wezel, Geneva, 13 March 1554, ibid., 29–32.
6. Calvin to the Brethren of Poitou, Geneva, 19 June 1554, ibid., 43–

45; Calvin to the Brethren of Poitou, 3 September 1554, ibid., 68–71.

7. Calvin to a Gentleman of Provence, Geneva, 6 September 1554, ibid., 71–74.
8. Calvin to the Swiss Churches, Geneva, 6 October 1554, ibid., 79–86.
9. Calvin to Lord John Grey, Geneva, 13 November 1554, ibid., 94–96.
10. Calvin to Bullinger, Geneva, 13 November 1554, ibid., 96–98.
11. Calvin to Peter Martyr, Geneva, 27 November 1554, ibid., 98.
12. Calvin to the King of Poland, Geneva, 5 December 1554, ibid., 99–109.
13. Calvin to John Wolf, Geneva, 26 December 1554, ibid., 110.
14. Calvin to the Duchess of Ferrara, [Geneva], 2 February 1555, ibid., 129–31.
15. Calvin to the Church of Poitiers, Geneva, 20 February 1555, ibid., 138–51.
16. Ibid., 145, 146.
17. Calvin to the Lords of Berne, Geneva, 15 February 1555, ibid., 137
18. Calvin to Bullinger, Geneva, 24 February 1555, ibid., 151–52.
19. Calvin to the Seigneurs of Berne, Lausanne, March 1555, ibid., 160–69; Calvin to the Pastors of Berne, Geneva, May 1555, ibid., 171–76.
20. Calvin to the Seigneurs of Berne, Geneva, 4 May 1555, ibid., 176–81.
21. Calvin to Farel, Geneva, 15 May 1555, ibid., 181–82.
22. Calvin to Bullinger, Geneva, about 9 o'clock, 5 June 1555, ibid., 185.
23. Calvin to Farel, Geneva, 10 October 1555, ibid., 235.
24. Calvin to Richard Vauville, [Geneva, November 1555], ibid., 236; see note.
25. Calvin to the Church of Frankfurt, Geneva, 22 December 1555, ibid., 240–43.

XIII. FERRARA 1555

1. Rodocanachi, *Renée de France*, 256–57.
2. Archives of State, Modena, Fontana, *Renata di Francia* 2:378.
3. Ibid. 2:380.
4. Ibid. 2:383.
5. Thomas McCrie, *History of the Progress and Suppression of the Reformation in Italy* (1856; reprint, New York: AMS Press), 238.
6. Harford, *Life of Michael Angelo Buonarroti*, 2:279.

7. Calvin to the Duchess of Ferrara, [Geneva], 10 June 1555, *Works*, ed. Bonnet, 6:187–89.

XIV. GENEVA 1556–58

1. Calvin to John Clauburger, Geneva, 24 June 1556, ibid., 281.
2. Ibid., 283–84.
3. Calvin to Bullinger, Geneva, 30 July 1556, ibid., 286– 89.
4. Calvin to Ambassador of the League, Geneva, 25 October 1556, ibid., 296–99.
5. Ibid., 309–12.
6. Ibid, 339.
7. Calvin to the Church of Angers, [Geneva], 19 April 1556, ibid., 363.
8. Calvin to the Women Detained in Prison at Paris, Geneva, September 1557, ibid., 363–66.
9. Calvin to the King of France, Geneva, October 1557, ibid., 372–77.
10. Calvin to Madame de Rentigny, [Geneva], 8 December 1557, ibid., 381–84.
11. Calvin to Mademoiselle de Longemeau, [Geneva], 14 December 1557, ibid., 390.
12. Calvin to the King of Navarre, [Geneva], 14 December 1557, ibid., 384–89.
13. Calvin to the Church of Paris, [Geneva], 5 January 1558, ibid., 390–93.
14. Calvin to the Church of Meaux, [Geneva], 5 January 1558, ibid., 393–94; in 1546 sixty persons in Meaux were arrested for celebrating the Lord's Supper in Reformed fashion. Fourteen were burned at the stake.
15. Calvin to the Church of Dieppe, [Geneva], 5 January 1558, ibid., 395–96.
16. Calvin to the Marchioness of Rothelin, [Geneva], 5 January 1558, ibid., 396–98.
17. Calvin to the Duke of Württemberg, Geneva, 21 February 1558, ibid., 400–405.
18. Ibid., 416n.
19. Calvin to Madame de Rentigny, [Geneva], 10 April 1558, ibid., 416–418.
20. H. M. Baird, *History of the Rise of the Huguenots of France* (reprint, New York: AMS Press, 1970), 2:252, 253; Theodore Beza, *Histoire ecclesiastique des eglises reformees au royaume de France* (Paris: Baum, 1883–89), 1:144.
21. Calvin to Monsieur d'Andelot, [Geneva], 10 May 1558, ibid., 418–21.
22. Calvin to the King of Navarre, [Geneva], 8 June 1558, ibid., 424.

23. Calvin to Monsieur d'Andelot, [Geneva], 12 July 1558, ibid., 437–40.
24. Ibid., 437–38n.
25. Ibid., 450n.
26. Calvin to Monsieur d'Andelot, [Geneva], July 1558, ibid., 450–53.
27. Ibid., 445n.
28. Calvin to the Marquis de Vico [Galeazzo Caracciolo], [Geneva], 19 July 1558, ibid., 440–46.

XV. FERRARA 1555–58

1. Rodocanachi, *Renée de France*, 273.

XVI. THE FIFTH LETTER

1. Calvin to the Duchess of Ferrara, [Geneva], 20 July 1558, *Works*, ed. Bonnet, 6:447–50.

XVII. GENEVA 1558–60

1. Calvin to the Admiral de Coligny, Geneva, 4 September 1558, ibid., 466.
2. Calvin to Madame de Coligny, [Geneva], 4 September 1558, ibid., 469.
3. Calvin to the Brethren of Metz, [Geneva], 10 September 1558, ibid., 470–72.
4. Calvin to the Ministers of Neuchâtel, Geneva, 26 September 1558, ibid., 474.
5. Calvin to Farel, Geneva, September 1558, ibid., 475–77.
6. Calvin to Melanchthon, Geneva, 19 November 1558, ibid., 482–83.
7. Calvin to William Cecil [Lord Burleigh], Geneva, 29 January 1559, ibid., 7:15–17.
8. Calvin to William Cecil, Geneva, May 1559, ibid., 46–48.
9. Calvin to Martin Miconius, Geneva, 23 February 1559, ibid., 25.
10. Calvin to the Prisoners of Paris, [Geneva], 18 February 1559, ibid., 18–20.
11. Calvin to Madame de Coligny, Geneva, 27 February 1559, ibid., 29–31.
12. Calvin to Peter Martyr, Geneva, 2 March 1559, ibid., 31–33.
13. Calvin to the Duke de Longueville, Geneva, 26 May 1559, ibid., 44–46.
14. Calvin to John Knox, Geneva, 7 November 1559, ibid., 73–76.
15. *Encyclopaedia Britannica*, 11th ed., s.v. "Calvin."

16. Calvin to John Sturm, Geneva, 23 March 1560, *Works*, ed. Bonnet, 7:91.
17. Calvin to Bullinger, Geneva, 11 May 1560, ibid., 104–6.
18. Calvin to Peter Martyr, Geneva, 11 May 1560, ibid., 106–7.
19. Calvin to the Church of Montelimar, Geneva, April 1560, ibid., 98–99.
20. Calvin to Peter Martyr, Geneva, 11 May 1560, ibid., 107.
21. Calvin to Sturm and François Hotman, Geneva, 4 June 1560, ibid., 108–10.
22. Calvin to Nicholas des Gallars, Geneva, 16 June 1560, ibid., 114–15.
23. Calvin to the Earl of Bedford, Geneva, June 1560, ibid., 115–17.
24. Calvin to the Waldenses, Geneva, 1 July 1560, ibid., 117–21.

XVIII. FERRARA 1559–60

1. State Archives, Modena, Rodocanachi, *Renée de France*, 300.
2. Calvin to Madame de Cany, [Geneva], 24 July 1554, *Works*, ed. Bonnet, 6:45–47. Madame de Cany, Peronne de Pisseleu was the sister of Francis I's mistress, Anne de Pisseleu, Duchess d'Etampes. Madame de Cany was converted to Protestantism by Laurent de Normandie, a boyhood friend of Calvin's who lived at Noyon and who came to Geneva at Calvin's invitation. Madame de Cany's chateau was on the Oise, near Noyon. Calvin wrote often to her (see letters dated 8 January and 29 April 1549, 7 June 1553, and 24 July 1554).
3. Calvin to Madame de Budé, [Geneva], 20 [?] 1546, ibid., 5:90–93.
4. Calvin to Madame de Rentigny, [Geneva], 8 December 1557, ibid., 6:381–84.
5. Calvin to an Italian Lady, [Geneva], [1553], ibid., 450–53.
6. Calvin to the Duchess of Ferrara, Geneva, 5 July 1560, ibid., 121–23.
7. Rodocanachi, *Renée de France*, 313.
8. Ibid., 315.

XIX. GENEVA—FRANCE 1560–61

1. Calvin to Sulzer, Geneva, 1 October 1560, *Works*, ed. Bonnet, 7:131.
2. Calvin to Bullinger, Geneva, 1 October 1560, ibid., 133.
3. Ibid., 136.
4. Calvin to Bullinger, Geneva, 14 October 1560, ibid., 142–44.
5. Calvin to Bullinger, Geneva, 1 November 1560, ibid., 145.

6. Rodocanachi, *Renée de France*, 320n.
7. Calvin to Sturm, Geneva, 5 November 1560, *Works*, ed. Bonnet, 148.
8. Calvin to Sulzer, Geneva, 11 December 1560, ibid., 151.
9. Calvin to Sturm, Geneva, 16 December 1560, ibid., 152.
10. Calvin to the Ministers of Paris, Geneva, December 1560, ibid., 154–58.
11. Gustave Baguenault de Puchesse, ed., *Lettres de Catherine de' Medicis* (Paris: Imprimerie nationale, 1901), 1:181.
12. Henri Daniel-Rops, *The Protestant Reformation* (Garden City, N.Y.: Doubleday, 1961), 1:513; Louis Batiffol, *The Century of the Renaissance* (New York: G. P. Putnam's Sons, 1935; reprint, New York: AMS Press, 1967), 194.
13. Rodocanachi, *Renée de France*, 328.
14. Calvin to the King of Navarre, Geneva, 16 January 1561, *Works*, ed. Bonnet, 7:161–62.
15. Calvin to the Queen of Navarre, Geneva, 16 January 1561, ibid., 162–64.
16. Calvin to the Admiral Coligny, Geneva, 16 January 1561, ibid., 165–66.
17. Calvin to the King of France, Geneva, 28 January 1561, ibid., 167–70.
18. Rodocanachi, *Renée de France*, 336.
19. Ibid.
20. Calvin to the Admiral Coligny, Geneva, 16 January 1561, *Works*, ed. Bonnet, 7:165.
21. Calvin to the Admiral Coligny, Geneva, 16 April 1561, ibid., 181–82.
22. Baguenault de Puchesse, *Lettres de Catherine de' Medicis*, 1:597.
23. Calvin to the Church of Sauve, Geneva, July 1561, *Works*, ed. Bonnet, 7:206.
24. Calvin to the Church of Aix, Geneva, 1 May 1561, ibid., 186–88.
25. Calvin to Ambrose Blaurer, Geneva, May 1561, ibid., 191–92.
26. Calvin to Bullinger, Geneva, 24 May 1561, ibid., 189.
27. Calvin to the Admiral de Coligny, Geneva, May 1561, ibid., 192–93; Calvin to the Admiral de Coligny, Geneva, 11 July 1561, ibid., 202–4.
28. Calvin to the Church of Nîmes, Geneva, 1 June 1561, ibid., 197–200.
29. Calvin to the Church of Sauve, Geneva, July 1561, ibid., 205–7.
30. Calvin to the King of Navarre, Geneva, May 1561, ibid., 195.
31. Calvin to Peter Martyr, Geneva, 17 August, 1561, 208–10.
32. Calvin to Sulzer, Geneva, 23 August 1561, ibid., 210–12.

XX. GENEVA—FRANCE 1561–62

1. Rodocanachi, *Renée de France*, 337; *Corpus Reformatorum* 18:590.
2. Rodocanachi, *Renée de France*, 346.
3. Calvin to the Admiral Coligny, Geneva, 24 September 1561, *Works*, ed. Bonnet, 7:221–25; Calvin to Madame de Coligny, Geneva, 24 September 1561, ibid., 225–26; Calvin to the Comtesse de Roye, Geneva, 24 September 1561, ibid., 227–28.
4. Calvin to Theodore Beza, Geneva, 24 September 1561, ibid., 229–30.
5. Ibid., 233n.
6. Calvin to Beza, Geneva, 1 October 1561, ibid., 234; Calvin to Beza, Geneva, 31 November 1561, ibid., 242.
7. Archives of State, Modena.
8. Calvin to the Queen of Navarre, Geneva, 24 December 1561, *Works*, ed. Bonnet, 245–47.
9. Calvin to the King of Navarre, Geneva, 24 December 1561, ibid., 247–52.
10. Calvin to Monsieur de Colonges, Geneva, 10 January 1562, ibid., 252–54.

XXI. VASSY AND AFTER 1562–63

1. Rodocanachi, *Renée de France*, 379.
2. Ibid.
3. Calvin to the Baron des Adrets, Geneva, 13 May 1562, *Works*, ed. Bonnet, 7:272–74.
4. Calvin to Bullinger, Geneva, 15 August 1562, ibid., 276.
5. Calvin to Sulzer, Geneva, 6 December 1562, ibid., 280–82.
6. Calvin to Bullinger, Geneva, 27 December 1562, ibid., 283.
7. Rodocanachi, *Renée de France*, 375; Beza, *John Calvin* 2:559; Jacques-Auguste de Thou, *Histoire universelle* 16 vols. (Paris: 1734) 4:231; Beza, *Histoire ecclesiastique* 2:559.

XXII. LETTERS FROM GENEVA SPRING 1563

1. Rodocanachi, *Renée de France*, 378.
2. Archives of State, Modena, Fontana, *Renata di Francia* 2:.
3. Calvin to Bullinger, Geneva, 8 April 1563, *Works*, ed. Bonnet, 7:297.
4. Ibid., 301.
5. Ibid., 298–301.
6. Calvin to the Comtesse de Roye, Geneva, April 1563, ibid., 302.

7. Calvin to the Marchioness of Rothelin, Geneva, April 1563, ibid., 303–4.
8. Calvin to Monseigneur de Crussol, Geneva, 7 May 1563, ibid., 304–5.
9. Calvin to Madame de Crussol, Geneva, 8 May 1563, ibid., 306–7.
10. Calvin to the Prince of Condé, Geneva, 10 May 1563, ibid., 310.

XXIII. THE EIGHTH LETTER

1. Calvin to the Duchess of Ferrara, Geneva, 10 May 1563, ibid., 313–16.
2. The court called Renée's castle an "hôtel Dieu," comparing it to the charity hospital across from Notre Dame in Paris.

XXIV. JUNE 1563—JANUARY 1564

1. Calvin to Monsieur de Soubise, Geneva, 25 May 1563, *Works*, ed. Bonnet, 7:317.
2. Calvin to the Queen of Navarre, Geneva, 22 March 1562, ibid., 266–68; Calvin to the Queen of Navarre, Geneva, 20 January 1563, ibid., 290–94.
3. Calvin to the Queen of Navarre, Geneva, 1 June 1563, ibid., 318–20.
4. Ibid., 320n.
5. Calvin to Bullinger, Geneva, 2 July 1563, ibid., 321.
6. Ibid., 320–23.
7. Calvin to Bullinger, Geneva, 19 July 1563, ibid., 323–24.
8. Calvin to Bullinger, Geneva, 29 July 1563, ibid., 325–26.
9. Calvin to Monsieur de Crussol, Geneva, 31 July 1563, ibid., 326–28.
10. Calvin to the Admiral Coligny, Geneva, 5 July 1563, ibid., 328–30.
11. Calvin to the Duchess of Ferrara, Geneva, ibid., 260–62. Bonnet dates this letter in February 1562, saying that it was written "a short time before the massacre of Vassy," see 260n. But this would have been while Anne of Este was in Joinville awaiting the birth of her third child and before her husband had precipitated the war which followed the massacre at Vassy.
12. Calvin to Bullinger, Geneva, 9 September 1563, ibid., 334–36.
13. Calvin to the Prince of Condé, Geneva, 17 September 1563, ibid., 339.
14. Alvarotti to Ercole II, Archives of State, Modena, Rodocanachi, *Renée de France*, 390.
15. Calvin to Bullinger, Geneva, 20 October 1563, *Works*, ed. Bonnet, 7:338.

16. Calvin to Bullinger, Geneva, 20 October 1563, ibid., 340.
17. Calvin to Bullinger, Geneva, 2 December 1563, ibid., 345–48.
18. Rodocanachi, *Renée de France*, 385.
19. *Works*, ed. Bonnet, 7:348n.
20. Ibid., 352n; *Corpus Reformatorum* 20:208.

XXV. THE NINTH LETTER

1. Calvin to the Duchess of Ferrara, Geneva, 8 January 1564, ibid., 348–51.
2. This was a gold piece which Louis XII had struck during his war with Pope Julius II. On it were engraved the words *Perdam Babylonis Nomen*. Babylon, in this case, was the papacy.

XVI. JANUARY—FEBRUARY 1564

1. Louis-Marie La Haye, *Lettres du Cardinal di Santa Croce ecrites pendant su nonciature en France* (1848), letter 45, 260; Rodocanachi, *Renée de France*, 397.
2. Ibid., 398.
3. Calvin to the Duchess of Ferrara, Geneva, 24 January 1564, *Works*, ed. Bonnet, 7:352–58.
4. Was he too weak to finish the letter or is the last page simply missing?

XXVII. MARCH 1564

1. Archives curieuses de l'histoire de France, 5:399ff., Dupuy Collection, vol. 86, Bibliothèque Nationale.
2. Is this request to burn her letters the reason we have only this one from Renée to Calvin?

XXVIII. GENEVA APRIL—MAY 1564

1. Calvin to the Duchess of Ferrara, Geneva, 4 April 1564, *Works*, ed. Bonnet, 7:360–61.
2. Calvin to Bullinger, Geneva, 6 April 1564, ibid., 362–63.
3. Calvin to Farel, Geneva, 2 May 1564, ibid., 364.
4. Calvin's Testament, Geneva, 25 April 1564, ibid., 365–68.

EPILOGUE

1. Archives of State, Modena.

Select Bibliography

Armstrong, William P. *Calvin and the Reformation*. Grand Rapids: Baker Book House, 1980.

Aubespine, Claude de. *Histoire particulière de la court de Henri II*. Vol. 3, Archives curieuses de l'histoire de France. Paris, 1834.

Bainton, Roland H. *Hunted Heretic: The Life and Death of Michael Servetus, 1511–53*. Boston: Beacon Press, 1953. Reprint. Peter Smith, 1978.

———. *The Reformation of the Sixteenth Century*. Boston: Beacon Press, 1956.

———. *Women of the Reformation in France and England*. Minneapolis: Augsburg Publishing House, 1973.

———. *Women of the Reformation in Germany and Italy*. Minneapolis: Augsburg Publishing House, 1971.

Baird, Henry M. *History of the Rise of the Huguenots of France*. 2 vols. New York: Charles Scribner's Sons, 1879. Reprint, New York: AMS Press, 1970.

Barton, F. Whitfield. *Olympia*. Philadelphia: Fortress Press, 1965.

———. *The Sage and the Olive*. Philadelphia: Muhlenberg Press, 1953.

Batiffol, Louis. *The Century of the Renaissance*. New York: G.P. Putnam's Sons, 1935. Reprint. New York: AMS Press, 1967.

Bayle, Pierre. *Dictionaire historique et critique*. Rotterdam: Chez M. Bohm, 1720.

Beveridge, Henry, and Jules Bonnet, eds. *Selected Works of John Calvin: Tracts and Letters*. Translated by David Constable. Philadelphia:

Presbyterian Board of Publication, 1858. Reprint. Grand Rapids: Baker Book House, 1983.

Beza, Theodore. *Histoire ecclesiastique des eglises reformees au royaume de France.* Paris: Baum, 1883–89.

———. *The Life of John Calvin.* Translated by Henry Beveridge. Philadelphia: Westminster Press, 1909.

Blackburn, William. *History of the Christian Church from Its Origins to the Present Time.* Cincinnati: Walden and Stowe, 1879.

Bonnet, Jules. *Vie d'Olympia Morata.* Paris: M. Ducloux, 1862.

———., ed. *Lettres de Jean Calvin.* Paris: Librairie de Ch. Meyraeis, 1854.

Bouchet, Henri. *Les femmes de Brantôme.* Paris: Maison Quantin, 1890.

V. L. Bourrilly, ed. *Le journal d'un bourgeois de Paris sous le règne de François I, 1515–36.* Paris: A. Picard et fils, 1910.

Brantôme, Pierre de. *Oeuvres complètes.* 12 vols. Paris: Société de l'histoire de France, 1894–96. Reprint. New York: AMS Press.

Bratt, John H. *The Heritage of Calvin.* Grand Rapids: William B. Eerdmans, 1973.

Breen, Quirinus. *John Calvin; a Study in French Humanism.* Grand Rapids: Wm. B. Eerdmans Publishing Company, 1931. Reprint. Hamden, Connecticut: Shoestring Press, 1968.

Burckhardt, Jacob. *Civilization of the Renaissance in Italy.* 2 vols. London: G. Allen & Unwin, 1890. Reprint. New York: Harper & Row.

Calvin, John. *Commentaires sur le livre des Psaumes.* Edited by Karl Barth and Charles Gagnebin. Paris: 1948.

Cambridge Modern History. New York: Macmillan, 1907.

Cartwright, Julia. *Isabella d'Este, Marchioness of Mantua, 1474–1539.* London: John Murray, 1903.

Chiappini, Luciano. *Guida di Ferrara.* Rome: Terni, 1970.

Church, Frederick. *The Italian Reformers, 1534–64.* New York: Columbia University Press, 1932.

Collins, Ross. *Calvin and the Libertines of Geneva.* Toronto: Clarke and Irwin, 1968.

Corpus Reformatorum, vols. 8, 11, 14, 18, 20, 22.

Creighton, Mandell. *History of the Papacy during the Period of the Reformation.* London: Longmans, Green, 1882. Reprint. New York: AMS Press,

Crespin, Jean. *Histoire des martyrs persécutés et mis à mort pour la vérité de l'évangile.* Toulouse: Benoit, 1889.

D'Aubigne, J. H. Merle. *History of the Reformation in Europe in the Time of John Calvin.* London: Longmans, Roberts, Green, 1876.

Delaborde, Henri. *Gaspard de Coligny admiral de France.* 3 vols. Paris: Firmin-Didot, 1880.

De La Ferrière-Percy, Hector, ed. *Lettres de Catherine de Médicis.* Vols. 1–5. Paris: Imprimerie nationale, 1901.

De La Planche, Regnier. *Estat de France sous François II.* Paris: Henneschet, 1836.

De Maulde-Le-Clavière, Rene. *The Women of the Renaissance: A Study of Feminism.* New York: G.P. Putnam's Sons, 1905. Reprint. Folcroft, Pennsylvania: Folcroft, 1978.

Denieul-Cormier, Anne. *The Renaissance in France, 1488–1559.* London: Allen and Unwin, 1969.

Doumergue, Emile. *Jean Calvin, les hommes et les choses de son temps.* 7 vols. Geneva: Slatkine Reprints, 1969.

———. *Le caractère de Calvin, l'homme, le système, l'Eglise, l'Estat.* Geneva: Slatkine Reprints, 1970.

Durant, Will. *The Renaissance.* The Story of Civilization, Part 5. New York: Simon and Schuster, 1953.

———. *The Reformation.* The Story of Civilization, Part 6. New York: Simon and Schuster, 1957.

Fontana, Bartolommeo. *Renata di Francia, duchessa di Ferrara, sui documenti dell' Archivio estense, de' medico, del Gonzaga, e dell' Archivio secreto Vaticano.* 3 vols. Rome: Forzani, 1887– 93.

Forneron, Henri. *Les ducs de Guise et leur époque.* Paris: E. Plon et cie, 1877.

Grant, Arthur J. *The Huguenots.* London: T. Butterworth, 1934. Reprint. Hamden, Connecticut: Shoestring Press, 1969.

Guerdan, René. *La vie quotidienne à Genève au temps de Calvin.* Paris: Hachette, 1973.

Guizot, François. *History of France from the Earliest Times to the Year 1848.* 8 vols. London: 1881. Reprint. New York: AMS Press, 1969.

Hackett, Francis. *Francis the First.* New York: Literary Guild, 1935.

Harford, John. "Memoirs of Vittoria Colonna, Marchioness of Pescara." In *The Life of Michael Angelo Buonarroti,* vol. 2. London: Longman, Brown, Green, Longmans and Roberts, 1858.

Harkness, Georgia. *John Calvin, the Man and His Ethics.* New York: Gordon Press, 1977.

Henry-Bordeaux, Paule. *Louise de Savoie, régente et "Roi" de France.* Paris: Plon, 1954.

Herminjard, Aimé L. *Correspondance des réformateurs dans les pays de langue Française.* 9 vols. Geneva: H. Georg, 1864–97.

Herrick, Samuel E. *Some Heretics of Yesterday.* Boston: Houghton, Mifflin and Co., 1884.

I. M. B. *Memorials of Renée of France, Consort of Hercules II, Duke of Ferrara.* London: 1859.

Jourda, Pierre, *Marguerite d'Angoulême, duchesse d'Alençon, reine de Navarre.* Turin: Bottega d' Erasmo, 1966.

Kelly, Caleb G. *French Protestantism, 1559–62.* Baltimore: Johns Hopkins Press, 1918.

Lavisse, Ernest. *Histoire de France.* Vol. 5. Paris: Hachette, 1903.

Mackinnon, James. *Calvin and the Reformation.* New York: Russell & Russell, 1962.

Marot, Clément. *Oeuvres complètes.* Paris: Garnier, 1879.

Mayer, Claude A. *Clément Marot.* Paris: Pierre Seghers, 1964.

————. "Le départ de Marot de Ferrara." *Bibliothèque d'Humanisme et Renaissance,* 18 (1956).

————. *La religion de Marot.* Geneva: E. Droz, 1960.

McCrie, Thomas. *History of the Progress and Suppression of the Reformation in Italy.* 1856. Reprint. New York: AMS Press.

Michelet, Jules. *History of France.* New York: Appleton, 1880.

Monter, E. William. *Calvin's Geneva.* New York: Wiley, 1967.

Montfaucon, Bernard de. *Les monumens de la monarchie françoise.* Vol. 4. Paris: J.M. Gandouin, 1732.

Muratori, Lodovico. *Annali d'Italia.* Part 2. Modena: 1714.

Noyes, Ella. *The Story of Ferrara.* London: J.M. Dent & Co., 1904.

Palm, Franklin C. *Calvinism and the Religious Wars.* New York: H. Holt and Co., 1932.

Parker, Theodore H. L. *John Calvin, a Biography.* London: J. M. Dent & Sons, 1973.

Potter, George R., and M. Greengrass. *John Calvin.* London: Edward Arnold, 1983.

Prescott, William H. *History of the Reign of Ferdinand and Isabella the Catholic.* Edited by C. Harvey Gardiner. Carbondale, Illinois: Southern Illinois University Press, 1962.

Puchesse, Gustave Baguenault de, ed. *Lettres de Catherine de' Medicis.* Vol. 6–10. Paris: Imprimerie nationale, 1901.

Rodocanachi, Emmanuel. *Renée de France, Duchesse de Ferrare, une protectrice de la Réforme en Italie et en France.* Paris: Paul Allendorff, 1896.

Roeder, Ralph. *Catherine de Medici and the Lost Revolution.* New York: Viking Press, 1937.

Roelker, Nancy. *Queen of Navarre; Jeanne D'Albret, 1528–1572.* Cambridge, Massachusetts: Belknap Press of Harvard University Press, 1968.

Rothrock, George. *The Huguenots, a Biography of a Minority.* Chicago: Nelson-Hall Co., 1979.

Sedgwick, H. D. *The House of Guise.* New York: The Bobbs- Merrill Co., 1938.

Sichel, Edith. *Women and Men of the French Renaissance.* London: Constable, 1905.

Sismondi, Jean de. *Histoire des Français.* Vols. 16, 17, 18, 23. Paris: Treuttel et Würtz, 1821–44.

————. *History of the Italian Republics in the Middle Ages.* London: G. Routledge, 1906.

Smith, Preserved. *The Age of the Reformation.* New York: H. Holt and Company, 1920. Reprint. New York: AMS Press.

Spitz, Lewis W. *Renaissance and Reformation Movements.* 2 vols. St. Louis: Concordia Publishing House, 1980.

Stickelberger, Emanuel. *Calvin, a Life.* Trans. by David G. Gelzer. Richmond: John Knox Press, 1954.

Stoddart, Jane. *The Girlhood of Mary Queen of Scots.* London: Hodder and Stoughton, 1908.

Sutherland, Nicola Mary. *The Huguenot Struggle for Recognition.* New Haven: Yale University Press, 1980.

Thou, Jacques-Auguste de. *Histoire universelle.* Vol. 26. La Haye: Chez H. Scheurleer, 1740.

Walker, Williston. *John Calvin, the Organizer of Reformed Protestantism.* New York: G. P. Putnam's Sons, 1906. Reprint. New York: AMS Press, 1972.

Whitehead, A. W. *Gaspard de Coligny, Admiral of France.* London: Metheun, 1904.

Zweig, Stefan. *The Right to Heresy: Castellio against Calvin.* Trans. by Eden and Cedar Paul. New York: Viking Press, 1936.